OXFORD
Children's
HISTORY
OF THE
WORLD

OXFORD

Children's

HISTORY

OF THE

WORLD

Neil Grant

OXFORD

UNIVERSITY PRESS

OXFORD
UNIVERSITY PRESS

Great Clarendon Street, Oxford OX2 6DP

Oxford University Press is a department of the University of Oxford.
It furthers the University's objective of excellence in research, scholarship,
and education by publishing worldwide in

Oxford   New York

Auckland   Cape Town   Dar es Salaam   Hong Kong   Karachi
Kuala Lumpur   Madrid   Melbourne   Mexico City   Nairobi
New Delhi   Shanghai   Taipei   Toronto

With offices in

Argentina   Austria   Brazil   Chile   Czech Republic   France   Greece
Guatemala   Hungary   Italy   Japan   Poland   Portugal   Singapore
South Korea   Switzerland   Thailand   Turkey   Ukraine   Vietnam
Oxford is a registered trade mark of Oxford University Press
in the UK and in certain other countries

British Library Cataloguing in Publication Data

Data available

ISBN: 978-0-19-911574-7

3 5 7 9 10 8 6 4 2

Printed in China by Printplus

CONSULTANTS

Mike Corbishley

Dr. Narayani Gupta

Dr. Rick Halpern

Dr. Douglas H. Johnson

Rosemary Kelly

James Mason

Contents

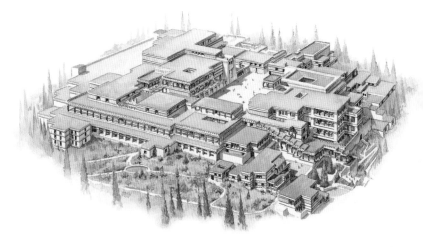

How to use this book

This book divides the history of the world into five chronological sections, beginning with ancient times and ending with the world today. The sections are divided into double-page spreads, each on a different subject. At the end of each section there is a Timeline. This shows at a glance the developments in different regions of the world during the period covered by the section. There is also a Who's Who page, which gives short biographies of the most important people of the period. At the end of the book there is a Glossary of important words, and an Index.

The text is divided into short blocks, each with its own heading. They describe one part of the main subject of the spread.

The title describes the subject of the spread, like a newspaper headline.

The first paragraph sets the scene, explaining what the spread is about and why it is important.

The coloured line shows which section you are in.

Dates here show the time in history when the events took place.

The Rise of Science

People began to understand more about nature and the universe as a result of scientific discoveries in the 17th century. The invention of instruments such as the telescope and the microscope made these advances possible. Galileo's observations proved that the Earth moves around the Sun, and Newton explained why.

Science in the East

Before this time, science in China, India and Islamic countries was more advanced than in Europe. The Chinese were especially good at technology. More than 1,000 years ago they invented the abacus (the first calculator), clocks, rockets, paper and printing. They knew more about medicine than people in other countries.

The Hindus in India were ahead in mathematics. They invented the idea of 0 (zero) and the numbers we use today. In Islam, the caliphs of Baghdad encouraged science, as long as it did not contradict religious teaching. Arab astronomy and geography were the best in the world. The Arabs took their mathematics from the Hindus. They translated and studied the work of ancient Greek scholars, who had been forgotten in Europe.

▷ Scholars in this 16th-century observatory in Constantinople (Istanbul) are using instruments for taking measurements of the stars. At the back are a cross-staff, a quadrant and an astrolabe, all used by travellers to work out where they were from the position of the stars. The study of the stars was important in Islam. It helped the Muslims to work out the direction of Mecca from wherever they were, so they knew in which direction to pray.

▷ When Galileo heard how a Dutchman had invented the telescope in 1608, he immediately made one himself. With it he saw that the surface of the Moon was rough and uneven.

1500 - 1700

Learning about the universe

Before the 17th century, science was held back by the Christian Church, which punished anyone whose ideas disagreed with its teaching. Copernicus, a Polish monk, wrote a book on astronomy which denied the Church's belief that the Earth was the centre of the universe. He dared not publish it until he was dying, in 1543. Nearly 100 years later, an Italian called Galileo got into trouble for teaching Copernicus's ideas. He knew Copernicus was right because he had looked at the sky using a telescope. He saw that Jupiter has moons that move around it, just as our Moon moves around the Earth. Changes in the appearance of the planets showed that they were circling the Sun. Galileo's telescope solved many mysteries. He showed that the planets seem larger than the stars because they are nearer, and that the Milky Way is not just a sheet of light, but billions of separate stars.

However, Galileo could not explain why some planets move around others. It was an English scientist, Isaac Newton, who discovered the law of gravity which he explained in a book, known as Newton's *Principia* ('principles'), one of the greatest science books ever written. Newton saw that the orbit of the Moon depends on the same force that makes an apple fall to Earth – the force of gravity.

△ When Robert Hooke made his microscope he was able to see a tiny flea clearly enough to make this detailed drawing.

Studying living things

The most sensational discoveries of the Scientific Revolution were in mathematics, physics and astronomy, but people also made important advances in other sciences, especially biology. A book on the human body by a Flemish doctor called Vesalius (1543) described the organs of the body, with brilliant drawings based on his dissections. This helped William Harvey, an Englishman, to understand how the blood circulates through the body (1628). Many discoveries followed Leeuwenhoek's invention of a better microscope. Robert Hooke, an Englishman, was the first to describe the cells of living things.

Sensational discoveries

1608 First telescope made by Lippershey.
1628 Harvey shows how blood circulates.
1658 Huygens makes pendulum clock.
1662 First study of statistics.
1673 Leeuwenhoek's microscope can magnify 200 times.
1676 Römer calculates speed of light.
1687 Newton publishes his theory of gravity.

Scientific societies
Universities began to take science seriously. Gresham College, London (1575) had lectures in astronomy. Sir Isaac Newton (right) studied mathematics and science at Cambridge University, England. From 1660 scientific societies or clubs, like the English Royal Society and the French Academy of Science, were founded. By bringing scientists together to discuss their ideas, they encouraged scientific progress.

93

Fact boxes list key events associated with the subject.

Photographs and illustrations show paintings, objects, places, people and scenes from the past.

Captions describe the illustrations and how they relate to the main text.

Coloured boxes give more details about major events or important people linked to the subject.

Many pages also have a map, to show the country or region where the events took place.

What is history?

History is the story of us, human beings. Everyone who has lived and everything that has happened are part of history. But history is not only what happened in the past. The word also means the study of the past, through old written records and other kinds of evidence.

Why are we interested in the past?

Why do we study history? One reason is that we enjoy it. A good story is even better if it is true, and history is full of good stories, though they can be terrible too. A more serious reason is to understand ourselves and the world we live in. To understand events happening now, we need to know their causes. We cannot understand the present if we know nothing about the past. History helps to explain why things are the way they are.

△ A Chinese temple.

▽ King Alfred's jewel, found in the marshes of Somerset, England.

Of course, history books cannot tell us everything about the past, not even everything that is recorded. A history of the world has to pick out the people and events that changed the world. Since ancient times, great civilisations have appeared in different continents and regions. Usually, only three or four existed at the same time. While they lasted, they changed the lives not only of their own people, but of their neighbours too. This book is mostly about those great civilisations, and the changes they caused.

People of the past

History is about people. It is about the important people, such as rulers, thinkers, scientists, explorers, writers and artists, who made an impact in their time and often beyond it. But it is also about ordinary people and their everyday lives. We want to know how they lived and what they thought.

△ Cleopatra, Queen of Egypt.

How do we know about the past?

A historian depends on evidence from the past to reconstruct the story. Evidence may be in written records, such as government papers, personal letters between friends, or even tombstones. In the earliest times no written records were kept, and many countries have few written records until recent centuries. Fortunately there are other kinds of evidence to help us find out about the past.

The first is objects. Archaeologists find evidence of the past in objects buried in the ground long ago. For example, the 4,000-year-old civilisation of the Indus Valley in south Asia was completely unknown 80 years ago. Now, thanks to archaeology, we know how the Indus people lived, what they ate, even the toys their children played with. Other evidence can be found in paintings, drawings and photographs. Both historians and archaeologists can be greatly helped by science. Radio-carbon dating can tell the age of any object that once formed part of a living thing, such as a piece of paper that was made from a tree, or leather from an animal.

If history can tell us about the past and help us understand the present, can it tell us something about the future too? Not really. History may give us hints, but things never happen in exactly the same way twice.

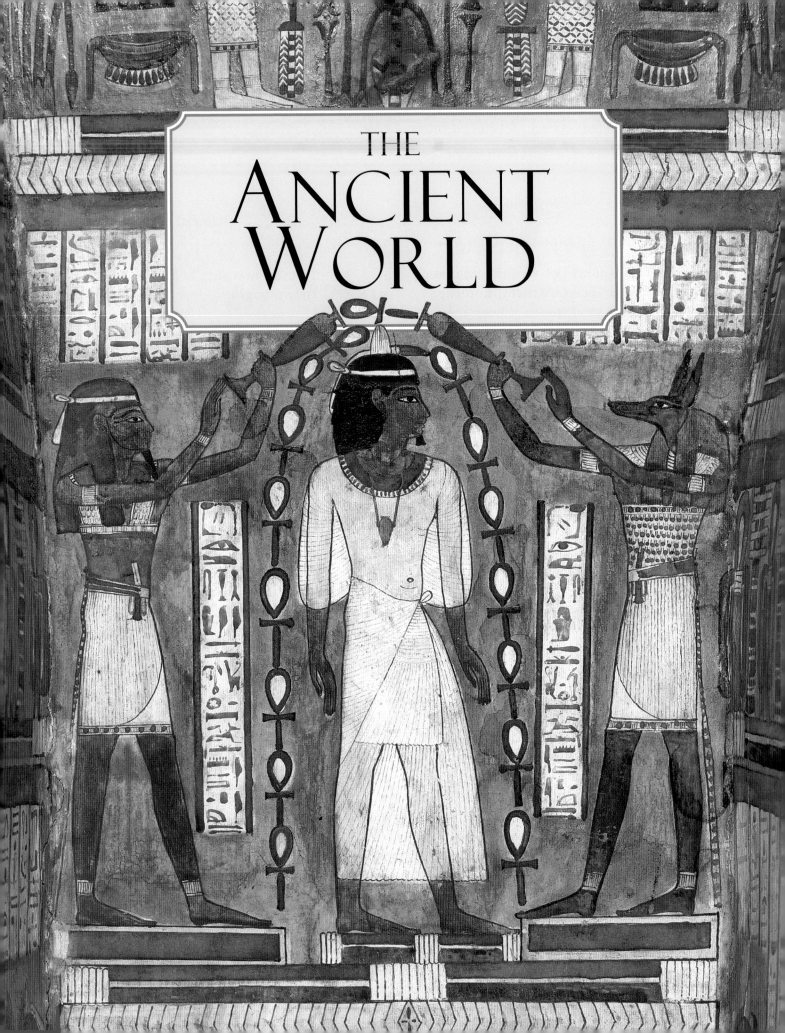

THE
ANCIENT
WORLD

Early Human Beings

Our earliest ancestors first appeared on the Earth about 5,000,000 years ago. Modern humans, who looked like us, developed more recently, only about 40,000 years ago. They lived a simple life, hunting animals, and picking fruits and vegetables.

Humans spread across the world

Humans today do not all look alike. But we are all related. Everyone in the world today is probably descended from one small group of people.

Our earliest ancestors lived in east Africa. Their descendants spread to south and west Africa and, over many thousands of years, throughout the world. They walked across the narrow 'bridge' of land that divides the Mediterranean and the Red Sea from Africa, into Asia and Europe.

The Earth was much colder then, and the Arctic ice stretched south to where Paris and New York are today. Because so much water was frozen, sea levels were lower, and people crossed from Siberia to Alaska on foot. They moved slowly south through North, then South America. People from south-west Asia reached Australia by raft. Others set out by boat and settled on distant Pacific islands. Almost the last land to be settled was New Zealand, where the Maoris' ancestors arrived between 2,000 and 4,000 years ago.

▷ Beginning in Africa, humans spread across the world. The differences in appearance we see today are the result of chance and local conditions. All peoples are closely related. There is only one human race.

Our earliest ancestors

The scientific name for modern humans is Homo sapiens ('wise man'). Homo sapiens evolved from earlier humans, such as Homo erectus ('upright man'). The earlier humans were descended from human-like creatures called hominids. One of the earliest hominids was Australopithecus. Neanderthals were another form of Homo sapiens. They became extinct.

| Australopithecus, early hominid | Homo erectus 'upright man' | Neanderthal man | Homo sapiens, modern man |

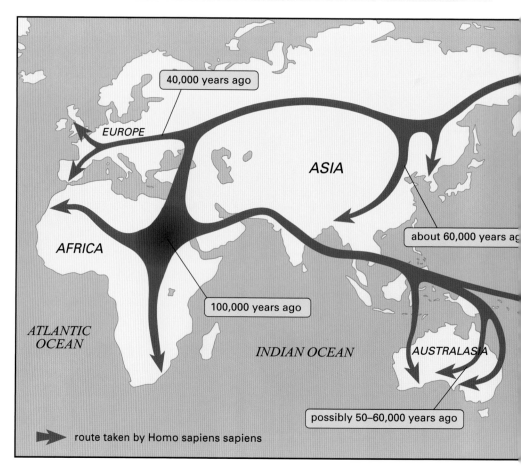

40,000 years ago

EUROPE

ASIA

about 60,000 years ag

AFRICA

100,000 years ago

ATLANTIC OCEAN

INDIAN OCEAN

AUSTRALASIA

possibly 50–60,000 years ago

➤ route taken by Homo sapiens sapiens

Hunters and gatherers

Early humans hunted animals and gathered wild plants for food. They also used the animal skins to make warm clothes. Their bigger brains, speech and agile hands gave humans an advantage over other animals. They lit fires and used tools. As they often moved in search of food, they made only simple shelters. We know that these people buried their dead carefully in graves, so they probably had some kind of religion. On the walls of caves they made wonderful paintings of animals. Perhaps these were a magic charm to give them luck in the hunt. As time passed, their skills increased, but human life changed little for 30,000 years.

▷ Neanderthal hunters in Europe trapped large animals, like this woolly rhinoceros, by digging big holes which they hid with branches.

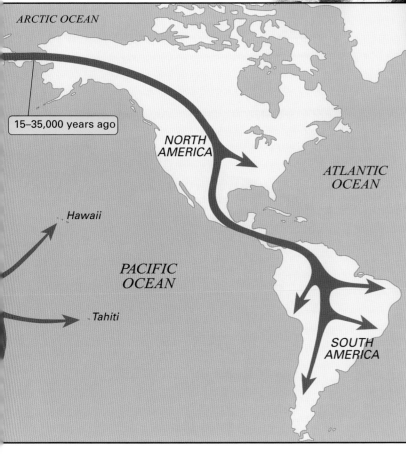

ARCTIC OCEAN

15–35,000 years ago

NORTH AMERICA

ATLANTIC OCEAN

Hawaii

PACIFIC OCEAN

Tahiti

SOUTH AMERICA

◁ Early humans made tools from wood, bone and stone. Flint was the most useful. It could be made into a hard chopper.

The end of the Ice Age

About 11,000 years ago the climate grew warmer. People moved further north, into lands uncovered when the ice melted. In these new lands they had to learn new habits and new crafts to survive. They made bows and arrows, fishing nets, and canoes from tree trunks. Life began to change more quickly.

The First Farmers

About 10,000 years ago the lives of some humans began to change. Instead of travelling in search of food, they settled down and learned how to grow food and keep animals. This gave them time to develop new skills, such as making pots, weaving cloth and using metals to make better tools.

Early farm animals

Hunters often followed wandering herds of wild animals, which gave them meat for food and skins for clothes. As they gained control over these herds, the animals became partly tame. Europeans were riding horses and Africans were keeping cattle even before people began to grow crops. Many early animals looked different from the farm animals we have today. This early pig looks more like a wild boar.

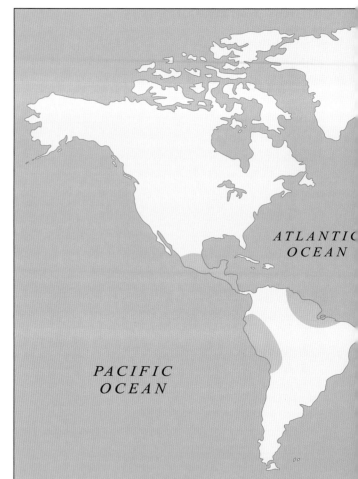

The first crops

Farming began about 10,000 years ago, after the end of the Ice Age. In some regions, people settled in one place, they collected the seeds of wild grasses, and learned to grow the ones which produced the largest grains. Different crops grew better in different parts of the world.

These first farmers lived in warm countries. They settled near big rivers because they needed a good supply of water. The very first farmers probably lived beside the Euphrates and Tigris Rivers in the Middle East, in a region called the Fertile Crescent. This region was much wetter than it is today, and crops grew well there. From there, farming spread very slowly to Europe and Africa. Meanwhile, people had begun farming in other parts of the world.

▽ The earliest pottery was made by hand. The potter's wheel was only invented thousands of years later. The first plough was just a pointed stick, which broke up the ground but did not turn the soil over.

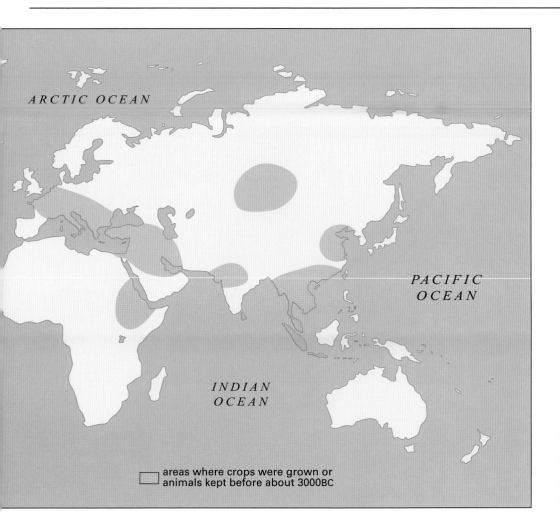

ARCTIC OCEAN

PACIFIC OCEAN

INDIAN OCEAN

☐ areas where crops were grown or animals kept before about 3000BC

The start of trade

As people began to make better use of the land, they produced more crops than they needed. This led to the growth of trade, as people exchanged the goods they had for the goods they needed. People living by the sea, for example, would have had plenty of fish but not enough wood for building. They could trade their fish for timber from a settlement further inland. Expert potters might trade with neighbours who made fine cloth.

◁ The first farming regions. In the Fertile Crescent the main cereal crop was wheat. In the Far East it was millet, later rice, and in tropical America it was maize (sweet corn). In regions where it was too dry or the soil was not good for growing crops, people remained hunter-gatherers or herdsmen into modern times.

Early crafts

When people became farmers they had a better food supply, so the population grew and began to settle in villages. Farming took less time than hunting and gathering food, which meant people had more time to develop crafts. The oldest crafts were making clothes, tools and pots. People made pots of baked clay 8,000 years ago. They also made woollen clothes, using wool from their sheep. The cloth was woven on a loom. People also made jewellery and ornaments.

▽ Different peoples learned to work in metal at different times. In China, it started much later than in the Near East. This Chinese bronze cooking pot was made in about 1700 BC.

Metalwork

Early farmers worked with wood or stone tools. Metal made better tools, but was hard to get. People found rocks with metal ore inside, and heated them to get the metal out. The ore melted and drained out. The first metal people learned to work with was copper, but this was too soft to make good tools. When they mixed it with tin, they made bronze, which was harder. Iron was best, but was more difficult to make. It came into use only about 4,000 years ago.

Early Cities

Settlements grew into towns and cities, where thousands of people lived, doing many different jobs. Some people became rich and powerful, but most were poor and forced to work very hard.

The growth of cities

The earliest cities in the world were built by people who had the most advanced farming, crafts and trade. Ordinary houses in the cities were made of cheap materials, such as mud bricks and thatch. Important buildings, like temples, were often built of stone. Remains of these buildings have been found, so we can imagine how they looked. The first region to develop cities was Sumer in southern Mesopotamia (modern Iraq). The cities were small states ruled by a king and nobles. The king also controlled all the settlements and farms in the region.

▷ The largest building in the Sumerian city of Ur was a ziggurat, a pyramid made up of huge platforms. On top was the temple where people believed Nana, the god of the city, lived. Because Sumer did not have much stone, even this building was made of mud bricks.

People start to write

People needed to write so that they could keep records. Early forms of writing used little pictures of objects. The Sumerians were the first to use symbols, like our letters. They wrote on clay tablets with a pointed tool. Because of the shape of the writing we call this cuneiform, which means wedge-shaped. This clay tablet records what crops were being grown in Sumer. Later, people began to write down religious stories.

Rulers and subjects

In the early city states there was a huge difference between the king, nobility and priests at the top of society, and the labourers and slaves at the bottom. In the middle were government officials, craftsmen and merchants. Although most people had to work from dawn until dusk, they had time off at religious festivals.

Ancient religion

The largest buildings in ancient cities were the temples. Religious beliefs developed from people's need to explain things they did not understand. For example, they realised that the Sun was important to life, so they believed the Sun was a god. Nana of Ur was a Moon god. Evidence from burial sites shows us that people believed in another life after death, and were buried with a religious ceremony.

Mathematics

The Sumerians were good at mathematics, probably because they needed to measure land. They invented a system of measuring in units of 60. The 60 minutes in an hour come from this system.

Arts in the early cities

Life in ancient cities was a struggle for many people, but richer people with leisure enjoyed music and art. They even played board games. Archaeologists have found many rich and beautiful objects at Ur made of gold, silver and stone. These show the great skill of the Sumerian jewellers and metalworkers.

◁ This ram or goat tied to a tree is made of gold, shell and lapis lazuli (a blue stone). It was made at Ur about 4,500 years ago, probably for a religious ceremony.

War between the cities

As far as we know, hunter-gatherers did not fight wars. Wars probably began when people first lived in large, permanent settlements. Sumerian cities were often at war with each other. The people built large, mud-brick walls to protect themselves.

◁ This scene shows the story of a king of Ur winning a battle. It starts on the bottom row with chariots charging at the enemy, and ends on the top row with the king inspecting his prisoners.

Ancient Egypt

The ancient Egyptians formed the first true nation 5,000 years ago. Their civilisation lasted for almost 3,000 years. The pyramids, built 4,500 years ago, are still standing at Giza. They remind us of the skills and wealth of Egypt's ancient civilisation.

Pharaoh and people

The king of Egypt, called the pharaoh, was all-powerful. In fact he was a god to the Egyptians, and had his own temple. Gods and temples were looked after by priests. The priests and officials (called scribes) also ran the government. Below them in society came the farmers, craftsmen and workmen, including slaves. Ordinary people had to work for the pharaoh, building huge palaces and temples, as well as working in the fields.

Although most people were poor, they had holidays and ate well. They could catch fish in the Nile, and hunt birds and animals in the Nile Delta. They also grew crops. The fields were fertilised with mud from the Nile. People used the Nile to water the plants. Farmers grew many different vegetables, grapes for wine, grain to make bread and beer, and flax to make linen clothes. They kept most of the types of animal found on farms today.

▷ The River Nile flooded every year, creating a strip of rich farmland beside it. The surrounding deserts and sea kept Egypt safe from attack.

Mediterranean Sea

Nile Delta

LOWER EGYPT

Giza
Memphis

Nile

• Tell el Amarna

Red Sea

UPPER EGYPT

Valley of the Kings •• Karnak
Luxor

Aswan •

Abu Simbel

▽ The Nile was Egypt's heart and its highway. Here, people take water from the Nile. Boats carry people across the river. Men with nets fish from the riverbank and boats.

Royal riches

This coffin was made for the pharaoh Tutankhamun, who died aged 18 in about 1352BC. It is made of 110 kg of solid gold. The coffin was inside two larger wood coffins, decorated with gold-leaf. When Tutankhamun's tomb was found in 1922 it was full of beautiful treasures, including the throne he used when he became king at the age of nine. Tutankhamun was the only pharaoh whose tomb was not robbed in the centuries after his death.

Life after death

Most of what we know about the ancient Egyptians comes from their tombs. They believed in another life after death, where the dead would need their bodies. So the bodies of important people were preserved, in a complicated process called mummification. The mummy was buried in a stone tomb, along with things that the dead person might need in the afterlife, such as food and money. One pharaoh's tomb contained a model brewery, so he could drink beer in the next life.

Tombs also contained records of the dead person's life, in the form of pictures and writing. Egyptian writing used little pictures as symbols, called hieroglyphics. They also wrote on a form of paper, called papyrus, which they made from reeds.

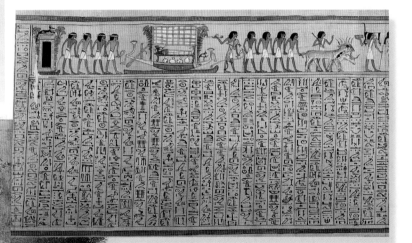

△ This page from the *Book of the Dead* shows the funeral of a man called Ani. Underneath is written a spell to help Ani in the afterlife.

3000 years of civilisation

3100BC	Egypt united by the pharaoh Menes.
2600-2160BC	The Old Kingdom. Pyramids built.
2160-2040BC	Central government breaks down.
2040-1700BC	Middle Kingdom. Egypt united again.
1700-1570BC	Egypt invaded by foreigners.
1570-1070BC	New Kingdom. Egypt at its greatest.
1070-600BC	Egypt broken into small states.
332BC	Egypt conquered by Alexander the Great.

Mesopotamia

For more than 2,000 years, empires rise and fell in Mesopotamia (modern Iraq). Many different peoples came to the region, some as conquerors, some as slaves. There were several empires at different times, but each one was affected by the ideas and customs of the Sumerians.

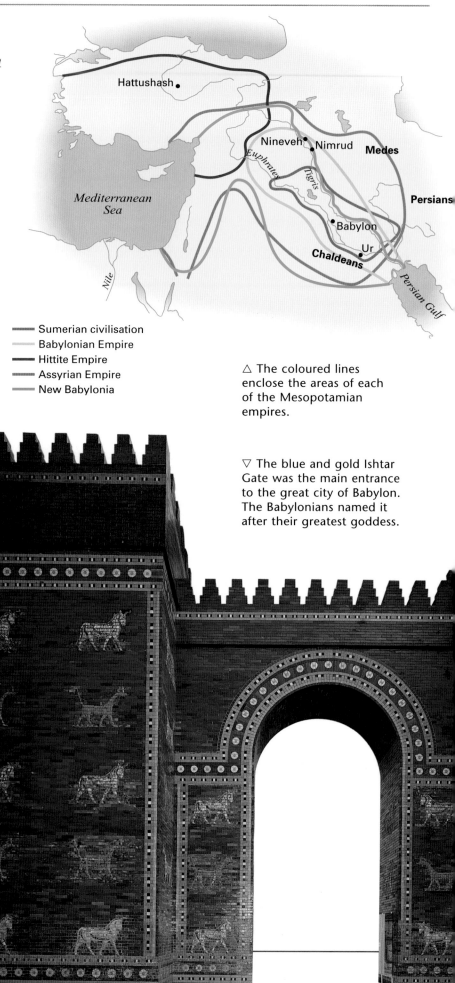

Babylon

The rulers of Babylon took control of many other cities in Mesopotamia. Their empire, Babylonia, was the greatest empire of ancient Mesopotamia. It ruled the whole region only for short periods, but it was never forgotten. It included the old cities of Sumer, and Babylonians inherited Sumerian inventions such as cuneiform writing and wheeled carts. Their arts and crafts were in the same style.

Babylon was built in about 1900 BC on the Euphrates River. It was a beautiful city, famous for its gardens and waterways. Canals were used for transport, and to take water out to the fields. Some were built on causeways, above ground level. Babylon was a rich and busy city, a great centre of trade. Money in the form of silver bars was borrowed and lent. Official records were kept of property and business, and wages were set at fixed rates. The temples of the gods of trade were used for business meetings. To control everything, King Hammurabi, Babylonia's most important ruler (1792-1750 BC), produced a system of laws. These were the first laws ever written down. They were also strict. Many crimes were punished by death.

— Sumerian civilisation
— Babylonian Empire
— Hittite Empire
— Assyrian Empire
— New Babylonia

△ The coloured lines enclose the areas of each of the Mesopotamian empires.

▽ The blue and gold Ishtar Gate was the main entrance to the great city of Babylon. The Babylonians named it after their greatest goddess.

The Hittites

The Hittites came from southern Turkey. They were a warlike people, who used iron weapons, and they were the greatest power in Mesopotamia in about 1400-1200 BC. Although they destroyed Hammurabi's magnificent city, the Hittites were quick to copy Babylonian ideas. They had many skills, and some of them spoke eight languages. They had their own laws, which were less severe than Hammurabi's. But the Hittites were too ambitious. Their empire finally collapsed because they fought too many opponents at once.

Assyria

The black-bearded Assyrians were even more successful warriors than the Hittites. They conquered the Hittites in the 8th century BC, and took over their empire. Their well-trained soldiers were experts in chariot warfare. As they were quite a small nation, they also hired foreign soldiers to fight for them.

▷ The Assyrians were experts at using chariots in battle. They used the same skills when hunting. This carving shows King Ashurnasirpal II hunting lions. It once decorated his palace at Nimrud.

The Assyrians were not just gifted in warfare. Their cities were splendid. The walls of their mighty palaces were covered with sculptures showing the deeds of their kings. In the palace at Nineveh, archaeologists have discovered a large library of clay tablets. Among them was the world's oldest written story, the tale of the hero Gilgamesh.

New Babylonia

As Assyrian power faded, Babylon rose again, ruled by the Chaldeans, from the south. The Babylonian king, Nebuchadnezzar (605-562 BC), completely defeated the Assyrians in 608 BC. The new empire, New Babylonia, lasted for less than 100 years, but it was a brilliant time in Mesopotamian civilisation. The Chaldeans are especially remembered as skilled astronomers. They could tell when an eclipse of the moon would happen.

▷ A silver cup found in the Persian city of Ecbatana. Like other early artists, the Persian silversmiths and goldsmiths were especially good at representing animals.

The Persian empire

The Medes helped the Chaldeans fight the Assyrians. The Medes were one of the Iranian peoples from the east who had often swept into Mesopotamia. Another Iranian people were the Persians. In 547 BC the Persian king, Cyrus, united the Medes and Persians. With amazing speed, he created the largest empire that the world had ever seen. It included all the lands of earlier Mesopotamian empires, and stretched from the Mediterranean to modern Pakistan.

The powerful Persian Empire brought many benefits to its conquered peoples. The most important of these was peace, as the empire was not challenged for 200 years. Farmers could work in their fields without being attacked, merchants traded without fear. Although the Persians were savage in battle, their government was fair and tolerant.

Ancient China and India

Two early centres of civilisation developed in Asia. Like the civilisations in Mesopotamia and Egypt, they depended on the good farming land provided by great river valleys. The centre of the first Chinese civilisation was beside the Huang He. The other civilisation was in the valley of the Indus, in what is now Pakistan.

China

The first cities and states in the valley of the Huang He (Yellow River) were started by powerful families, or dynasties, by about 1600 BC. Very soon there were signs of the beliefs and customs that would continue in China for over 2,000 years. They had a strong belief in law, and a religious respect for their ancestors, whose spirits were supposed to influence the gods. Other early developments were chopsticks to eat with, the use of money, and a system of picture writing. They produced works of art in bronze, ivory and jade (a hard green stone).

Craftsmen were also making fine goods, such as pottery and silk, for which China would be famous 2,000 years later.

Life in the Huang He valley was not peaceful. There were wars between the small city-states, until the Qin dynasty finally united the Chinese people in 221-206 BC. The Qin ruler took the title of emperor, to show he ruled over the lesser kings.

The terracotta army

The first Qin emperor, Shihuangdi, was a harsh and powerful ruler who tried to take his power beyond the grave. Nearly 10,000 soldiers with their weapons and horses guarded his tomb near the Qin capital, Xi'an. But these were not real soldiers. They were life-size models made of baked clay (terracotta). In an amazing discovery, archaeologists found the emperor's tomb and his hidden army in 1974.

The Han dynasty

The Qin dynasty was followed by the Han dynasty (206 BC - AD 220). This was the first 'golden age' of imperial China. China became the most advanced country in the world, and the Han capital, Ch'ang-an, was the world's greatest city. Inventors discovered how to make porcelain and paper. Government officials had to pass examinations, and they ruled well and honestly. Han armies increased the size of the empire, and merchants traded outside its borders.

▽ The Great Wall of China is the largest building in the world. It is over 2,000 km long, 9 metres high and up to 5 metres wide. It was built to stop nomadic tribes in the north raiding China's rich cities and villages. The first Qin emperor strengthened it by joining the parts already built. Thousands of ordinary people were forced to work on it. Many died in accidents or from disease or overwork.

Confucius

Confucius was a great Chinese teacher, who lived about 500 BC. In later times, his teaching became a religion, but what he really taught was how to live in a civilised way. Confucianism was mostly about life on Earth. The Chinese believed in spirits and demons, but they had no all-powerful gods, no heaven or hell.

The Indus Valley

Of all the ancient civilisations, the one in the Indus Valley is the least well known. Although it lasted a thousand years, it was rediscovered only 150 years ago, by engineers building a railway. No one so far has been able to understand its written language. The mud-brick cities, which were built before 2000 BC, are still being studied by archaeologists.

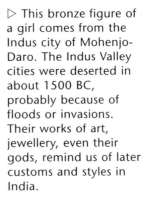

▷ This bronze figure of a girl comes from the Indus city of Mohenjo-Daro. The Indus Valley cities were deserted in about 1500 BC, probably because of floods or invasions. Their works of art, jewellery, even their gods, remind us of later customs and styles in India.

The people of the Indus Valley did not build huge temples or palaces. Their cities were carefully laid out, with roads and sewers. Some houses even had lavatories. Their largest buildings were storehouses for grain, which were huge so their harvests must have been good. They traded crops for copper, and they even had some contact with Mesopotamia. As well as food crops, they also grew cotton – they may have been the first people to do this.

The Mediterranean

The first European civilisation developed on the island of Crete in the middle of the Mediterranean Sea. It is called the Minoan civilisation, after its legendary king Minos. The Minoans were a sea-going people and grew rich through trade.

▽ This wall painting from the palace at Knossos shows acrobats vaulting over the back of a charging bull. This custom was probably connected with a religious ceremony. Bulls were the most powerful animals known, and they played a part in the beliefs of many early peoples.

The Minoans of Crete

The Minoans lived on the fertile island of Crete. They traded with Egypt, Greece and Spain, and although they had no army, their ships ruled the sea. Their biggest city, Knossos, built before 2000 BC, had no city walls, which shows that the Minoans had no fear of invasion. Knossos had space for over 20,000 people, more than lived in Babylon. It had paved roads, and the water and sewage system was even better than in the Indus cities. However, the rich civilisation of the Minoans was forgotten until archaeologists found its remains less than 100 years ago.

We cannot read the Minoan language, so we have to learn about the Minoans from what archaeologists have found in Crete. As well as jewellery and pottery, there are lifelike wall paintings which tell us a lot about Minoan life. We know that the Minoans were ruled by kings, who lived in big, airy palaces. The most important figure in Minoan religion was a goddess. We do not know her name, but she is often pictured holding snakes, which were a sign of long life and good health.

The Phoenicians

The Phoenicians were great seafarers from the coast of Lebanon. Until about 1200 BC they were ruled by powerful neighbours, such as Egypt. They never formed a single state, and their cities, including Sidon and Tyre, had their own rulers.

The Phoenicians were skilful craftsmen and traders. Although their country was small, it was fertile, producing grapes, olives and building timber. The tall cedars of Lebanon supplied timber to Mesopotamia and Egypt. The Phoenicians' most valuable export was a purple dye made from shellfish. They also traded goods from Africa and India. Like the Minoans, they set up colonies around the Mediterranean. The greatest was Carthage in north Africa, which became a great power in the Mediterranean after the Phoenicians' homeland was conquered by the Assyrians in the 7th century BC.

▷ Phoenician craftsmen made this perfume bottle by building it up in coils of molten glass. They may also have been the first to discover how to make glass vessels by blowing into a lump of molten glass on the end of a tube.

◁ The magnificent royal palace at Knossos was five floors high. It had thousands of rooms and covered an area as big as two soccer pitches. It was ruined by a huge volcanic explosion that destroyed the Minoan cities in about 1450 BC.

The first alphabet

The Phoenicians' greatest invention was their writing. They were the first to represent a sound with a single shape, which we would call a letter. This was the basis of our alphabet. Words were made up of several different shapes. This was different from Chinese writing where one shape represents a whole word.

Voyages of trade and exploration

The Phoenicians developed tough little sailing ships, in which their sailors and merchants made long voyages. They sailed as far as Britain to buy tin, and they made long exploring voyages. An Egyptian pharaoh hired them to sail around Africa, though we do not know if the Phoenicians ever completed such a long voyage.

Another Phoenician did sail around the bulge of West Africa and captured some creatures he described as small hairy people. They may have been chimpanzees.

The Mycenaeans and Greeks

Mycenaeans from mainland Greece took over Crete in about 1450 BC. Their civilisation in Greece lasted nearly 300 years, before it was overcome by the invasion of a northern people, the ancestors of the ancient Greeks.

Mycenae

The Mycenaeans were a stronger and more warlike people than the Minoans. They took over the Minoans' trade and colonies, and solid gold objects found in Mycenaean graves tell us they were very wealthy. They were less skilful craftsmen than the Minoans, and their cities were more strongly fortified. Each city had its own king. The kings were supported by landowning warriors, who ruled over the peasants and slaves. Although the cities were separate, in times of trouble they sometimes united. Mycenae, the city which gave its name to the whole people, was smaller than Knossos.

△ A gold mask (made after death) found in a Mycenaean grave by the archaeologist Heinrich Schliemann in 1876. Schliemann liked to think it portrayed the mythical Mycenaean king, Agamemnon.

◁ The Aegean world, about 2000-1200 BC.

The Trojan war

Some historians think that the Mycenaeans went to war with the city of Troy in Asia Minor in the 12th century BC, probably over trade. This may have been the war described by the poet Homer, although he said it began when the Trojans kidnapped a princess. No one knew whether Troy really existed, until archaeologists discovered its remains in the late 19th century. There had been at least nine ancient cities on the site. When one was destroyed, another was built on the ruins. Remains of the different cities are found in layers, with the oldest at the bottom. Homer's Troy was probably the seventh city. Evidence shows that this was destroyed in about 1200 BC, just at the time that the siege in Homer's story took place.

The ancestors of the Greeks

Wars between their cities weakened the Mycenaeans, and so they were unable to stop invasions from the north. Among these invaders were a people known as Dorians, who were ancestors of the Greeks. Although their civilisation was less advanced, the invaders probably had better weapons made of iron. That gave them an advantage over the Mycenaeans, who used bronze. The Mycenaean cities were destroyed, and their treasures vanished. The art of writing was lost, and we know very little of what happened next in Greece, until the rise of Greek civilisation in about the 8th century BC.

▽ In Homer's story, the Greeks captured Troy by hiding some men in a huge wooden horse. They pretended to leave, and tricked the Trojans into hauling the horse inside the city walls.

Homer

The poet Homer, who lived in the 8th century BC, was the first great European writer. His two epics (long stories in verse), the Iliad and the Odyssey, tell the story of the siege of Troy and the adventures of the hero Odysseus (or Ulysses). The Greeks thought of Homer's heroes as their ancestors, but they were probably Mycenaeans. Although Homer was telling stories handed down over centuries, rather than history, we now know that Troy did exist and that there was a Trojan war.

The ancient Greeks

Some Mycenaeans fled from the invaders and settled in Ionia, on the west coast of Asia Minor (Turkey). Here they built strong cities, each ruled by a warrior king supported by nobles. On the Greek mainland, the invaders took over much of the south. Independent cities, with their own kings and gods, were also formed here and throughout Greece. Sometimes a ruthless leader, called a tyrant, seized power, and in many cities a struggle took place between rulers and people. By 500 BC, the ordinary citizens in a few city-states had some power. Athens, the largest city-state, was a true democracy.

People were proud of their own city, and neighbouring cities often made war on each other. But when, in the late 6th century, all of Greece was threatened by the growing Persian Empire, the rival cities, led by Athens and Sparta, joined forces and fought against the Persians. Their victory in this war united the Greeks and encouraged the development of the great civilisation of Classical Greece.

Classical Greece

The history of Western civilisation begins in Classical Greece in the 5th-4th centuries BC. The Greeks invented democracy, most kinds of literature, Western science, and even the Olympic Games. Greek ideas guided Europeans for 2,000 years.

The Greek city-states

The Greek city-states were communities, whose people had their own customs. These people thought of themselves as Greek, and they all spoke the same language, but their first loyalty was to their city. The city-states had different types of government. Sparta had a king and warrior nobles, while Athens was a democracy. Every male citizen who had been born in Athens voted and took part in government. Slaves and women could not vote, but women had some rights, and slaves could become free.

▷ Crowds approach the entrance to the Acropolis, the religious centre of Athens. At top right is the Parthenon, the temple of Athena, patron goddess of the city.

Greek art and architecture

The Greeks developed a wonderful style of architecture, and their sculptors made beautiful works in marble. Some of the buildings are still standing today. Greek pottery was decorated with paintings, often showing scenes from everyday life (below). These pictures are very useful to historians, because they show Greek customs, clothes, furniture, weapons and other objects.

Greek ideas

The Greeks owed many ideas to earlier civilisations. They especially admired Egypt, and they took the alphabet from the Phoenicians. But the Greeks went far beyond these earlier people. Athens produced some of the world's greatest thinkers. Much of their knowledge was new, and has influenced Europe ever since. In subjects like mathematics and biology, the Greeks were the greatest experts in Europe for more than 2,000 years. The ideas of philosophers such as Plato and Aristotle are still studied today. Although wonderful thinkers, the Greeks were not true scientists because they did not do experiments. Many of their ideas were wrong. For example, Aristotle thought that everything in nature is made up of earth, fire, air and water.

△ A marble bust of the philosopher Diogenes, who is said to have lived in a tub as a protest against people's bad behaviour.

Greek literature and theatre

The first true poets and historians were Greeks. That is one reason why we know so much about the Greeks. For the first time we can learn about people from their books. The theatre as we know it began with the great Athenian playwrights of the 5th-4th centuries BC. Aeschylus, Sophocles and Euripides wrote tragedies and comedies that are still performed today.

▽ Actors in Greek plays wore masks. These pottery figures are wearing masks for a comedy. Comic plays made rude jokes about politicians. Actors had different masks for acting in tragedies.

Greek gods

The Greeks had many gods and goddesses, led by Zeus and his family (Athena, goddess of Athens, was one of his daughters). Many were 'adopted' by the Greeks from eastern countries, and others were local gods. In stories the gods had supernatural powers, but also behaved like ordinary people. They quarrelled, told lies and lived everyday lives. To us, these gods are only legends, but most Greeks believed in them. Religious beliefs strongly affected life in Greece. Someone about to make an important decision would first ask a god for advice by going to a prophet, or oracle. There was a famous oracle at Delphi.

The Peloponnesian War

The rivalry between Athens and Sparta ended in a civil war. Every city in the Peloponnese (the southern part of Greece) took part on one side or the other. After nearly 30 years, Athens was defeated, and never recovered. The great days of the city-states were ending. Athens had given up democracy during the war. The Greeks were still not united, and although Persia was no longer a danger, there were others. King Philip of Macedonia, north of Greece, was planning to conquer the city-states.

Alexander the Great

Alexander of Macedonia was a great soldier and leader, who spread Greek influence over a large area. His empire stretched from Greece in the west to India in the east.

Macedonia's ambitions

The Macedonians were related to the Greeks and spoke Greek. However, the Greeks thought they were 'barbarians', which meant foreigners, and not true Greeks. The Macedonians were ruled by a king and a small class of warrior nobles, who trained the citizens into a good army. King Philip, Alexander's father, started taking over the Greek city-states one by one. He was murdered before his plans were complete, but his son Alexander made himself ruler of all the Greeks.

Alexander was the most famous warrior of ancient times. He carried out his father's plan to lead the Greeks against Persia, and launched his invasion in 334 BC, when he was 21. It was the beginning of a campaign that lasted until his death in 323 BC, when he was only 32.

▷ Alexander defeated the Persian king Darius at Issus (now in Turkey). By conquering the Persian empire, he had won most of the world that people in the Mediterranean knew. But Alexander wanted to conquer still more lands.

Alexander's empire

After defeating the Persian king in battle, Alexander marched through Syria into Egypt. There the people welcomed him and called him a god. He defeated the Persians a second time, and their whole empire collapsed. The king was killed by his own men, and Alexander replaced him as ruler.

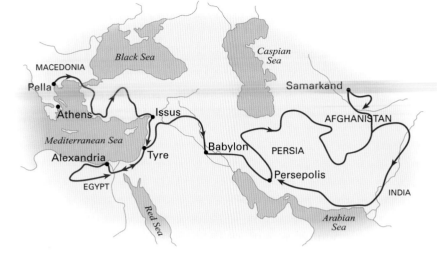

This did not satisfy Alexander. Like all conquerors, he found it difficult to stop, but he was also driven by a desire to learn about the whole world. He marched on across Afghanistan and into north-west India, defeating an Indian prince whose army contained 200 trained elephants. At last, his tired men, who had been fighting for eight years, refused to go further. Alexander agreed to return home, but first he persuaded his men to march down the Indus valley to the ocean, which the Greeks believed circled the Earth. From there he led the long march homewards, but he died in Babylon before he reached Greece.

△ Alexander's conquests depended on good organisation. Although he travelled very far, he was always in touch with Macedonia.

→ route taken by Alexander the Great

The Greek world

Alexander's empire did not last long after his death. The Mauryan kings of eastern India reconquered the Indian lands, and the rest of Alexander's empire was divided among his generals. They founded ruling families in Egypt and the Middle East. Three centuries later, the remains of Alexander's empire became part of the Roman Empire.

Alexander tried to unite the East (the world of the Mesopotamian empires) and the West (Greece and the Mediterranean region). His empire depended on the support of the people of the conquered lands. To win them over he accepted some of their customs himself. He married a Persian princess, and forced thousands of his soldiers to marry Asian women. But he also spread the influence of Greek civilisation. The people in the cities he built followed Greek customs and spoke Greek.

△ After his death Alexander became a legend. One eastern king even had Alexander's victory at Issus carved on the sarcophagus he was buried in. A thousand years after the death of Alexander, stories about him were eagerly read, although they were mostly untrue.

Alexandria

Many cities were founded by Alexander, and named after him. The most famous is Alexandria in Egypt, which became a great centre of learning. Euclid, the founder of geometry, and Archimedes (above), who invented the screw, studied at the city's library. Eratosthenes, who was the chief librarian about 200 BC, measured the size of the Earth.

The Roman Republic

The ideas and customs of Classical Greece passed to the next great Mediterranean power, Rome. Starting as a small city state, over 500 years the Roman Republic won an empire as large as that of Alexander the Great.

The Etruscans

The Etruscans, whose ancestors had come from the East, ruled north-west Italy. In this very fertile land, their kings and nobles grew rich. One city ruled by the Etruscans was Rome. In about 509 BC the Romans rebelled, and threw out the Etruscans. For the next 200 years the Romans were usually at war. They won towns from the Etruscans, and defeated neighbouring peoples, until they became the largest power in Italy.

△ In 218 BC Hannibal, a great Carthaginian general, surprised the Romans by invading from the north. He led his army, including some elephants, across rivers and the Alps.

The Romans could not beat him in battle, but Hannibal could not capture Rome. After 15 years, he was called home to defend Carthage from Roman attack.

The Republic

The Romans did not want another king. They formed a republic, led by two officials called consuls, who were elected every year. The Plebeians, the ordinary people, could vote, but the chief noble families, the Patricians, had the real power. Their representatives made up the powerful Senate, or governing council. The Romans had a strong sense of duty to their family, and also to their state. This made them patriotic and determined warriors. After conquering Italy, they defeated the North African city of Carthage and gained control of the Mediterranean.

▽ The Romans built public baths in every city. Although they liked to keep clean, they also believed in games and fitness. The baths were a kind of sports and social club, where friends or business partners would meet.

Roman religion

The Romans took much of their religion from the Greeks. The Roman god Jupiter is the same as the Greek god Zeus. As well as gods of the state, they worshipped family gods, who looked after the household or the farm.

Rich against poor

Fighting wars helped to keep Romans united, but trouble grew between the rich and powerful Patricians and the poor citizens, the Plebeians. The Plebeians won some victories. They were allowed to elect their own representatives, called tribunes, who formed their own assembly. But in the 2nd century BC the struggle between the classes brought Rome close to chaos. Government broke down, and many people on both sides were murdered. Civil war broke out in the next century between rival generals Marius and Sulla. Sulla won. He was a brutal ruler and no one was able to control him. He ruined the Republic.

◁ The Romans enjoyed cruel sports. Gladiators fought duels to the death, to entertain the Roman people. Sometimes they fought wild animals (left). Gladiators were often slaves or prisoners. There were a huge number of slaves in ancient Rome. At one slave sale, 150,000 people were sold in a day. A rebellion of slaves in 73 BC was crushed with great cruelty, after they had rampaged through southern Italy.

The end of the Republic

By the 1st century BC the Roman army had become the most powerful force in the Republic. It helped give Rome its first emperor. Soldiers in distant places were loyal to their own generals, not to Rome. After Sulla died, other generals struggled for power. The winning general was Julius Caesar, who had conquered Gaul (France) and invaded Britain. He defeated his chief rival, Pompey, and took power. Caesar's rule lasted only five years. He was murdered by a group of jealous senators, who were afraid that he was going to make himself a king. The murder caused another civil war, which was won by Caesar's friend Mark Antony and his nephew, Octavian. The winners then quarrelled. Octavian defeated Antony and became Rome's first emperor, known as Augustus.

▽ Cleopatra, the last queen of Egypt, used her beauty as a weapon in politics. She fell in love with Julius Caesar and they had a son. Later, she fell in love with Mark Antony. The defeat of Antony by Octavian in 31 BC ended Egypt's independence, and Cleopatra killed herself.

The Roman Empire

For 600 years the Romans ruled most of Europe, North Africa, and part of the Middle East. Roman law, ideas and customs influenced European civilisation for more than a thousand years after the Roman Empire had ended.

Roman rule

When they built their empire, the Romans killed many people and destroyed the customs and beliefs of many more. But most people of the conquered lands welcomed Roman rule and their more advanced standard of living. People in lands as far apart as Britain and Palestine were proud to be Roman citizens. Under Roman rule, people enjoyed fair government and peace. Two things especially held the empire together. One was Latin, the Roman language, which was spoken by educated Europeans for centuries. The other was Roman law, which was simple to understand and enforced fairly. In countries such as France, Roman law is still the basis of the legal system. Taxes were not too heavy, and the protection and good government of Rome allowed trade and farming to prosper. However, even the best Roman governors used their power to make themselves rich.

The emperors

Because Roman emperors had enormous power, much depended on their character. Some were fair and intelligent men like Augustus, the first emperor (above). Others were selfish and half-crazy like Nero, the fifth emperor, who was said to have set Rome on fire out of spite. The emperor was supposed to be elected, but in fact he was either the heir of the previous emperor or, in later times, the winner of a struggle between rival generals.

▽ A grand procession through Rome of the treasure taken during the capture of Jerusalem in AD 70.

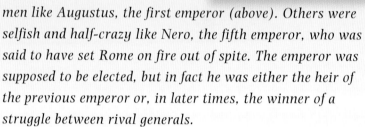

▽ The Roman Empire in AD 117.

BRITAIN
GERMANY
ATLANTIC OCEAN
GAUL
ITALY
SPAIN
Rome
Pompeii
Byzantium
Black Sea
ASIA MINOR
MESOPOTAMIA
GREECE
Carthage
Mediterranean Sea
Jerusalem
AFRICA
Alexandria
LIBYA
EGYPT

— Hadrian's Wall

◁ The Pont du Gard, the great aqueduct over the valley of the River Gard in southern France, was built 2,000 years ago to carry fresh water to the Roman city of Nîmes.

Arts and technology

Roman civilisation owed a lot to the Greeks, but Rome had its own great writers, such as Virgil, Horace and Ovid. Romans were highly skilled, not only at organising an empire, but also in building and engineering. They thought their empire would last forever, and wanted their buildings to last as long. Many of them have lasted to the present day. Roman buildings had arches and domes, and were built with brick and concrete as well as stone. Palaces and rich men's villas had underfloor heating, which was useful in colder provinces such as Britain. The Romans also excelled in some crafts, particularly glass and mosaics.

The beginning of the end

The empire continued to expand until the time of Hadrian (AD 117-138), who decided it was already too big. He used the army for jobs like road building instead of conquest. From the 3rd century, 'barbarian' peoples from the north-east began to settle inside the empire. The imperial government had grown weak, Rome was no longer prosperous and, like all empires, the Roman Empire was running out of energy. It was later divided in two: a Western Empire ruled from Rome, and an Eastern Empire ruled from Constantinople (Byzantium).

The 'Barbarians'

In the 5th century, whole peoples from eastern Europe began to move west. The Huns, who came from furthest east, were the first to start moving. In the end, these 'barbarian' invasions destroyed both the Roman Empire in Europe and the Gupta Empire in India.

The Barbarians and the Romans

The Romans, like the Greeks, called all foreigners 'barbarians'. The Germanic peoples who invaded the empire lived a simple life, but they were not savages. Some had been in contact with Rome for many years. They knew Roman customs and they admired the Empire, especially its wealth. They would have liked to take it over, but they were too disorganised to manage an empire. In the end they helped to destroy it. The movement of peoples from east to west was not new. The Celts in France and Britain had originally come from central Europe.

The Goths

The Goths were a farming people living by the Black Sea when the Huns invaded the region. They were allowed to enter the Roman Empire, but soon fell out with the Romans. In AD 378 they defeated the Romans in battle at Adrianople and killed the emperor Valens. They invaded Italy, but a Vandal general held them back for a while. The Romans could no longer defend themselves, and the Goths captured Rome in AD 410. The Goths were not just a fighting people. They also made beautiful objects like this silver buckle.

▷ The Huns, Visigoths, Ostrogoths and Vandals spread across Europe. The Huns also invaded Persia and India, and pushed European tribes further west. The Angles and Saxons settled in Britain.

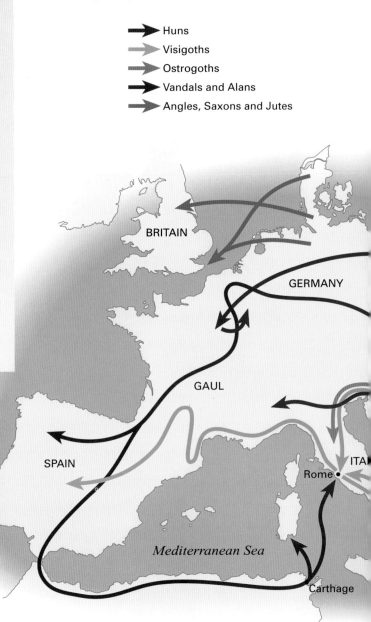

→ Huns
→ Visigoths
→ Ostrogoths
→ Vandals and Alans
→ Angles, Saxons and Jutes

BRITAIN

GERMANY

GAUL

SPAIN

ITA

Rome •

Mediterranean Sea

Carthage

The Huns

The Huns were a group of wandering tribes, who kept cattle but grew no crops. They also lived by hunting and gathering and, sometimes, by raiding settlements. They were brilliant horsemen, and their children learned to ride as soon as they could walk. The 'Black' Huns were the first people to move west in the 5th century, when they spread into eastern Europe, pushing other tribes, such as the Alans and Goths, further west. Another group, the 'White' Huns, turned south and invaded Persia, where they killed the emperor. They moved on into India, where they destroyed Gupta civilisation and set up their own kings. The Huns killed tens of thousands of people, and were renowned for their cruelty.

◁ A Hun horseman. Some people believed that Hun and horse were parts of one animal! The Huns used a short but deadly bow, easy to shoot from a horse. It was made from strips of wood, bone and sinew which had to be glued together when the weather was not too warm or too cold.

The end of Roman Empire

The Vandals, who came from north Germany, invaded Gaul in the early 4th century. They were driven south into Spain by the Visigoths (western Goths), and finally settled in Roman North Africa. They made Carthage their capital, and controlled the Mediterranean. In AD 455 the Vandals sailed across to Italy, captured Rome and took all the treasure they could carry.

Meanwhile, the Huns launched their greatest attack under their leader, Attila. In AD 447 they besieged Constantinople, capital of the East Roman or Byzantine Empire, but they agreed to leave the city for three tons of gold. They conquered much of the Empire and invaded Italy, but disease and hunger forced them out before they could capture Rome. However, they caused enough destruction to finish off the Roman Empire. The last emperor was deposed in AD 476 by Odoacer, a 'Barbarian' general who had at one time fought on Rome's side.

Black Sea

Constantinople

GREECE

▷ This mosaic shows a Vandal outside Carthage in North Africa. Vandal Africa was destroyed by the Byzantine general, Belisarius, in the 6th century

The Byzantine Empire

The Roman Empire in Europe collapsed in the 5th century AD. The Roman Empire in the East, called the Byzantine Empire, survived for a thousand years. It developed into a civilisation that was quite different from Europe.

Byzantium

The Roman emperor Constantine decided to make Byzantium his eastern capital in AD 330, and he changed the city's name to

▷ In Constantinople, Justinian built the Church of St Sophia, the largest and most beautiful Christian church of that time. When the Ottomans captured Constantinople in 1453, they turned St Sophia into a mosque.

Constantinople (now Istanbul). It controlled trade routes between Europe and Asia and, while Rome was getting weaker, it grew into the largest and richest city in Europe. Its massive city walls are still an impressive sight.

The Byzantine emperors still called themselves 'Romans', and dreamed of reconquering Rome's Western Empire. After Odoacer defeated the last emperor of Rome, the Byzantine emperor, Zeno, paid the Ostrogoths to overthrow him. They succeeded, but to Zeno's annoyance, the Ostrogoth leader made himself ruler, and built a fine capital at Ravenna, in north-east Italy.

Orthodox Christianity

Constantine had made Christianity the religion of the Roman Empire, and so Byzantium was a Christian state. Religion was a part of government and of everyday life. The emperor was God's representative. In pictures he was shown with a halo, like a saint. In Europe the Pope led the Roman Catholic Church, but the Church in Byzantium had no religious leader. It used the Greek language, not Latin, and had different ceremonies. Growing arguments about religious customs drove the Roman and Byzantine Churches further apart. In AD 1054 they became completely separate. Byzantium also had its own style of religious art. Its most famous art works are icons (religious images) like this one of the Archangel Michael.

Justinian the Great

Under the Emperor Justinian, called 'the Great' (AD 527-65), the dream of restoring the old Roman Empire almost came true. Belisarius and other Byzantine generals reconquered North Africa, most of Italy and part of Spain. However, the Byzantines spoke Greek instead of Latin, and the Europeans thought they were foreigners, not 'Romans'. The Byzantines soon lost the reconquered lands, and Byzantium steadily lost contact with Europe.

Justinian ruled with his strong and intelligent wife, Theodora. He was the most successful Byzantine emperor, but he was less successful as a ruler after his wife's death. To us, his greatest achievement was not his brief conquests, nor even St Sophia, but his code of law. This preserved the laws which the Romans had made, for the future benefit of Europe.

The empire under siege

The Byzantine Empire was never as strong as it had been under Justinian. In spite of wonderful achievements in art and learning, the Byzantines were not good governors. They did not look after the peasants, who provided their food and fought in their armies. The emperors had many enemies abroad. In the 7th century the empire seemed about to collapse, but it was saved by a great general and emperor, Heraclius, who defeated the Slavs and Persians. But before his death a new, more powerful enemy appeared – the armies of Islam.

△ Byzantine artists were particularly famous for their mosaics. This one shows the Empress Theodora, wife of Justinian, with her attendants and officials.

From the 11th century, Constantinople was failing and its empire shrinking. The Byzantines were still fine artists and scholars. They kept alive ancient learning that Europe had forgotten. But, like ancient Rome a thousand years before, the Byzantines could no longer defend themselves. They had to hire foreign soldiers to help them. The Byzantine Empire finally ended when the Ottoman Turks captured Constantinople after a great siege in 1453. The last emperor died fighting, and a fine civilisation died with him. After the fall of Constantinople, Russia became the leading Orthodox country. The Russian tsars saw themselves as the heirs of the Byzantine emperors.

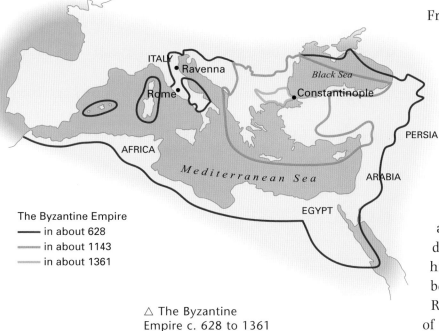

The Byzantine Empire
— in about 628
— in about 1143
— in about 1361

△ The Byzantine Empire c. 628 to 1361

Religion

In history, religion has been one of the strongest influences on the way people think and behave. Most of the world's great religions began 2,000 years ago or more. Only Islam is more recent. All of these religions began in either India or the Middle East.

Hinduism

The oldest of current religions is Hinduism, which developed in India more than 4,000 years ago and spread to south-east Asia. Unlike most other religions, it had no founder or prophet, and no elaborate organisation. Its holy writings, the *Mahabharata* and *Ramayana*, were written more than 1,500 years ago. Hinduism has many different customs and beliefs, and hundreds of different gods. The main teaching of Hinduism is that people should do their work well and honestly, and live a morally good life. In ancient times Hinduism existed in India along with Buddhism and, later, with Islam. There were conflicts between the religions, but people mostly lived together peacefully.

▽ The Great Stupa at Sanchi, India, was begun by the Emperor Asoka, who helped to spread Buddhism. Stupas were Buddhist temples and contained relics.

△ The Hindu god Shiva dances in a circle of fire. Shiva the Destroyer is one of the three aspects of God. The others are Brahma (the Creator) and Vishnu (the Preserver).

Buddhism

Buddhism was founded by Siddhartha Gautama, called the Buddha, a prince who lived in north India about 2,500 years ago. The suffering of ordinary people inspired him to give up his princely life. He spent the rest of his days meditating and teaching. Buddha taught that all living creatures are reborn in another form, so all living things should be respected. The cycle of dying and being reborn ends when a person reaches a state of 'enlightenment'. This means he has overcome all selfish desires. Buddhism developed many different branches. It was eventually absorbed into Hinduism in India, but its teachings spread all over central and eastern Asia, including China and Japan.

Judaism

The Israelites, later called Jews, were a small group of people in Palestine whose religion developed more than 3,000 years ago. The most important idea in Judaism is the belief in a single, all-powerful God, who created the world and everything in it. Prophets, such as Abraham and Moses, told the people about God's instructions. The prophets were the real leaders of the Jews who, for most of their history, were ruled by greater powers such as Babylon and Rome. After Jewish rebellions in the 2nd century AD, most Jews were driven from Palestine and scattered across Europe and the Middle East. They kept their religion during the centuries of exile, but did not regain their homeland until the creation of Israel in 1948.

◁ Christians use a cross as a symbol because Christ was executed on a cross. This cross is made of gold, silver and jewels.

Christianity

Christianity developed as an offshoot of Judaism, following the teachings of a man called Jesus. Jesus Christ was born in about 4 BC ('Christ' means Saviour). His followers believed he was the Son of God. He stood up for the poor and he attacked the Jewish religious authorities. He promised a future kingdom of God, where the poor and humble would be rewarded. His powerful teaching worried the Jewish religious authorities and the Roman rulers, and he was executed in about AD 29. Christians believe that he came back to life and was taken to Heaven. They expect him to return one day to rule over the kingdom of God on Earth. More and more people became Christians, even though they were persecuted in the Roman Empire. However, in AD 313 the Emperor Constantine made Christianity the official religion of the empire. In the next few centuries, Christianity spread all over Europe, governed by a powerful organisation headed by the Pope in Rome.

▽ The prophets taught the Israelites to obey God. In one Bible story, when the Israelites began to worship a foreign god, Baal, the prophet Elijah challenged the priests of Baal, to see if God or Baal could set an altar on fire.

The Ten Commandments

The Ten Commandments were ten rules for living, written in stone. They were said to have been given by God to Moses on the top of Mount Sinai, while the Jews were making their long journey back from exile in Egypt to their homeland in Palestine, in about 1300 BC. The history of the Jews is written in the Old Testament, which also forms part of the Christian Bible.

The Americas

In the Americas civilisation developed later than in Asia and Europe. Different peoples and empires rose and fell in Central America over the centuries, but some traditions were passed on from one people to the next.

American civilisations

The first large cities were built more than 2,000 years ago. They were ruled by powerful kings, supported by warrior-nobles and priests. They appeared in two regions, in Central America and in South America west of the Andes Mountains.

The Olmecs were one of the earliest peoples in Mexico. They grew maize as their main crop, and were skilful sculptors, especially in jade. Their greatest centre, La Venta, was at its most important 900-400 BC. Most of its large buildings were temples, built on earth platforms. Later peoples continued that tradition.

△ This Mayan clay figure is of a god. It was used as an incense burner.

The Golden Age of the Maya

The 6th century AD was a time of wars, and many different peoples established powerful centres in the Americas. The greatest were the Maya, in southern Mexico and Guatemala. Mayan civilisation took its traditions from the Olmecs. It was at its height about AD 300-1000, but it had not completely disappeared when the Spanish arrived in 1520. Mayan cities were centres of religion, and priests controlled much of everyday life. Their huge stone temples in the form of ziggurats were 60 metres high. The cities were independent powers, but were joined by good roads. Most of the people lived in villages, growing crops in fields that they cleared in the forest. The Maya were experts in some subjects, such as astronomy and mathematics. They had an accurate calendar and a written language. But they had no metal tools, and they never used the wheel.

◁ The Olmecs are known for their carving. This axe was made out of jade, for use in religious ceremonies.

The Aztecs

By the 15th century there were two great civilisations in the Americas, the Aztecs in Mexico and Incas in Peru. These were true empires, including different groups of people with different languages. The Aztec capital, Tenochtitlán, was a beautiful place with gardens, towers and canals. It was built on an island in a lake and reached by causeways from the shore. Over 500,000 people lived there. Other people of the Aztec empire lived in farming villages. They produced good crops of maize, although they had no ploughs, carts or animals to pull them. The bloodthirsty Aztec gods needed human victims, so the Aztecs fought many wars to capture prisoners for sacrifice.

▽ Tenochtitlán, the Aztec capital, had large ziggurats which dominated the city like the ones built in ancient Mesopotamia. At the top of the largest ziggurat (on the left) was a pair of temples. One was to the rain god, Tlaloc, the other was to Huitzilopochtli, god of sun and war. The remains of the city are now under the modern Mexico City.

The peoples of North America

The natives of North America lived in thousands of different groups, who spoke hundreds of different languages. The people of the Great Plains in the west were hunters, who lived off the buffalo herds and lived in tepees (tents). In other places, people farmed and lived in permanent villages. Some Pacific-coast people built wooden houses decorated with carvings and paintings, while the Pueblo people of the south-west made houses of adobe (mud bricks). Most peoples were ruled by kings and priests, who were usually the cleverest men of the tribe. They had many gods and spirits of nature, and celebrated festivals with singing and dancing.

The Incas

The Incas controlled most of South America west of the Andes. Their empire included about 8 million people. The chief cities were built high in the Andes mountains, and were connected by paved roads. Relay runners kept the rulers in touch with local affairs. All property belonged to the state, and was shared out among the people. Private life was governed by strict rules. Two people could not marry without government approval. Under Inca law, a blind man had to marry a blind woman. Special help was given to the old and sick, but this was not a 'welfare state'. The rulers, not the people, came first.

The Ancient World

For most of this period, we have no written records. Even after the invention of writing, the records are few and not always reliable. Most of our knowledge depends on the work of archaeologists, who have discovered such things as the remains of ancient cities.

	BEFORE 4000 BC	**4000-3000 BC**	**3000-2000 BC**	**2000-1000 BC**
AMERICAS	**c.14,000** People reach Alaska from Asia and spread to South America by 12,000. **c.6000** A form of maize is grown in Peru and Mexico. **c.6000** Llamas (right) are used as pack animals in Peru. **c.5000** Fishermen in California make large canoes.	**c.4000** North American hunters build temporary villages of grass huts. **c.3500** Pacific fishing villages in South America grow cotton for cloth. **c.3500** Pottery is made from Mexico to Peru. **c.3500** North American hunters use weighted spear throwers.	**c.3000** Most people in Central America live in settled villages. **c.2500** Maize is the chief food crop in Mexico and Central America.	**c.1800** Ancestors of the Inuit settle in Arctic Canada. **c.1800** Temple-towns are built in South America. **c.1100** The Olmec civilisation is established in southern Mexico.
EUROPE	**c.38,000** Human beings reach southern Europe. **c.20,000** Hunters paint animals on cave walls in France and Spain. **c.10,000** Shelters are made of animal bones in Russia. **c.5000** Farming spreads from the Middle East.	**c.4000** Stone graves are made in Britanny, France. **c.4000** Crop-growing begins in Britain and Ireland. **c.3500** Ploughs are used in parts of Europe. **c.3500** Farmers in Germany build wooden houses on stilts.	**c.3000** Objects are made of bronze, cast in moulds in the Mediterranean region. **c.3000** The stone village of Skara Brae is built in the Orkney Isles, Scotland. **c.2700** The building of Stonehenge (left) begins in England. **c.2200** Bronze becomes common through most of Europe.	**c.2000** The Minoan civilisation begins in Crete and lasts until c.1450. **c.1600** The Mycenaean civilisation begins in Greece and lasts until c.1200. **c.1200** Celts from central Europe move to the west.
ASIA and OCEANIA	**c.6000** Signs of farming exist in the Indus valley. **c.6000** Pigs are kept in northern China. **c.5000** Farmers in south-east Asia and China learn to grow rice. **c.5000** Hand-painted pottery is made in central China.	**c.4000** Fruit trees are grown in northern China. **c.4000** Large villages in northern China are laid out according to a plan. **c.4000** Chinese craftsmen develop new kinds of pottery.	**c.3000** Chinese farmers use ploughs. **c.3000** Chinese potters increase production with the potter's wheel. **c.3000** Metal objects are made in south-east Asia. **c.2400** Towns appear in the Indus valley. **c.2200** Farm animals in the Indus valley include zebu (hump-backed cattle).	**c.1760** The rich Shang kingdom exists in Henan, China, and lasts until c.1125. **c.1500** Polynesian settlers reach Tonga and Samoa by boat (left). **c.1500** Elaborate bronze vessels are made in Shang China. **c.1450** The Indus valley towns are destroyed by earthquakes and invasion.
AFRICA and MIDDLE EAST	**c.40,000** Human beings (*homo sapiens*) are living in Africa. **c.8000** The first city of Jericho is built. **c.7500** Houses of mud bricks are made in Mesopotamia. **c.6000** Herdsmen tame wild cattle in North Africa. **c.6000** Channels are dug to water crops, cloth is woven for clothes and clay pots are made for cooking. **c.5500** The first metal tools (copper) are made in Mesopotamia. **c.5000** People in the Nile valley (Egypt) grow grain and keep animals.	**c.4000** Dams and reservoirs are made in Iran. **c.4000** Mesopotamian farmers use simple ploughs (left). **c.4000** Sharp stone knives with bone handles are made in Egypt. **c.3500** Large temples are built in Mesopotamia. **c.3500** Sailing boats are used on the Nile. **c.3200** The Sumerians develop the earliest form of writing. **c.3100** Menes unites Upper and Lower Egypt as one kingdom.	**c.3000** The wheel is in use for transport in Mesopotamia. **c.2800** People bury their dead at Zimbabwe, south-east Africa. **c.2700** Pyramids (below) are built as tombs for Egyptian kings. **c.2600** Egypt trades with the Middle East.	**c.2000** Some iron tools and weapons are made. **c.1780** Hammurabi publishes his laws. **c.1780** The Hyskos, foreign kings, rule Egypt until c.1550. **c.1600** The Hittites capture Babylon. **c.1400** The Phoenicians develop an alphabet. **c.1100** The Hebrews leave Egypt and return to Palestine.

Thanks to modern science, we can find out surprising details about people's lives in these far-off times, even what they ate and what illnesses they had. But some things we will never know.

1000–500 BC

c.1000 Olmec sculptors make mysterious, giant-size stone heads (below).
c.850 Chavin de Huantar becomes a big religious centre in Peru.
c.700 The Olmecs leave their chief city of San Lorenzo.
c.600 The Oaxaca civilisation replaces the Olmecs.

c.800 Homer composes the *Iliad* and the *Odyssey* in Greece.
776 The first Olympic Games are held.
c.600 Greek merchants settle at Marseilles, France.
509 The Romans create their republic.
508 Democratic government begins in Athens.

c.1000 Invaders called Aryans spread across northern India.
c.1000 The people of the Jomon culture produce the first-known works of Japanese art.
557 King Cyrus unites the Medes and the Persians.

c.940 King Solomon of Israel builds the first temple in Jerusalem.
c.900 The kingdom of Kush is created in the Sudan.
c.900 Clay heads (left) are made by the people of the Nok culture in Nigeria.
814 The Phoenicians found Carthage in North Africa.
c.600 King Nebuchadnezzar builds the Hanging Gardens of Babylon (right).

500 BC–AD 1

c.500 The Zapotecs, successors of the Oaxaca, begin their ceremonial capital of Monte Albán, southern Mexico.
c.300 The Maya population in Central America begins to increase sharply due to improved farming methods.

479 The Greeks defeat a Persian invasion.
438 The Parthenon is built in Athens.
431 The Peloponnesian War begins, ending with Athens defeated in 404.
49 Julius Caesar conquers Gaul.
27 Augustus become the first Roman emperor.

c.480 Two great religious leaders die: Buddha (below) in India, Confucius in China.
322 Chandragupta founds the Mauryan empire in India.
221 The Qin dynasty unites China.
110 The Chinese open the Silk Road across central Asia.

332 Alexander the Great conquers Egypt. In 331 he conquers the whole Persian empire.
c.300 Jewish traders settle in Egypt and Syria.
c.300 The library of Alexandria, Egypt, is founded.
c.300 Bantu-speaking tribes from West Africa begin to spread east and south.
168 The temple in Jerusalem is destroyed by Syrian rulers of Israel.
146 The Romans conquer Carthage.

AD 1–500

c.100 Teotihuacán becomes the largest centre in Mexico.
c.200 The Maya begin to use a form of writing (right).
c.250 The Maya come under the rule of godlike kings and build huge stone temples.

69 The Emperor Vespasian begins building the Colosseum (below) in Rome.
79 The Roman town of Pompeii is buried by a volcano.
117 The Roman empire reaches its greatest extent.
410 Alaric and the Goths capture Rome.
476 The last Roman emperor in the West is deposed.

c.100 The Chinese learn how to make paper.
c.100 The first people settle in Hawaii.
c.150 Buddhism spreads in China.
220 The Chinese empire is divided after the end of the Han dynasty.
c.350 The Huns begin invading India.
c.480 The Gupta empire in India begins to break up.

133 Jews flee to other countries after a failed rebellion.
c.200 An Arab people in Jordan build Petra (right) in Greek style.
330 Constantinople becomes the capital of the Eastern Roman (Byzantine) empire.
396 St Augustine, Christian teacher, becomes Bishop of Hippo in Algeria.
c.400 The empire of Aksum controls most of highland Ethiopia and the Blue Nile valley.
400 The Huns invade Iran.
c.430 The Vandals settle in North Africa.

500–600

c.550 Mayan civilisation reaches its greatest development.

527 Justinian becomes Byzantine emperor and regains much of the old empire in the West.

535 The last Gupta ruler in India dies.
581 China is reunited under the Sui dynasty.
571 Prince Shokotu begins to organise the imperial government in Japan.
594 Buddhism becomes the chief religion of Japan.

c.570 Nubia, in north-east Africa, becomes Christian.
579 The Sassanid Empire of Persia reaches its greatest extent.

Who's Who

Alexander the Great (356-323 BC), king of Macedon. He led a Greek army against the Persians and in 13 years conquered an empire that stretched from Greece to India. His empire did not last long after his death, but it spread Greek ideas in Asia and brought Eastern influences into the Mediterranean world.

Archimedes (died 212 BC), Greek inventor. He invented a water pump which used the principle of the screw. Another famous discovery, made in his bath, was the 'Archimedian principle', that the weight lost by a body in water equals the weight of the water the body displaces.

Aristotle (384-322 BC), Greek philosopher. He had a school in Athens and was for a time tutor to Alexander the Great. He lectured and wrote on many subjects, from plays and poetry to politics and plant life. He is still considered one of the world's greatest thinkers, nearly 2,000 years after his death.

Augustus (63 BC-AD 14), first Roman emperor. Born Octavian, he was the nephew and heir of Julius Caesar. He became ruler of the Roman world after defeating his rival, Mark Antony, and was given the title Augustus ('Exalted') by the Senate in 27 BC. His reign was a golden period, especially for literature and architecture.

Caesar, Julius (100-44 BC), Roman ruler. He conquered Gaul (France) and invaded Britain (55 and 54 BC). The most powerful man in the empire, he marched into Italy (49 BC) against orders from the Senate. He defeated his rival, Pompey, and became dictator. He was murdered by a group of jealous noblemen.

Cleopatra (69-30 BC), queen of Egypt. She was supported by the Roman leader, Julius Caesar, and later by his chief supporter, Mark Antony. At the battle of Actium (31 BC), her ships deserted Antony, who was defeated by the forces of Octavian (Augustus). Having failed to win over Octavian, she killed herself.

Constantine (died AD 337), Roman emperor. He became sole emperor in 324 after defeating several rivals. He founded an eastern capital of the empire at Byzantium, renaming it Constantinople after himself. He made Christianity a legal religion, calling the Council of Nycaea (AD 325) to settle differences in Christian beliefs.

Cyrus the Great (died 529 BC), founder of the Persian empire. After uniting the Medes and the Persians, he conquered Babylon in 539 BC. He was more generous than most conquerors and allowed the Jews, held captive in Babylon, to return home. His dynasty, the Achaemaenids, ruled the huge Persian empire until 331 BC.

Heraclius (died AD 641), Byzantine (East Roman) emperor. The Byzantine Empire was in a state of collapse when Heraclius became emperor in 610. He built up the amy and in six years defeated all enemies, including the Persians, who had almost captured the city. In the 630s he was unable to stop new invaders, the Arabs.

Hadrian (AD 76-138), Roman emperor from 117. Travels throughout the empire convinced him that it was too large to defend. He fixed its eastern border at the River Euphrates and its northern border at Hadrian's Wall in Britain. He admired Greek civilisation, and built many fine buildings in Rome and other places.

Hannibal (247-183 BC), Carthaginian general. In 218 BC he invaded Italy by crossing the Alps from Spain with an army including elephants. He defeated the Romans in Italy, but could not capture Rome. After 15 years in Italy, he returned to defend Carthage from a Roman attack and was defeated at the battle of Zama (202 BC).

Hippocrates (died 377 BC), Greek doctor. Called the 'father of medicine', he lived on the island of Cos and his taught students to rely on facts and examination. Most of what we know of him is legend, and he may not be the author of the ancient code of good behaviour for doctors called the 'Hippocratic oath'.

Justinian (AD 483-565), Byzantine (East Roman) emperor. With his wife Theodora, he reigned over a brilliant court. He is remembered best for his collection of Roman law and his buildings, especially the Church of St. Sophia. His generals and his barbarian allies won back most of the western empire for a short time.

Pacal (AD 603-683), Mayan king of Palenque, 615-683. During the reign of Pacal and his son, Palenque controlled many other Mayan cities. Fine buildings were erected in Palenque, including a 20-metre tower. Pacal, who was only 5 feet tall, was still leading his army when he was 70.

Pericles (died 429 BC), leader of Athens. His intelligence and character made him the greatest man in Athens, and the brilliant artists he employed made the city more beautiful. He foresaw the coming war with Sparta (431 BC) and made plans for it that were at first successful, though he died of plague before it began.

Ptolemy (2nd century AD), Greek scholar of Alexandria. The study of astronomy and geography in Europe was based on his writings until the 16th century. He believed that the Earth is the centre of the universe, and thought it smaller than it really is. This influenced Columbus's voyage to America in 1492.

Rameses II (?1290-1224 BC), king of Egypt. One of the greatest warrior pharaohs, he is remembered for his war against the Hittites in Syria, and for his massive buildings. They included the Temple of Amun at Karnak, the largest religious building in the world, and the Temple of Abu Simbel, with giant statues of himself.

Taharqa (reigned 690-664 BC), king of Egypt. He belonged to the 25th Dynasty, Kushites from Nubia in the south. Taharqa reigned during a period of prosperity, and he built many temples and monuments. Growing rivalry with Assyria led to defeat soon after his death, and the Kushite kings gave up Egypt.

THE
MIDDLE
AGES

The Arabs and Islam

In the 7th century a new power appeared in the Middle East – the Arabs. They were inspired by the teachings of the Prophet Muhammad, and conquered an empire larger than the Roman Empire.

Muhammad and Islam

Muhammad was born in the 6th century in Arabia. Arabia was mostly desert, with many small towns built beside oases. Muhammad grew up in Mecca, which was a great trading city. Muhammad believed he was inspired by God to create a new religion. His message was this: there is only one God (Allah), and Muhammad is his prophet. Muhammad's teachings annoyed Mecca's wealthy merchants. He and his followers were attacked, and Muhammad was forbidden to preach. So in 622 they moved to the rival city of Medina. This journey is called the Hejira. It marks the beginning of Islam. In the Muslim calendar it is year 1.

Islam is not just a religion, it is a whole way of life, with people united by their faith in Allah. The followers of Islam are called Muslims. The teachings of Muhammad are recorded in the Koran, the holy book of Islam. After Muhammad's death (632), the Arabs set out to conquer the Middle East and North Africa for Islam. Many peoples, including the Christians of Egypt and Syria, welcomed Arab rule, which was not harsh. People of different religions were not usually persecuted.

◁ This is the courtyard of the great mosque at Damascus in Syria, first built in 705-715. Muslims soon developed their own type of religious building, with a dome, minaret (a tower for calling people to prayer) and a large space inside for prayer.

The spread of Islam

The leader of Islam was called the caliph. He was a ruler as well as a religious leader. There were quarrels about who should be caliph, and in 656 the third caliph was murdered. Islam then split into two branches, Sunni and Shi'a. After a civil war, the Umayyads in Syria took control. They ruled from Damascus for nearly 100 years.

The Abbasid family, with Shi'ite support, overthrew the Umayyads in 750. They shifted the centre of Islam from Syria to Iraq, and moved the capital to Baghdad. Islam was no longer an Arab empire. Other peoples, especially Persians, played leading parts. The army became a force of trained slaves, called Mamelukes. The caliphs grew more powerful. There were roughly four classes of people in Islam. At the top were Arab Muslims, followed by non-Arab Muslims, then people of other religions and, at the bottom, slaves.

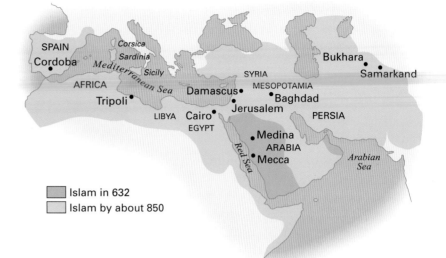

Islam in 632
Islam by about 850

The golden age of Islam

Under the caliphs, a brilliant new civilisation developed. With its libraries and observatories, Islam was superior in knowledge to Christian Europe. Its scholars studied the learning of ancient Greece, as well as Egypt, the Middle East and Asia. It was also better governed, and less intolerant. Every Muslim who could afford it had to go on a pilgrimage to Mecca, and merchants travelled to India and China to buy luxuries. On these journeys they learned more about the world. Islam also produced fine new styles in art and architecture.

△ Although Islam grew by conquest, many peoples welcomed it.

▷ Islamic scholars wrote beautiful books by hand and artists illustrated them with intricate miniature paintings. Islamic art was a mixture of Arab, Turkish and Persian traditions.

Court life

Some of the stories of the 'Arabian Nights' are set in the court of Harun ar-Rashid. At his court could be seen the most amazing riches, like this silver bowl (below), and the finest musicians, artists and scholars in the world. Islamic craftsmen invented a brilliantly painted new form of pottery, called 'lustreware'.

The last caliph

After the death of the Abbasid caliph Harun ar-Rashid (809), the empire began to break down. By the 10th century the caliphs had little power. A branch of the Umayyad family set up their own caliph in Spain. The Shi'ite Ismailis conquered Egypt and built Cairo. The Seljuk Turks captured Baghdad in 1055. The last Abbasid caliph was thrown out by the Mongols in 1258.

The Rise of the Chinese Empire

Under the early Tang emperors, the Chinese Empire grew larger and richer than it had been under the Han. Although Tang rule ended in chaos, Chinese civilisation flourished again during the Song dynasty.

The Tang dynasty

After many years of civil war and foreign rule, China was reunited by the Sui emperors (581-618), followed by the Tang (618-906). The Tang dynasty was the most successful in ancient China. The emperor was called the 'Son of Heaven'. He strengthened his control by using loyal, trained officials to run the central government, rather than untrustworthy nobles. Tang emperors had the Great Wall repaired, and enlarged the empire far into central Asia, until they were stopped by the Arabs in 751. There was one female Tang ruler, the Empress Wu.

▽ This beautiful horse with a polo player shows the skill of Tang artists. It is made of porcelain. The Chinese loved horses, and had figures like this buried with them. As early as the 1st century BC, Chinese emperors sent expeditions to buy horses from breeders in central Asia.

The Tang capital, Ch'ang-an, was the world's largest city. There you might see monks from Tibet, merchants from Arabia, and travellers from the Middle East, Korea and Japan. The population of China grew. According to a census it was over 50 million by 754. Country people were better off than they had been before, although landlords held complete power over the peasants. A series of rebellions by the peasants eventually destroyed the Tang dynasty, and China split into many small kingdoms.

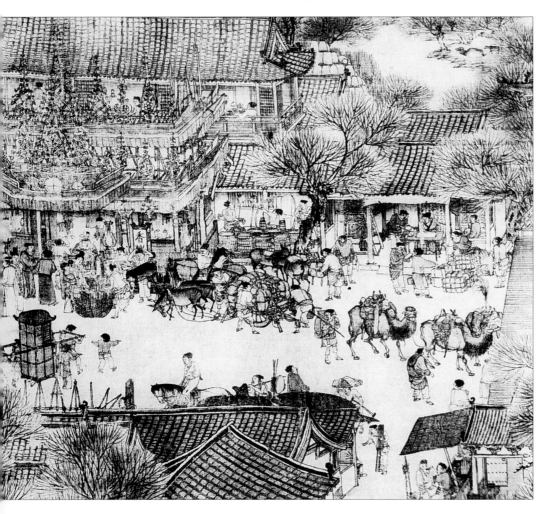

◁ This busy street in a Chinese city was drawn in about 1100. Chinese cities were large. Over a million people lived in Hangzhou. It took 200 tonnes of rice a day to feed them all.

The Silk Road

Chinese craftsmen produced beautiful goods, such as silk fabric, which people wanted to buy. As a result, trade developed between China and other countries. From the 3rd century BC to the 15th century AD, China was linked to the west by the Old Silk Road. This long and dangerous road stretched from the Great Wall to Iran. It passed along the edge of the Takla Makan Desert, 1,000 km of nothing but sand, then crossed the Tian Shan mountain range. One branch went south, over the high Pamir Mountains into India. Traders from many countries met along the Road.

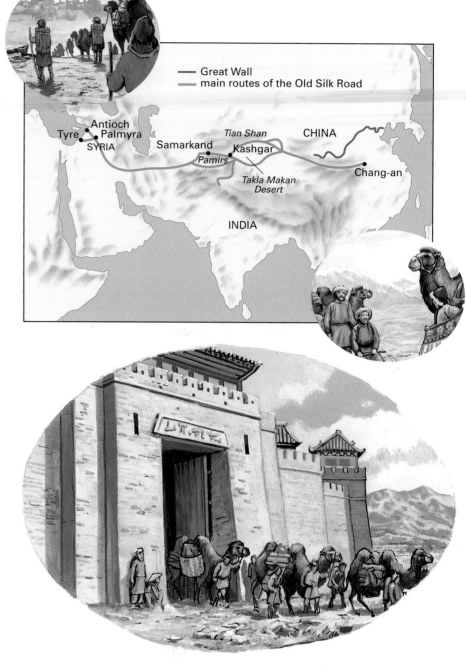

Buddhism

Buddhism became very popular in China during the hard times before the Sui reunited the country. Buddhists built tens of thousands of temples and monasteries. Buddhism was so popular that it threatened the old religions of Confucianism and Taoism, and even the power of the emperor. In 845 the Emperor Wu Zong closed many temples and monasteries. This harsh treatment soon stopped, as Buddhism no longer threatened the emperor's rule.

The Song dynasty

Fifty years after the end of the Tang dynasty, the Song reunited the small kingdoms of China. This was a wonderful age for poetry, arts and learning. The blue-and-white pottery which later became popular in Europe, was just one new development. Among the others were landscape painting and calligraphy (the art of writing with an ink brush). Chinese knowledge of science was also advanced: books were printed, and engineering and medicine were taught in government schools. Water-powered machines were used in industry, and two crops of rice each year kept the Chinese well fed.

Although it had gunpowder, Song China (960-1279) was not a great military power. The empire was far smaller than under the Tang. After 1127 the Song lost control of the north, and in 1279 China was conquered by the Mongols.

△ Goods passed along the Silk Road from China to Central Asia. From there, they went to the Mediterranean and, in the end, reached European markets. On the way they were bought and sold several times. Above, a gate in the Great Wall, and scenes of caravan travel.

The Rulers of Japan

The Japanese were never invaded, for they lived on islands, protected by the sea. Although the Japanese learned many of their customs from China, their civilisation was very different.

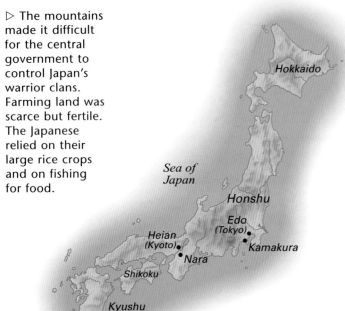

▷ The mountains made it difficult for the central government to control Japan's warrior clans. Farming land was scarce but fertile. The Japanese relied on their large rice crops and on fishing for food.

▽ The Kamakura Buddha is over 13 metres high, and made of bronze. Buddhism, especially the form called Zen, was a powerful influence on Japanese civilisation.

Emperors and shoguns

Japan has had a monarchy for longer than any other country. The first emperor of Japan lived over 2,000 years ago. However, a system of central government began only under Prince Shotoku Taishi (572-622), based on the system in Tang China. At this time most Japanese lived in the southern islands. Another people, the Ainu, lived in the north. Their descendants still do.

Shotoku made Nara the capital. He also encouraged Buddhism, which became a great influence on Japanese civilisation, though it never destroyed the older religion, Shinto. In 794, the Emperor Kammu moved the government to Heian (Kyoto), to get away from the Buddhists in Nara. But there it fell under the influence of powerful clans. For many centuries these mighty families provided the real rulers of Japan, the 'shoguns'. Shoguns were military rulers. The emperor was supposed to be a god, but in reality he had very little power over his people.

Japanese arts

The nobles had plenty of leisure time, which they used to practise and enjoy the arts. They wrote poetry in beautiful script, which they learned from the Chinese, and illustrated it with delicate landscape painting. Under Buddhist influence, the Japanese made art forms out of such activities as paper folding (origami) and gardening. Gardens made from rocks and pebbles, with no plants, were designed as a picture to be seen from the house. Japan's special form of theatre was the Nō drama. Nō plays were like ceremonies, with dancing and chanting. Actors wore masks, and there was no scenery.

△ A Kabuki play. Theatre was one of the liveliest Japanese arts. Besides the Nō drama, more popular plays developed in the towns in the 17th century. Kabuki was one form. Bunraku was another, involving puppets.

Japanese and Europeans

Europeans first visited Japan in 1543. By then the Ashikaga shogunate had collapsed, and Japan was ruled by local lords, called 'daimyo'. The daimyo were amazed by European technology, especially guns which they were eager to buy. European missionaries converted many people to Christianity. Soon after this, Japan was reunited by three great daimyo. One of them, Tokugawa Iyeasu, set himself up as a shogun in 1603 and ruled all Japan. He distrusted all foreign ideas, drove out the Europeans and even killed many Japanese Christians, after they rebelled against him.

The samurai

'Samurai' means a servant. A samurai was a warrior. Like a knight in Europe, he fought for his local lord. His life was controlled by a strict code of behaviour, called 'bushido', which was influenced by Zen Buddhism. Honour, loyalty and courage were the great samurai virtues. A samurai preferred death in battle to surrender. A samurai who lost his honour would kill himself with his own sword. Under the Tokugawa, samurai became officials and governors, as well as warriors, but their code of behaviour lived on.

Mauryan and Gupta India

India is protected by sea and the Himalayan Mountains. Invaders could reach it only from the north-west. Over the centuries, many conquerors entered by that route and won empires in northern India.

The Mauryan Empire

Soon after Alexander's invasion of India in 327 BC, Chandragupta Maurya became king of Magadha, a large kingdom in the valley of the Ganges. He made it the centre of a huge empire. Under Mauryan rule, farmers and villagers lived well. Trade grew because good roads were built, including the main highway of northern India, later called the Grand Trunk Road. Mauryan government was well-organised. A good system for collecting taxes meant that the emperor did not have to make war to gain treasure. The greatest Mauryan ruler was Asoka (273-232 BC), Chandragupta's grandson. He was a great warrior, but he grew tired of killing, and became a peace-loving Buddhist. Along the roads Asoka planted banyan trees to give shade, and stone pillars, beautifully decorated and inscribed with his laws and messages of goodwill and justice.

▷ Empires in ancient India covered a different area from the modern state. Asoka's empire stretched from Afghanistan to the Bay of Bengal.

⬭ Mauryan Empire in about 232 BC
▢ Gupta Empire in about 410
— Mauryan highway

▽ A farming village in Gupta times. Carts like this were used by the Indus Valley people 4,000 years ago. They are still used today.

△ This sculpture from a Hindu temple shows the god Vishnu sleeping on the serpent-god Ananta.

The Gupta Empire

After Asoka, the Mauryan Empire broke up into smaller states. A new empire was created by the Guptas in the 4th-6th centuries AD. This was the 'golden age' of Indian civilisation. Magnificent temples were built. Dancing and music flourished, and sculpture and painting were at their best. Great literature was written in Sanskrit, the ancient Indian language. Mathematicians used algebra and invented the decimal system. They first had the idea of a number 0, or zero. Hinduism influenced a new form of Buddhism, called Mahayana. It was less strict and more open to new ideas. Although the Gupta Empire was destroyed by the Huns in the 6th century, the Gupta civilisation lived on in India.

Castes

The Hindu caste system was based on religious beliefs. Hindus believed that when the world was created, everyone was divided into four classes. The Brahmin were priests and scholars, the Khatriya were warriors and princes, the Vaishya were craftsmen and merchants (like the man weighing his goods, above), and the Sudra were the labourers. The caste system began in Mauryan times, and later many more castes developed. The poorest people had no caste. They were the 'untouchables'. It was almost impossible for a person to change his caste, or marry someone of another caste. This kept people in their place, but it also gave them a sense of belonging.

The Muslims in India

Arabs had traded with eastern Indian states for centuries. They built mosques there in the 9th century. Much later, Islam reached north India from central Asia. An Afghan conqueror, Muhammad of Ghor, made himself sultan of Delhi in about 1200. The Delhi sultans were the greatest power in India for the next 200 years, but this was not a true empire. It was made up of independent states which paid taxes to the rulers in Delhi. Muslim rule almost ended Buddhism in India, but Muslims and Hindus lived together, although not always peacefully. The Delhi of the sultans was destroyed by the Mongols, who captured the city in 1398.

Southern India

Once, most of India was occupied by people sometimes called 'Dravidians'. The invaders of northern India pushed many of them south. Here they formed independent kingdoms, such as the Tamil states in the far south, and the Cheras in Kerala. These Hindu kingdoms often fought each other. Many Indian ideas and customs spread from south India to Sri Lanka, Myanmar (Burma) and south-east Asia.

Medieval Africa

Africa was a continent of villages, towns and small kingdoms. Many people lived around the coasts and in the Sahel, the region south of the Sahara Desert and north of the tropical forest. In West Africa, large empires rose and fell, while rich city states developed along the east coast.

West African empires

Most African peoples south of the Sahara were farmers and cattle herders. A wide variety of crops was grown, and new crops from Asia and elsewhere spread quickly through the continent. Cattle and other animals were kept in many different regions and climates.

Most African kingdoms were small. However, several African kingdoms became so powerful that they conquered their neighbours and created large empires. In West Africa there were three different empires, but they did not exist at the same time. When one kingdom grew weak, another one took over. The first West African empire was called Ghana. Its power was greatest in about the 10th century.

Attacks by Muslims from the north ruined Ghana. In the 13th century it was replaced by the larger empire of Mali. Because Mali's rulers were Muslims themselves and had a strong army, the danger from northern Muslims ended. Visitors reported that Mali was rich and peaceful, with little crime, but in the 15th century it too was conquered. The new empire belonged to the Songhay, former subjects of Mali, from Gao on the Niger. Theirs was the largest African empire yet.

▷ African states had no clear borders, and government control grew weaker far from their centres. The three great West African empires existed at different times. Another large empire, Kanem-Borno, lay to the east of Songhay. The ports on the east coast had Muslim rulers, and grew rich on trade with Arabia and the Middle East.

◁ Sculpture was the finest of the African arts. The bronze heads from Benin (Nigeria) are especially famous. This one was made in the 16th century.

⬭ Ghana
⬭ Mali
⬭ Songhay
⬭ Kanem-Borno

⬭ Karanga
— trade routes

Trade across the Sahara

The riches of the West African rulers came from gold. When Sultan Musa of Mali made the pilgrimage to Mecca, he took 1.5 tonnes of gold for travel expenses! Gold was traded for salt from the Sahara salt pans. Salt was very difficult to get so it cost as much as gold. Merchants from North Africa brought cloth, horses and iron weapons across the Sahara in exchange for gold and slaves, which they sold in the Mediterranean region. Even European kings who had never heard of Africa had coins made from West African gold. Most Africans used other objects, such as cowrie shells or pieces of iron, as money.

◁ This extraordinary church was carved out of solid rock by early Christians at Lalibela in Abyssinia (modern Ethiopia) before 1000. Abyssinia became a Christian country as early as the 4th century, when missionaries from Syria converted the king to Christianity. The country remained an independent, Christian kingdom until the 20th century.

▽ Many people crossed the Sahara in ancient times. Traders joined together in large groups called caravans, with hundreds of camels carrying their goods. They travelled in caravans to protect them from attack by the blue-veiled Tuareg, the roving nomads of the desert.

Great Zimbabwe

These stone buildings, built 700 years ago, are the ruins of Great Zimbabwe in what is now modern Zimbabwe. The outer wall was built of granite blocks. It was 250 metres long and up to 10 metres high. When it was built Great Zimbabwe was the centre of the Karanga trading empire. As in West Africa, gold was the reason for its wealth. The gold was mined by women in mines deep in the forest. After it was refined, the gold was carried down to the coast and shipped to trading ports such as Sofala.

The Birth of European Nations

Between the 5th and 10th centuries, European tribes formed Christian kingdoms ruled by warrior kings. The most successful were the Franks. Their king Charlemagne created an empire that was the foundation for some of the nations of Europe today.

land inherited by Charlemagne in 771
additional land gained by Charlemagne by 814

△ Charlemagne fought Lombards in Italy, Saxons in Germany, Muslims in Spain, and many others.

Charlemagne and the Pope

Charlemagne united the Franks under his rule in 771, and increased his empire by wars of conquest. He was a skilful ruler as well as a great conqueror. He forced the people he conquered to become Christians. His court at Aachen became the centre of learning and art in Europe. The greatest authority in medieval Europe was the Church, headed by the Pope in Rome. The Church expected everyone to follow its teaching. It owned a lot of land, and the Pope had great authority, but he had no army. He needed an ally, a powerful ruler who would support the Church, with force if necessary. The Pope found that ally in Charlemagne.

On Christmas Day 800, the Pope crowned Charlemagne Emperor in Rome. He became a ruler like the old Roman emperors, although his was a Christian empire.

◁ The first great revival of European art since Roman times took place under the Frankish kings (called Carolingians). This ivory sculpture was made as part of a book cover, in about 800.

▷ The finest buildings in Europe were the monasteries that followed the rule of St Benedict (480-547). The largest was at Cluny, in France. Only one tower of the old building survives.

After Charlemagne

After Charlemagne died (814), his empire was split up among his descendants. The two biggest parts later became the nations of France and Germany. The idea of a Christian empire lived on. In the 10th century the German king, Otto I, was crowned by the Pope. He took the title Holy (meaning 'Christian') Roman Emperor, though he controlled only what is now Germany and Italy. The title was held by German kings for nearly 1,000 years.

The Anglo-Saxons

In the 5th and 6th centuries Angles, Saxons and other tribes from northern Germany invaded England. They formed several small kingdoms and became Christians. In the 9th century, the Vikings overran all these kingdoms except one, Wessex. The King of Wessex, Alfred the Great, defended the south of England successfully. After his death (899), the whole of England (though not Scotland, Wales or Ireland) was united under the kings who came after him.

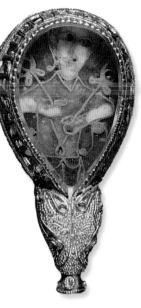

△ Alfred was England's Charlemagne. He encouraged education and learning, and created a system of law. This jewel portrait probably belonged to him. He may have lost it in marshes while dodging the Vikings.

The Church

Priests were part of everyday life in Christian Europe, from royal court to poor village. The parish priest was often the only person in the village who could read. His sermons were the only source of news and information.

Monasteries were great centres of Christian civilisation. As well as praying, monks farmed the land and cared for the sick (there were no other hospitals). Some were teachers and scholars. The only records of these times were written by monks. Bede wrote the first history of the English in 731.

Women could not be priests, but they could become nuns in their own religious houses. A nun could rise to be an abbess, a powerful person in the district. Well-born women without a husband often became nuns.

Some of the finest examples of Carolingian art were illustrated copies of religious books. One monk might spend many years working on a single book. The illustration above shows the Pope consecrating the Abbey of Cluny in 1095.

The Vikings

In the 8th-10th centuries, bands of people from Scandinavia left their homes to search for land and wealth. We call them Vikings. Some of them were robbers, but others were traders or colonists.

Raiders

The Vikings came from Denmark, Norway and Sweden. They were a farming people but, because they lived close to the sea, they were also skilful sailors. They may have decided to leave their homes because good farming land was scarce. The Vikings first attacked northern Europe as raiders. As fierce fighters and non-Christians, they terrified peaceful people, killing some and capturing others to sell as slaves. They often attacked monasteries, which were not well-protected, and carried off valuable objects such as gold crosses. Other Vikings sailed up rivers to attack inland cities. In 845, 100 ships sailed up the Seine to Paris. The king gave them 3,000 kg of silver to go away.

▷ The Vikings had a form of writing made up of signs, or letters, called runes. The families of famous people made rune stones like this one to describe their deeds. This one in Sweden was written in memory of a dead son.

◁ Viking longships were the finest ships in Europe. They were light but strong, made of oak or pinewood, and could bend a little, which allowed them to survive the rough northern seas. They were mainly powered by oars, but also had a sail and could go as fast as 10 knots (20 kph). Longships were warships, and perfect for surprise attacks. They could sail in shallow water and land on a beach.

Traders and travellers

Viking merchants from Sweden crossed the Baltic Sea to Russia in the 9th century. They set up trading posts there among the Slav tribes. They played some part in creating Novgorod and the first Russian state. Some Swedish merchants travelled by boat, down Russian rivers to the Black Sea and the Caspian. Riding camels, they travelled to Constantinople, where some found work and settled. Many Swedes joined the Byzantine emperor's personal guard. Other Swedish merchants travelled as far as Baghdad in Persia.

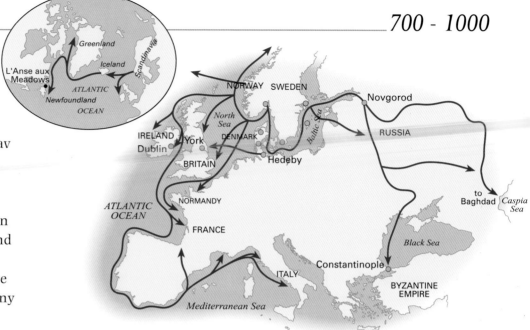

△ The Vikings travelled as far as Baghdad and Newfoundland. In Iceland, the Norwegians founded a new European nation. At first it was governed by an assembly of chiefs, Europe's first 'parliament'.

- ● important Viking settlement
- → Viking routes

Settlers

After the early raids on northern Europe, the Vikings left Scandinavia in larger numbers. They were looking for land where they could live, farm and trade. They conquered half of England, and almost destroyed the Celtic civilisation of Ireland, founding new kingdoms in York, Dublin and other places. The French king gave Normandy to a large group of Vikings, who promised to defend his kingdom against other Vikings. The descendants of this group were the Normans, who became a great power in Europe in the 11th century.

Vikings from Norway sailed far into the Atlantic. They found lands where no one lived, and settled in the Faroe Islands and Iceland. From here, they explored further west and settled in Greenland. They even sailed to North America, but did not settle there because the local people drove them off.

Everyday life

In most of Scandinavia, the Vikings built houses of wood. In Iceland and Greenland, which had few trees, they used stone and chunks of turf. Houses had no chimney nor windows, just a door. Inside was one large room where people lived and worked and children played games (until told to play outside). Sometimes they slept here too, on the raised parts at the sides of the room. Women cooked on an open fire, and a hole in the roof let out the smoke.

Lords and Priests in Europe

*In the 11th to 15th centuries, most ordinary people in Europe,
as in other continents, made their living from farming.
Their lives were ruled by the lord who owned the land,
and by the teaching of the Church.*

Feudalism

After the Vikings, there were no more great invasions in Europe. The continent settled down into kingdoms. The king was the 'owner' of his kingdom, and gave land to the nobles in exchange for their support, especially in war. The nobles in turn gave land to lesser lords in exchange for their service.

We call this system 'feudalism', the arrangement of people promising loyalty and service in return for land and protection. Not everyone obeyed these arrangements. There was plenty of fighting between nobles, and nobles sometimes rebelled against their king.

The Normans were the most successful feudal power in the 11th century. They fought all over Europe and in 1066 they invaded England and defeated the English king at the battle of Hastings. Their leader, William the Conqueror, set up a strong feudal system, supported by the powerful castles of his lords.

The Church and the king

The greatest authority in Europe was the Church, which was ruled by the Pope. Kings and lords ruled people's bodies, but the Church ruled their souls. People feared that if they disobeyed Church teaching, they would go to hell when they died.

The Church was rich and powerful. Kings and nobles promised to support the Church, but kings did not like sharing their power. The division of power between the Church and the King caused problems. Bishops were powerful lords as well as priests. But should they obey the King, or the Pope? This question caused many quarrels, especially between the Pope and the Holy Roman Emperor. In England, Archbishop Thomas Becket and King Henry II argued about the rights of priests, and this led to Becket's murder in 1170.

▽ In the 12th century, stone castles were built all over Europe. They usually followed a simple plan. A large central building, called the keep, stood in a bailey or courtyard, protected by walls and towers. This castle has two baileys and a moat, for extra protection.

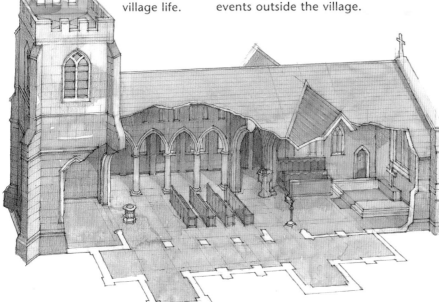

▽ The loudest sound in the countryside in the Middle Ages was the sound of church bells. The church was the centre of village life.

Everyone was supposed to go to services, but only the priest understood them, as they were in Latin. Only priests and travelling friars knew about events outside the village.

Pilgrimage

Christians, like Muslims, made long journeys to holy places. This was called going on pilgrimage. All kinds of people became pilgrims. For some it was a kind of holiday. One of the most popular sites in Europe was Santiago de Compostella in Spain, where an apostle of Jesus was said to be buried. In England, pilgrims flocked to the shrine of Archbishop Becket in Canterbury. The holiest place was Jerusalem, but it was far away, and when the Turks captured the city, people could not visit it.

The Crusades

In 1096, the Pope appealed to Christian rulers to reconquer Jerusalem, which had been captured by the Seljuk Turks. The result was a long series of holy wars, called crusades, against the Muslims in Palestine. The First Crusade captured Jerusalem, and founded several small Christian kingdoms in the Middle East. However the Muslims fought back, and Christians gradually lost interest in crusading. By 1300 almost all the Holy Land was back in Muslim hands.

Crusades were also fought against the Muslims in Spain. These were more successful. By 1492, the last Muslim state in Spain had fallen.

▽ This 15th-century painting shows how later French artists imagined scenes of the Crusades. It shows the Muslim leader Saladin recapturing Jerusalem in 1187.

Everyday Life in Medieval Europe

Life in Europe between 1000 and 1500 was difficult. Most people were poor, they had to work hard, and they died young. But even poor people were able to enjoy themselves a few times during the year.

The life of peasants

Nobles, priests and monks made up only about a tenth of the population. The rest were peasants. Most peasants in the countryside lived as 'serfs' in villages or manors, which were owned by a lord (one lord might own many villages). Serfs worked on their lord's farm, and were allowed some land of their own in return. Although they were not slaves, serfs had few rights. They could not marry or leave their village without the lord's permission. The lord even had his own law court where he punished criminals and settled arguments.

Medieval homes and food

Most houses were built of timber, or sticks and mud. Few people could afford bricks or stone. Peasants' homes had few rooms, and the people often shared the space with farm animals. Even at the end of the 15th century, only the rich had glass windows or chimneys. Women usually cooked on an open fire, and a hole in the roof let out the smoke. Houses often caught fire.

Rich people ate meat every day, but for the peasants it was a luxury. They ate mostly porridge, some cheese, and thick vegetable soup. They grew their own grain and vegetables on the land their lord allowed them, as well as working on his land. They made their bread at home and baked it in the village oven. When times were hard, they made flour from acorns and soup from nettles.

△ A village's mill belonged to the lord. It ground all the people's grain, but they had to pay the miller.

▽ This picture shows peasants working on the harvest with the lord's representative watching over them. They are cutting the wheat with scythes.

Women and children

A woman from a good family could either marry or become a nun. If she married, her father chose her husband. Upper class marriage was a business, in which a contract was made between the husband and his wife's father. Wives were supposed to be obedient to their husbands (but sometimes the wife made the decisions). Poorer women worked in the fields and, more often, at home, looking after their children, preparing food, and making clothes.

Mothers often died when they had a baby, and families were lucky if one child in four survived. Children worked from an early age. Boys who were going to be knights or craftsmen began training at the age of eight. They went to live with the man who taught them. Girls learned from their mothers. Few peasant children went to school or could read. Schools were run by the Church, mainly to train priests or monks. As times changed, more boys – and a few girls – of noble families went to school.

The Black Death

The Black Death was an epidemic (large-scale outbreak) of plague, a disease carried by fleas on rats. It started in Asia in 1347, and spread across Europe in 1348-49. It was the greatest disaster Europe had ever suffered. In three years, nearly one-third of the population died. Many people believed that it was a punishment from God.

◁ The black figure with the scythe is Death. He stands on a plague victim.

Entertainment

Peasants rested on Sundays and on other holy days. They would visit feasts and fairs, where jugglers and singers performed, and useful services were available, such as pulling teeth. Boys and men practised archery, and played a rough form of football. Life was cruel, and people enjoyed cock-fighting and bear-baiting.

▽ A popular entertainment among medieval nobles was the joust or tournament. Knights competed against each other on horseback.

European Towns

In the 12th and 13th centuries more goods were produced, trade was increasing fast, and the old feudal arrangements were breaking down. The merchants who traded across Europe and even further became more important.

Caring for the sick
A doctor tries to find out what is wrong with his patient by examining his urine. The sick man must have been rich, as doctors were expensive. Their cures seldom worked because they did not know the causes of disease. Monks or nuns ran hospitals in some towns.

The rise of the merchants

In 1300 only a small number of people lived in towns. However, important changes were taking place there. Some merchants, bankers and skilled craftsmen, such as goldsmiths, were becoming richer than the lord who ruled the town. All over western Europe, craftsmen and merchants formed groups called guilds to protect their trade. They often managed to make their town independent of the local lord. In Italy and Germany especially, large towns were ruled by rich merchants, not by nobles. The richest place in Europe was probably Venice, in Italy. That city's wealth was based on trade with the East.

△ This beautiful Italian angel is a reliquary. Reliquaries were made to hold a 'relic', such as a bone from a dead saint. Pilgrims often travelled long distances to pray near a holy relic.

△ The difference between the country and the towns was less great than in later times. Even townspeople kept chickens and a pig, and grew vegetables, while in the country people made their own clothes and tools. In every town and village, the largest building was the church. The great cathedrals were the finest creations of all Christian art.

The growth of trade

The growth of trade was helped by the development of banking in the 14th century. Merchants were able to buy and sell on credit. Silk and other luxuries arrived from the East, but the largest trade was in wool and woollen cloth. The leading traders in northern Europe were in the Hanseatic League, a group of 150 north German towns, led by Hamburg and Lübeck, which traded with each other. They also had special trade agreements in cities such as London in England, Bruges in Flanders and Bergen in Norway.

Trading cities were by the sea or on major rivers, because goods were usually carried by ships. Even though ships were often wrecked, water transport was safer and quicker than using the roads.

The end of feudal life

As a result of war, famine and disease, the population of Europe decreased in the 14th century. This was a time of changes, and of problems. Wars and rebellions became more common. Even peasants rebelled against their lords. The old feudal arrangements were disappearing, and money was becoming more important. By the 15th century, most peasants were no longer serfs. They paid the lord rent for their land, and he paid them cash for their work. Kings paid professional soldiers to fight for them, instead of asking nobles to lead their peasants into battle.

The Mongols

The Mongols were the last of the nomadic, horse-riding peoples from central Asia who invaded the towns and farms of Asia and Europe. Under Genghis Khan, they conquered lands stretching from China to eastern Europe. It was the largest empire the world had seen, though it did not last long.

Warrior herdsmen

The Mongol tribes moved around the plain of east-central Asia with their herds of sheep, goats and cattle. The leader of one tribe, Genghis Khan, united them in about 1206. He dreamed of ruling the world, and under his leadership the Mongols conquered a large empire with amazing speed. The Mongols were swift and skilful horsemen, and planned their attacks carefully. Mongol leaders (called khans) would never start a battle without first carefully investigating the enemy's position, and then deciding on the best way to attack.

▽ The Mongols lived in large tents, called yurts. They were made of felt on a light wooden frame, and could be put up in less than an hour.

▽ A fierce battle between Mongol tribes. Until they were united by Genghis Khan, the different tribes sometimes fought each other. Mongols were excellent horsemen. Each man owned four or five horses, captured from the wild Mongolian herds. Often a man's best horse was buried with him. A warrior carried several throwing spears and a curved sword, but his best weapon was his bow. He could hit a target 300 metres away.

Marco Polo

The Mongol conquest reopened the old trade routes from Europe to the East. Adventurous Italian traders followed the Old Silk Road to China. One of these was a young man called Marco Polo. He met the Mongol emperor Kublai Khan in 1275 (shown in the painting below, where Marco Polo receives the emperor's golden seal). The emperor seems to have hired him as a government official. Marco Polo's Asian travels lasted 24 years, and when he returned to Italy he told his story to someone who wrote a book about them. These tales of a great, strange civilisation in the East astonished Europe. Some people thought the story was made up. Marco Polo certainly exaggerated, but we now know that many of the things that people doubted were true.

Mongol China

The Mongol conquest was a savage blow to Chinese civilisation, and caused dreadful destruction. Genghis Khan's grandson, Kublai Khan, became the first emperor of the Mongol dynasty in China (also called the Yuan dynasty). Kublai Khan was a wise and intelligent ruler. He kept Chinese customs, supported Buddhism, and improved trade. But he never trusted Chinese officials. He tried to spread his empire further and invade Japan, but the invasion was ruined by storms which sank his ships.

▽ The Mongol Empire at its largest. The Mongol invasions in Asia and Europe had surprisingly few lasting effects. Not even the language has survived anywhere outside Mongolia.

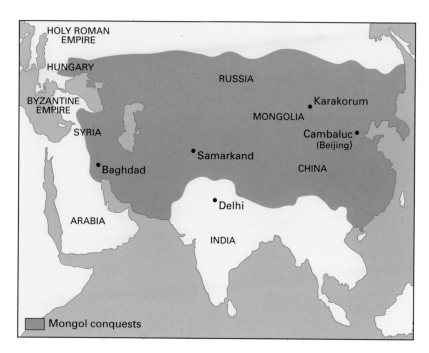

The end of the Mongol empire

After the death of Genghis Khan (1227), the Mongol empire was divided between his four sons. His son, Ogudai, became the Great Khan. The Mongols went on to invade Russia and Hungary, and might have conquered all Europe, but Ogudai died in 1241, and his brothers argued over who should replace him. The conquest of China was completed by Kublai Khan. The Great Khan's brother, Hülegü, invaded west Asia. He captured Baghdad and killed the caliph. But in 1260 a large Mameluke army defeated the Mongols in Palestine. That was the end of Mongol conquest. By 1300 the empire had broken up and was ruled by four separate khans.

Tamerlane

Mongol conquest was started again by Timur, or Tamerlane, in 1380-1405. Timur may have been a descendant of Genghis Khan. Like Genghis, he was a great war leader, and just as cruel. But he had no ability as a governor and did not create an empire. He conquered western Asia and destroyed the Khanate of the Golden Horde, which was ruled by one of Genghis Khan's descendants. He invaded India, and died while trying to conquer China.

The Medieval World

Over a thousand years separated the ancient world from the beginning of modern times. In that period new civilisations arose. The most powerful were based on religion: Christianity in Europe, and Islam, centred on the Middle East. In other regions, such as

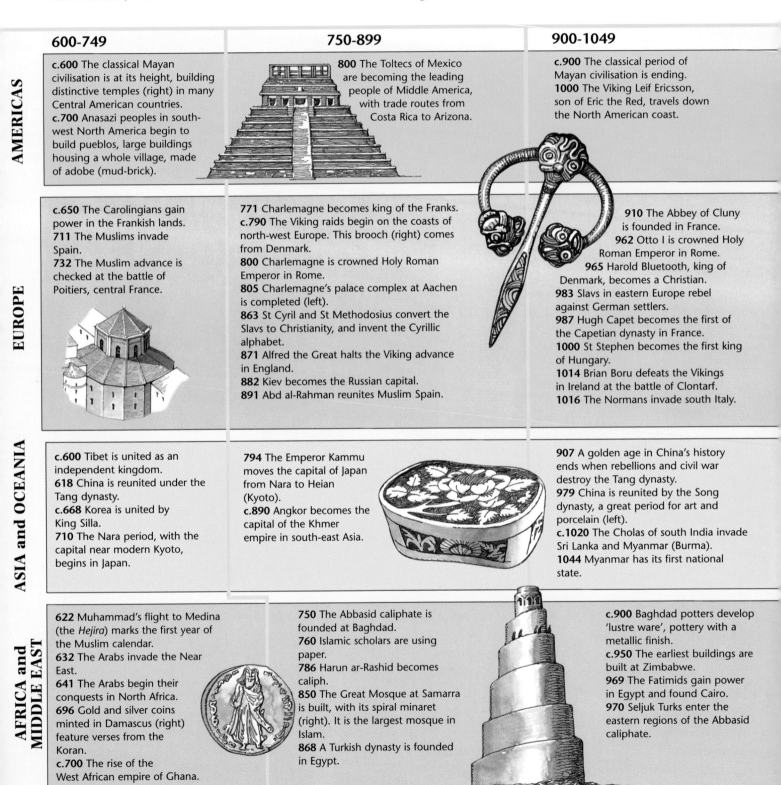

	600-749	**750-899**	**900-1049**
AMERICAS	**c.600** The classical Mayan civilisation is at its height, building distinctive temples (right) in many Central American countries. **c.700** Anasazi peoples in south-west North America begin to build pueblos, large buildings housing a whole village, made of adobe (mud-brick).	**800** The Toltecs of Mexico are becoming the leading people of Middle America, with trade routes from Costa Rica to Arizona.	**c.900** The classical period of Mayan civilisation is ending. **1000** The Viking Leif Ericsson, son of Eric the Red, travels down the North American coast.
EUROPE	**c.650** The Carolingians gain power in the Frankish lands. **711** The Muslims invade Spain. **732** The Muslim advance is checked at the battle of Poitiers, central France.	**771** Charlemagne becomes king of the Franks. **c.790** The Viking raids begin on the coasts of north-west Europe. This brooch (right) comes from Denmark. **800** Charlemagne is crowned Holy Roman Emperor in Rome. **805** Charlemagne's palace complex at Aachen is completed (left). **863** St Cyril and St Methodosius convert the Slavs to Christianity, and invent the Cyrillic alphabet. **871** Alfred the Great halts the Viking advance in England. **882** Kiev becomes the Russian capital. **891** Abd al-Rahman reunites Muslim Spain.	**910** The Abbey of Cluny is founded in France. **962** Otto I is crowned Holy Roman Emperor in Rome. **965** Harold Bluetooth, king of Denmark, becomes a Christian. **983** Slavs in eastern Europe rebel against German settlers. **987** Hugh Capet becomes the first of the Capetian dynasty in France. **1000** St Stephen becomes the first king of Hungary. **1014** Brian Boru defeats the Vikings in Ireland at the battle of Clontarf. **1016** The Normans invade south Italy.
ASIA and OCEANIA	**c.600** Tibet is united as an independent kingdom. **618** China is reunited under the Tang dynasty. **c.668** Korea is united by King Silla. **710** The Nara period, with the capital near modern Kyoto, begins in Japan.	**794** The Emperor Kammu moves the capital of Japan from Nara to Heian (Kyoto). **c.890** Angkor becomes the capital of the Khmer empire in south-east Asia.	**907** A golden age in China's history ends when rebellions and civil war destroy the Tang dynasty. **979** China is reunited by the Song dynasty, a great period for art and porcelain (left). **c.1020** The Cholas of south India invade Sri Lanka and Myanmar (Burma). **1044** Myanmar has its first national state.
AFRICA and MIDDLE EAST	**622** Muhammad's flight to Medina (the *Hejira*) marks the first year of the Muslim calendar. **632** The Arabs invade the Near East. **641** The Arabs begin their conquests in North Africa. **696** Gold and silver coins minted in Damascus (right) feature verses from the Koran. **c.700** The rise of the West African empire of Ghana.	**750** The Abbasid caliphate is founded at Baghdad. **760** Islamic scholars are using paper. **786** Harun ar-Rashid becomes caliph. **850** The Great Mosque at Samarra is built, with its spiral minaret (right). It is the largest mosque in Islam. **868** A Turkish dynasty is founded in Egypt.	**c.900** Baghdad potters develop 'lustre ware', pottery with a metallic finish. **c.950** The earliest buildings are built at Zimbabwe. **969** The Fatimids gain power in Egypt and found Cairo. **970** Seljuk Turks enter the eastern regions of the Abbasid caliphate.

South America and most of Asia, civilisation developed under a series of ruling peoples or dynasties. In spite of sharp differences, life in all these regions depended on simple farming, and changes happened very slowly.

1050-1199

c.1100 Anasazi people build the great pueblo of Mesa Verde, Colorado, which includes a 'palace' with 230 rooms.

1200-1349

c.1200 The Aztecs settle in central Mexico.
c.1300 The Hohokam people are building multi-storey buildings, like this one, in Arizona (left).
c.1345 The Aztecs found their capital, Tenochtitlán.

1350-1499

c.1380 The Inca empire of Peru expands into central Chile.
c.1450 Taino villages on Hispaniola (right) have 1000-2000 inhabitants.
1492 Columbus arrives in the Caribbean.
1497 John Cabot reaches Newfoundland from England.

1054 The Eastern (Byzantine) and Western (Roman) Churches are divided for good.
1066 The Normans conquer England.
1073 The power struggle between the Pope and the Holy Roman Emperor begins.
c.1077 The Bayeux Tapestry (right), showing scenes from the Norman conquest of England, is completed.
1096 The First Crusade, a Christian invasion of Palestine, sets out.
c.1100 The first universities are founded.

1236 The Mongols begin their conquest of eastern Europe.
1282 Prince Llewelyn of Wales dies in battle, bringing the end of Welsh independence from England.
1314 The Scots defeat the English at Bannockburn.
1348 The Black Death reaches Europe.

1378 The 'Great Schism' begins in the Church (rival popes).
1389 The Ottoman Turks conquer south-east Europe.
1397 The Union of Kalmar unites the Scandinavian kingdoms.
1453 The Ottoman Turks capture Constantinople.
1479 Christian Spain is united under Ferdinand and Isabella.
1480 Ivan III ends Mongol domination in Russia.
1492 The last Muslim state in Spain falls to the Christians.
1494 The French invasion of Italy begins a struggle for power with the Habsburgs.

---

c.1090 The Ananda temple (right) is built in the city of Pagan, Myanmar.
c.1100 The temple of Angkor Wat is built in Cambodia.
1126 The Song dynasty is driven from northern China.
1192 The Kamakura period begins in Japan, and Chinese monks teach Zen Buddhism.

1206 The Delhi Sultanate is founded. The Mongol conquests begin under Genghis Khan.
1264 Kublai Khan founds the Yuan (Mongol) dynasty in China.
c.1275 Marco Polo arrives in China.
1338 The Ashikaga shogunate begins in Japan.

1368 The Ming dynasty is founded in China.
1398 Tamerlane captures Delhi.
1428 A Vietnamese state gains independence from China.
c.1434 The Khmer capital of Angkor is abandoned after Thai attacks.
1498 Portuguese ships arrive in India.

1055 The Seljuk Turks capture Baghdad.
1071 The Seljuk Turks defeat the Byzantines at the battle of Manzikert.
1076 The Almoravids of North Africa conquer the empire of Ghana.
1096 Christian crusaders invade the Near East and capture Jerusalem.
1147 The last Almoravid ruler in Morocco dies.
1171 Saladin conquers Egypt from the Fatimids.
1188 Saladin conquers the Crusader states in the Near East.

c.1200 The rise of the empire of Mali. Hausa states are established in northern Nigeria.
c.1250 The rise of Benin.
1260 The Mamelukes defeat the Mongols in Palestine.
c.1300 The art of glassmaking reaches its peak under the Mamelukes (left).
1300 The Yoruba of Ife make marvellous heads in clay, stone or bronze (right).

1352 Ibn Battuta, the Moroccan traveller, visits Mali.
c.1400 The stone citadel of Zimbabwe is built.
1402 Tamerlane defeats the Ottoman Turks.
1415 The Portuguese capture Ceuta in North Africa.
c.1450 The rise of the empire of Songhai in West Africa.
1488 The Portuguese reach the East African coast by rounding the Cape of Good Hope.

Who's Who

Al-Idrisi (1100-66), Arab traveller and geographer. He was born in Morocco and studied in many Islamic centres, but worked mainly at the Christian court of the Norman King Roger II of Sicily. His most famous work was a silver globe of the world. Idrisi's maps show that the Arabs had a much greater knowledge of the world than the Europeans.

Alfred the Great (849-899), king of Wessex. His was the only English kingdom not conquered by the Viking armies, and he agreed to let them have half England while he ruled the other half. Alfred was a good governor, lawmaker, and educator. His successors drove the Vikings out and became kings of all England.

Asoka (273-232 BC), grandson of Chandragupta and greatest of the Mauryan emperors of India. His empire included nearly all of modern India, Pakistan, Bangladesh and Afghanistan. He became a Buddhist, and his Buddhist inscriptions on rocks and pillars all over India are a valuable record for historians.

Bede (the Venerable Bede, 673-735), English monk and historian. For most of his life he lived in the monastery of Jarrow in Northumbria, the northernmost Anglo-Saxon kingdom. He wrote many books, but his most famous is the *History of the English Church and People*, the first history of England.

Saint Benedict (about 480-547), Italian monk, and founder of the Benedictine order. Living as a hermit, he gained many followers and started a monastery for them at Monte Cassino in Italy. The rules he wrote for his monks were copied in monasteries all over Europe, and no other order was founded until the 11th century.

Chandragupta Maurya (died 286 BC), Indian emperor, founder of the Mauryan dynasty. As a young man, he met Alexander the Great. He seized the throne of Magadha, destroyed the last Greek outposts in India, and built an empire in northern India and Afghanistan. He gave up his throne to his son in 298 BC.

Charlemagne (742-814), king of the Franks and emperor of the West. Success in war made him ruler of a large part of Europe, and in 800 the Pope crowned him as a new Roman emperor. His court at Aix-la-Chapelle (Aachen) was the main centre of art and learning in Europe.

Eric the Red (died about 1005), discoverer of Greenland. Born in Norway, he went to Iceland as a young man when his father was banished. When Eric in turn was banished from Iceland for three years, he went exploring. He discovered good land in Greenland, where he founded a colony. His son Leif sailed to North America.

Genghis Khan (1167-1227), Mongol conqueror. Son of a local chief, he was named Temujin. He was later called 'Genghis Khan', meaning 'world ruler', because after a long struggle, he united the Mongols and conquered a huge empire. His success resulted from good managment and, although he could not read, he was a good governor and law-maker.

Harun ar-Rashid (764-809), caliph of Baghdad. Under him the caliphate reached its greatest power and wealth. He made Baghdad the centre of Arabic learning, and was in contact with Charlemagne and Tang China. He led his armies to victory over the Byzantines. But, by his death, the power of the caliph was shrinking.

Kublai Khan (1215-94), founder of the Yuan or Mongol dynasty in China. In 1260 he completed the conquest of Sung China begun by his grandfather, Genghis Khan. He understood and admired Chinese civilisation, and moved the Mongol capital from Karakorum to Beijing. The Yuan dynasty lasted until 1368.

Marco Polo (about 1254-1324), Italian traveller in Asia. He was only about 17 when he went to China with his uncles, who were merchants from Venice. He spent nearly 20 years in Kublai Khan's service, travelling all over his empire. On his return to Italy he was imprisoned in Genoa, where a fellow prisoner wrote down his story.

Muhammad (570-632), founder of Islam. An orphan, he was brought up by an uncle, and as a young herdsman learned the customs and language of the nomadic Bedouin. After years of study and thought, he became a teacher and prophet. He was driven out of Mecca but welcomed in Medina and, after a civil war, he became the leader of all Arabia.

Otto I (912-973), German king. He was crowned Holy Roman Emperor by the Pope in 962, reviving the idea of a Christian, European empire begun by Charlemagne. With their main centre of power in Germany, there were Holy Roman Emperors in Europe from 962 until 1806.

Saladin (Salah ad-Din, 1138-93), Muslim commander against the Crusaders. After making himself ruler of Egypt and Syria, he led a holy war against the Crusaders, recapturing Jerusalem and defeating the efforts of the Third Crusade to get it back. He was also a good governor, restoring Egypt's power and wealth.

Shotoku Taishi (573-621), Japanese ruler. As regent for his aunt, the Empress, he strengthened the imperial government and reduced the powers of the nobles. He was in contact with Tang China, and introduced the Chinese system of government, including Confucian and Buddhist ideas.

Wu Zetian (624-705), the only woman emperor of China. When her husband, a Tang emperor, died, she locked up her son and took power herself (690). A born politician, she encouraged good government and the arts. But she was – and needed to be – ruthless, spying on her ministers and having her opponents murdered.

Sundjata Keita (about 1210-60), king of Mali. He founded the Mali Empire by creating a large kingdom among the Mande people of West Africa. A tolerant ruler, he controlled trade routes across the Sahara and the supplies of West African gold. He is remembered as a great hero.

THE
EARLY MODERN
WORLD

Voyages of Exploration

In the 15th century, European sailors began to explore the oceans looking for new trade routes. By 1550 they had sailed around the world, visited every continent except Antarctica, and set up trading posts and colonies in Asia, Africa and the Americas.

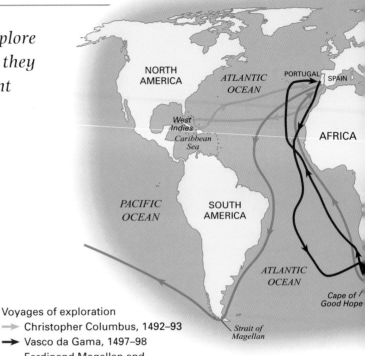

Voyages of exploration
→ Christopher Columbus, 1492–93
→ Vasco da Gama, 1497–98
→ Ferdinand Magellan and
  Juan Sebastian del Cano, 1519–22

Trade routes

Since ancient times, Europeans had imported luxury goods, such as silk and spices, from Asia. These goods passed through many hands to get to Europe, and were always expensive. The rise of the Ottoman Empire had closed many overland trade routes, so the Europeans wanted to find a route to the East by sea. No one knew if there was one. Ships had never sailed far from land. Many people still believed the Earth was flat, and thought ships could sail off the edge. Even people who knew that the Earth was round believed that it was much smaller than it is. No one had any idea that the Americas existed, so it was a complete surprise to Europeans when this 'new world' was found by explorers looking for new ways to the East.

European voyages
1488 Dias passes the Cape of Good Hope, South Africa.
1492 Columbus crosses the Atlantic.
1497 Cabot sails from England to Newfoundland.
1498 Vasco da Gama finds the route to India via East Africa.
1534 Cartier enters the St Lawrence River, Canada

△ The best route to India and the Far East was followed by Vasco da Gama. The western route was blocked by Columbus's 'New World'. Later captains, still believing that Asia lay close by, tried to find a way past or through it. In 1519 Ferdinand Magellan sailed around South America and became the first European to cross the Pacific Ocean. One of his ships reached home in 1522, having sailed around the world. But this route to the East was too long and dangerous to be useful.

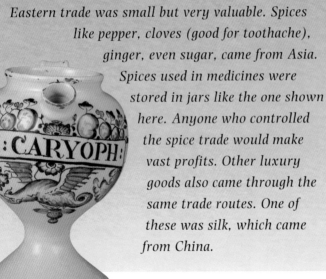

The spice trade
Eastern trade was small but very valuable. Spices like pepper, cloves (good for toothache), ginger, even sugar, came from Asia. Spices used in medicines were stored in jars like the one shown here. Anyone who controlled the spice trade would make vast profits. Other luxury goods also came through the same trade routes. One of these was silk, which came from China.

The Portuguese

The first explorers of the oceans were the Portuguese. Portuguese sea captains explored the West African coast, hoping to find the source of African gold and a route to the East. In 1487 Bartolomeu Dias reached the south-western tip of Africa, the Cape, opening the way to the Indian Ocean. Ten years later Vasco da Gama followed with a large, well-armed fleet. He visited the trading cities of East Africa, and from one of them, Malindi, an Arab pilot guided him across the Indian Ocean. A sea route from Europe to Asia had been found! In a few years, he and other Portuguese captains seized the Indian Ocean trade from Indian and Arab merchants. They pressed on to the spice islands of the Pacific.

▷ Columbus and his crew of 40 men sailed in the *Santa Maria*, a tough merchant ship about 30 m long. She was later wrecked in the West Indies, but Columbus also had two smaller ships. At sea, Columbus could work out his latitude (his position between north and south), but he had to rely on good guesswork for his longitude (his position between east and west).

Columbus

Christopher Columbus, an Italian captain, hoped to find a route to the East by sailing west. After other governments had turned him down, he got support from Spain. In 1492 he landed in the Caribbean. He believed he was on the edge of Asia, and called the islands he found the Indies, thinking they were the East Indies. They were later called the West Indies.

Spain set up colonies in the West Indies and began to explore the mainland. Hundreds of adventurous Spaniards arrived. Most hoped to find gold and make a fortune, but some were Christian missionaries who wanted to convert the local people. In 1499 another Italian captain working for Spain, Amerigo Vespucci, discovered the Amazon River. The new continent of America was named after him.

▷ The native peoples of the Americas had never seen guns, horses, or large ships. These Aztecs are fighting the Spaniards. On the left one of them wears a jaguar skin.

Other nations

The Pope declared that the world should be divided between Spain and Portugal. A vertical line was drawn through a map of the Atlantic. Spain had the Americas to the West, Portugal had Brazil and the East Indies. Other Europeans did not accept this. In 1497 John Cabot, an Italian captain working for England, reached Newfoundland. Between 1534 and 1536 a Frenchman, Jacques Cartier, discovered the St Lawrence River and reached what is now Montreal. Later, Cabot's and Cartier's voyages led to the setting up of English colonies in Massachusetts and Virginia, and French colonies in Canada.

The European Renaissance

In Europe by the 15th and 16th centuries people were becoming much more curious about the world around them. This was one reason for the voyages of exploration. People also developed new ideas about art, science and religion which led to big changes in Europe.

A rebirth of learning

Renaissance means 'rebirth'. It was a rebirth of interest in the art and learning of ancient Greece and Rome, which reached its peak in Italy at this time. For centuries, the Church had been the centre of learning and art, and the Classical civilisations had been mostly forgotten. Now scholars made new translations of the work of ancient writers. They discovered that these people, who had lived over 1,000 years earlier, often understood the world better than they did. This interest in ancient learning inspired humanist scholars to think for themselves, and led them on to great discoveries in art and learning. The scholars are called humanists because they were interested in people and in the world around them. It was a very exciting time, and people felt there was no limit to what they could discover or do.

▽ The cathedral of Florence, in Italy. This magnificent building was finished about 1436, and many famous Renaissance artists worked on it. The dome on the cathedral was designed by Filippo Brunelleschi, and was the first large dome built in Europe since the 6th century.

The spread of the Renaissance

The Renaissance flourished in different parts of Europe at different times. It reached its peak in northern Italy, the most advanced region in Europe. Wealthy merchants and princes of the city states, such as the popes in Rome or the Medici family of Florence, spent their money on beautiful buildings and works of art. They encouraged the best artists to make things for them.

Renaissance ideas spread all over Europe. In the Netherlands rich merchants also wanted paintings. Artists here developed the technique of oil painting. The most famous humanist scholar in Europe was a Dutchman called Erasmus.

△ Michelangelo painting the ceiling of the Pope's Chapel in Rome, with scenes from the Bible. One of the greatest geniuses of the Renaissance, Michelangelo was a sculptor, painter, architect (he designed most of St Peter's Basilica in Rome) and poet. The chapel's ceiling is larger than a basketball court, and it took Michelangelo over four years to paint it.

Printed books

The most important invention of the Renaissance was printing with metal type. This picture shows a Renaissance printer's workshop. The first metal type was used by Johannes Gutenberg, in Germany in the 1450s. Before that, books were written by hand or printed with wood blocks. Now they could be printed in many copies, more cheaply and quickly. New ideas could spread faster. Although scholars still wrote in Latin, some writers used their own language.

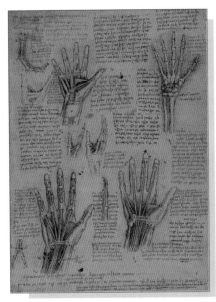

△ Leonardo's notebooks are full of drawings of marvellous machines, and studies of the human body, like this one. He wrote his notes in back-to-front writing.

Science

As people were interested in all kinds of knowledge, scholars would study many different subjects, not specialise in one area. Leonardo da Vinci, an Italian, was an example of 'Renaissance man'. He is remembered best as a painter, but he was also a military expert, engineer, and inventor. He dissected dead bodies to understand how bones and muscles work.

Literature

As in painting and sculpture, the subjects of literature became more realistic, and less based on religious stories. Plays were performed in specially built theatres, instead of in the street or in the courtyards of inns. These were the first permanent theatres since the time of the Romans. The plays of the English Renaissance writer William Shakespeare (1564-1616) were written to be performed in these theatres.

▷ William Shakespeare

The Reformation

For over 1,000 years there was one Christian Church in western Europe. It was ruled by the Pope in Rome. In the 16th century, some people, and some states, broke away from the Church, and Christians divided into Roman Catholics and Protestants.

▽ In 1517 Luther fastened 95 complaints about the Church on the church door (often used as a notice board) in Wittenberg, Germany. That act marks the beginning of the Reformation.

Complaints about the Church

Some Christians in the 16th century complained that all sorts of churchmen, from the Pope down to ordinary priests and monks, did not behave like Christians. The Pope ruled a large part of Italy, and he seemed more interested in power and wealth than in God. Bishops were often harsh landlords. Many priests were ignorant, lazy and dishonest. People began to protest about the way the Church was run, so they became known as Protestants. Although at first they wanted to stay in the Roman Catholic Church and improve it, in the end they formed their own new churches.

Martin Luther

Martin Luther (1483-1546), a German priest, was the first great reformer. He criticised the Pope for taking money from people in return for forgiving their sins. Luther believed that only God could forgive sinners. The Pope expelled Luther from the Church because of his criticisms. But Luther had many followers, including some German princes. These Lutherans left the Roman Catholic Church.

The Reformation spread. The reformers complained that church services and the Bible were both in Latin, the language of ancient Rome, which ordinary people could not understand. They thought the Church was keeping people ignorant so it could control them. Luther translated some of the Bible into German.

◁ John Calvin was a reformer who led the Protestants in Geneva, Switzerland. He taught that only those specially chosen by God, the 'elect', would go to heaven when they died. The 'elect' were Calvin's followers. Calvin's ideas spread even more widely than Luther's, especially in the Netherlands and Scotland.

The destruction of English monasteries

Some rulers gained power and wealth by rejecting the Roman Catholic Church and the Pope. When Henry VIII of England made himself head of a national Church, he increased his royal power. He closed down the monasteries, and took over their lands, which greatly increased his income. In the process, many pieces of religious art were destroyed.

The Counter-Reformation

After the Reformation, the Roman Catholic Church did reform itself. Strong popes demanded better behaviour from churchmen. A new religious order was founded, the Society of Jesus. Its members, called Jesuits, started schools and became missionaries to convert people to Roman Catholicism.

Religious wars

The divisions between Catholics and Protestants brought wars and persecution. In most countries the Church and government were closely linked. Rulers did not want their people to practise different forms of religion. They were afraid that if people did not obey the Church, they might decide not to obey the government either.

In France, where the king was a Catholic, there were civil wars between Catholics and Protestants (called Huguenots). These ended when the Huguenot leader became King Henri IV. He had to become a Catholic, but he gave the Huguenots freedom to worship as they wanted, in the Edict of Nantes, in 1598. Protestants in the northern Netherlands rebelled against their Spanish, Catholic rulers.

The Netherlands became independent from Spain in 1609.

The Thirty Years' War (1618-48) began as a war between Protestant German princes and the Catholic Holy Roman Emperor. It turned into a struggle for power between different European countries, with the powerful Catholic countries, Spain and France, fighting on opposite sides.

△ The Massacre of St Bartholomew's Eve. On 24 August 1572 the French king planned to assassinate leaders of the Huguenots in Paris. Things got out of hand, and tens of thousands of ordinary Huguenots were killed.

Spanish and Portuguese Empires

In the 16th century, Europeans spread their power around the world. The leaders were Spain and Portugal. Portugal gained control of the valuable spice trade. At the same time Spain founded an empire in the Americas and became rich from the silver discovered there.

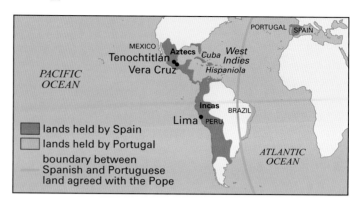

The Portuguese Empire

Once the Portuguese had gained control of the Indian Ocean, they moved farther east. They wanted to control trade with the Moluccas, known as the 'Spice Islands'. Their greatest empire-builder was Albuquerque. He built a large base at Goa in west India, and in 1511 he captured the important Malayan port of Malacca. In 1512 the Portuguese reached the 'Spice Islands', and in 1513 Albuquerque captured Ormuz, in south Persia. This gave the Portuguese control of the Persian Gulf. By 1556, the Portuguese had a base at Macao, China. To the west, Portugal claimed Brazil in the Americas. Portugal's main interest was in controlling trade – it did not want to colonise these new lands it claimed.

△ The line dividing the non-Christian world between Portugal and Spain was fixed in 1494.

▽ The battle for Tenochtitlán. The Aztec city was on an island in a lake, joined to the mainland by a causeway. The Spaniards destroyed the city and built what is now Mexico City.

CONQVISTA DE MEXICO POR CORTES. N.7

The Spanish Americas

Except for Brazil, the Americas 'belonged' to Spain. The Spanish conquests were organised by adventurers who hoped to make their fortune. Cortés, an official in Cuba, heard stories of a wealthy state deep inland. With 500 men he landed at Vera Cruz, Mexico, in 1517. The local people were willing to help him against the Aztecs who ruled them. Montezuma, the Aztec emperor, allowed the Spaniards into the city of Tenochtitlán, but trouble soon broke out. With the help of the other local people, the Spaniards captured Tenochtitlán, and the Aztec empire fell into Spanish hands. Cortés became ruler of what was called 'New Spain', an area larger than Spain itself.

The other great American empire was the Inca Empire in Peru. It was already weakened by a civil war, so it was conquered even more easily. Francisco Pizarro arrived in 1531 with only 180 men. The Inca ruler, Atahualpa, let them in, but they ambushed him and captured the capital, Quito. In the next few years Pizarro's followers took over the whole Inca Empire.

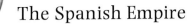

△ The Inca made wonderful objects of gold, like this llama. Atahualpa promised the Spaniards a hoard of gold if they would let him go. The Spanish took the treasure, but killed Atahualpa as well.

The Spanish Empire

The Spanish explored 'New Spain' looking for 'El Dorado', a legendary city of gold. During their search they killed many American people, but they never found the city. They did, however, find silver mines in Mexico and Peru. Every year, they sent home large fleets of ships loaded with silver. Spain became for a time the richest and most powerful country in Europe.

Spanish people were given large estates in America, and made the native Americans their slaves. Although the Spanish government and Christian missionaries tried to give the slaves some protection, many died from overwork and cruel treatment. Even more died of European diseases. To replace the native Americans, new slaves were brought from Africa.

△ At first, European traders bought furs from native hunters. Later, a new kind of hunter developed, the 'runners of the woods', part French, and part American.

New England and New France

Other European nations refused to accept the division of the world between Portugal and Spain. However, the English, French and Dutch did not settle in colonies in the Americas until over 100 years later. By then, Spanish power was weakening.

The French started settlements in 'New France' (south-east Canada) to exploit the valuable fur trade, but not many people settled there permanently. In 1682 a French explorer, La Salle, travelled from the Great Lakes, along the Mississippi to the Gulf of Mexico. He claimed the region for France. This threatened the English colonies, and England and France fought over land in North America until the French were defeated in 1763.

Some of the most profitable American colonies proved be the rich, sugar-growing Caribbean islands.

European Nations

In the 16th century, Europe was becoming a group of independent nations. Most were ruled by powerful kings. Their people began to feel they belonged to one nation, and that it was their duty to be loyal to their monarch.

'New monarchies'

In the 16th century rulers had more control than in earlier times. Kings chose their own ministers, who ran the country instead of powerful lords. The kings had royal courts to provide justice, and some had professional armies to control the country and fight foreigners. But kings also needed the support of their people. To get this they had to keep the country orderly and the people prosperous. They were helped by the fact that the population was growing, and so were trade and business. Kings supported business with special privileges.

The powerful Tudors

In the 15th century there was a long civil war in England over who should be king. The first Tudor king, Henry VII, won his crown in battle in 1485, and worked hard to make his throne secure. His son Henry VIII (above) increased his power when he made himself Supreme Head of the Church of England in 1534. Henry VIII's daughter, Elizabeth I, coped skilfully with dangers at home and abroad, even though people then did not believe a woman could rule successfully. English sailors such as Francis Drake challenged Spanish power in the New World, and managed to defeat the great Spanish fleet, the Armada, which tried to invade England in 1588.

In 1400 there was no single great power in Europe. The French king controlled only a third of France, because the king of England and the Duke of Burgundy owned large parts of the country. But by 1453 the English had been driven out, and in 1477 Burgundy was divided up and France took half of it. France became a strong and united kingdom. The same happened in other parts of Europe. In Russia, the Grand Duke of Muscovy became tsar of Russia, and in Sweden the strong Vasa kings made their country independent from Denmark.

△ The marriage of Ferdinand of Aragon and Isabella of Castile, in 1479, joined the two main Spanish kingdoms. When the last Muslim kingdom was defeated in 1492, Spain was united for the first time.

▽ The house of a rich English wool merchant in the 16th century. The wool trade was still the biggest business in Europe.

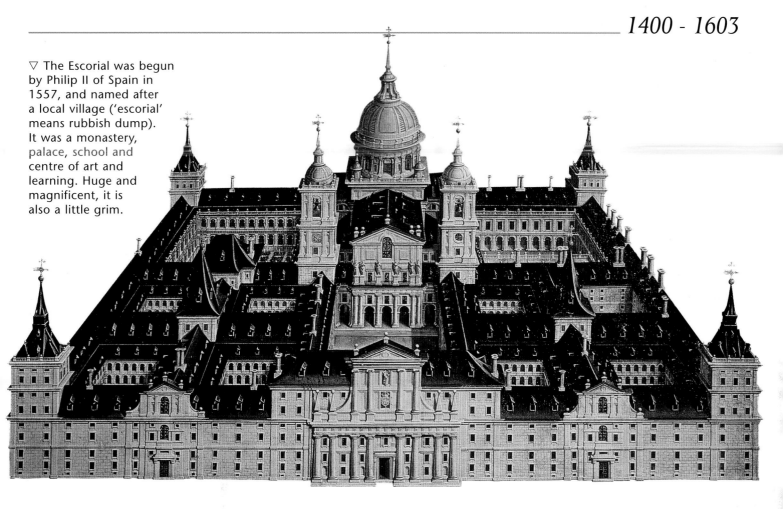

▽ The Escorial was begun by Philip II of Spain in 1557, and named after a local village ('escorial' means rubbish dump). It was a monastery, palace, school and centre of art and learning. Huge and magnificent, it is also a little grim.

Germany and Italy

Not all monarchs were as successful as the Tudors. The kings of Poland and Hungary built empires in the 15th century, but they did not last long, because the Ottoman Turks conquered south-east Europe and threatened Germany. The King of the Germans was the Holy Roman Emperor, but he could not control the German princes, who ruled as independent monarchs. One of the emperor's difficulties was that he had too many responsibilities. Charles V (emperor 1519-58) ruled over Italy, which was divided into several different states, as well as Germany and the Netherlands. He also ruled Spain and the Spanish possessions in America. This huge empire could not be run by one government. When Charles gave up his thrones, the empire went to his brother, and the Spanish crown to his son.

Spain

Under Charles's son Philip II, Spain was the greatest kingdom in Europe, thanks to its wealth from American silver. This wealth and power made them enemies, especially after Spain took over Portugal (1580). English and French ships attacked their empire. American silver drove up prices, and made Spaniards believe they need not work for a living, causing the country's decline in the 17th century.

The rise of bankers
Banks hardly existed before the 14th century, because the Church taught that lending money and charging interest was a sin. Banking started with merchant-bankers like the Medici in Italy, who bought and sold goods on credit. Banking was usually a family business, and some families became very rich. The most famous German bankers were the Fuggers of Augsburg, who made a fortune by lending money to the Emperor Charles V. But lending money to great monarchs was risky. They did not always pay it back.

The Persian Empire

The Safavid Empire of Persia (modern Iran) was the smallest of the three Islamic empires. It did not last long, but its arts were brilliant, and its influence has lasted to the present.

The divisions of Islam

In the 15th century, Islam covered a larger region than Christianity. It was divided into many groups, or sects. In the early 16th century, at about the same time as the Reformation in Europe, Islam went through a time of crisis. This was caused partly by the rise of the Safavids. They were Shi'ite Muslims from Azerbaijan, named after their founder, a Sufi named Safi al-Din. They became the greatest power in Persia, and in 1502 their leader, Ismail, made himself shah. Many years passed, and many battles were fought, before Ismail controlled the whole of Persia.

△ The Safavid Empire depended on a great leader, Abbas I, who united it and made it strong. It lasted over 100 years, but the Ottoman Empire lasted much longer.

▢ Safavid Persian Empire in 1628
▢ Ottoman Empire in 1683

Ismail I

Under Ismail, the Safavid Empire grew to an area larger than modern Iran. It included Persians, Turkmen, Arabs and other peoples. Ismail made his form of Shi'ism the religion of Persia (as it still is today). His followers believed he should be the head of all Islam. That was a threat to other Muslim rulers, especially the Ottoman sultan. The Ottoman Turks and the Persians were already quarrelling over land, so fighting became inevitable. When the Ottomans invaded, Ismail could not stop them seizing his land and killing thousands of people. People said that after this defeat, Ismail never smiled again. The fighting between the Safavids and the Ottomans continued for over 100 years.

△ A caravanserai was a kind of travellers' inn. It provided food and shelter for merchants' caravans. Shah Abbas made his people build good roads, bridges, and caravanseries, to assist trade.

Abbas the Great

The Safavid Empire was at its height during the rule of Shah Abbas (1586-1628). He created an army of trained soldiers, which drove out the invading Uzbeks, regained all the territory taken by the Ottomans, and captured Baghdad. These victories helped him to unite the peoples of Persia into one nation. Abbas was more tolerant than earlier rulers. He even allowed Christian missionaries into his empire. Europeans brought trade, but he was annoyed by the Portuguese, who controlled trade in the Persian Gulf. He recaptured Ormuz from them in 1622. Abbas is remembered for his skill in government and his encouragement of trade, industry and the arts. He ruthlessly protected his own power, but he created a rich and powerful country.

▽ Shah Abbas built a new capital at Isfahan, one of the world's most beautiful cities. It was a place of glittering mosques and minarets, pavilions, orchards, streams, and lively bazaars.

Carpets

People in many Asian countries made rugs and carpets, knotted by hand. Persian carpets, filled with flowers and animals, are perhaps the most beautiful.

Nadir Shah

Later Safavid rulers did not have Abbas's skill or intelligence. They wasted their time in plots and feuds. The empire was conquered by the Afghans in 1722, but in 1736 the throne was seized by Nadir Shah. He had been leader of a large band of robbers, but was a brilliant military leader. Nadir Shah was the last of the great Asian conquerors. He drove out Afghans, Turks, and others, and created an empire larger than the Safavids', conquering northern India. But he had no other skills. He was cruel and greedy, and in the end he was killed by his own soldiers.

The Ottoman Empire

The Ottoman Turkish Empire was the greatest power in the world in the early 16th century. It included parts of three continents: Asia, Africa and Europe. For most Muslims, the Ottoman sultan was the leader of all Islam.

The rise of the Ottomans

When the earlier empire of the Seljuk Turks was attacked by the Mongols (1243), the Ottomans took over. During the 14th century they rapidly gained land, mostly taken from the Byzantine Empire. In 1453 the Ottomans captured Constantinople. This, finally, marked the end of the 1,100 year-old Byzantine Empire. Under Selim the Grim (1512-20) the Ottomans added Egypt, Syria and part of Safavid Persia to their empire.

▷ The key to Ottoman success was the world's first professional army, the Janissaries. They were mostly Christians from peasant families, who were taken to Constantinople when they were boys and educated to be Muslim soldiers. They lived by their own rules in their own barracks. They were very loyal to the sultan, who gave them special privileges. In later times, however, their strength and independence made them a threat to weaker rulers.

▽ To win more land in south-east Europe, the Turks had to take Constantinople. They finally captured it in 1453, with the aid of a giant cannon (it was not really much use as it could only fire once every few hours).

Suleiman the Magnificent

Ottoman power and wealth was greatest under Suleiman I (1520-66). Europeans called him 'the Magnificent', because they were impressed by his splendid court. Suleiman's subjects called him 'the Lawgiver', because he was a good governor. The Ottoman Empire under Suleiman was prosperous as well as powerful. It had a large population and plenty of rich farm land. There were good hospitals and schools, and little crime. Although Suleiman was a Muslim, he accepted people of other religions. He employed Greek-speaking Christians from the old Byzantine Empire, and appointed Christian governors in the newly conquered Balkans (south-east Europe). Suleiman was also a good war leader. His armies captured Aden and Algiers, and took the fortress of the Knights of St John on the island of Rhodes. In 1525 they won Hungary. They even threatened the heart of Europe, by besieging Vienna in 1529.

▷ Suleimaniyeh, the Mosque of Suleiman in Istanbul. Suleiman employed the great architect Sinan to build mosques, palaces, schools and hospitals throughout the empire. The mosque still stands today, a reminder of the golden age of the Ottoman Empire.

The Ottoman navy

One weakness of all the great Muslim empires was that they had no navy to match their armies. Suleiman found a man to create one: Kheir-ed-din, called 'Barbarossa' ('red beard') by Europeans. He was a North African captain, famous for his raids against Christian ships and towns in the Mediterranean. With Suleiman's support, he built a powerful navy of war galleys, which gave the Sultan command of the eastern Mediterranean.

The decline of the Ottomans

Many of the sultans who came after Suleiman were poor leaders. They concentrated on quarrels within their large court, instead of on government, trade and industry. The population kept growing, but the empire's wealth did not. In 1571 a combined Christian fleet defeated the Ottoman navy at the battle of Lepanto, so the Ottomans lost control of the Mediterranean. The empire sometimes became powerful again under good rulers. In fact it was at its largest in the late 17th century, when the able Kuprili family served as chief ministers and the Ottoman armies again besieged Vienna (1683). But the empire could not keep that strength. The Ottomans lost most of their lands in Europe and Africa in the 19th century, and the last sultan was finally deposed when the modern Turkish Republic was founded in 1922.

Mughal India

The third great Muslim empire of the 16th century was the empire of the Mughals. They united most of India and ruled for more than 200 years.

Akbar

'Mughal' comes from the name 'Mongol'. Babur ('Tiger'), who was the first of the Mughal emperors, was a descendant of the Mongol conqueror, Tamerlane. Babur conquered Afghanistan and began the conquest of India in 1525. His grandson, Akbar (1556-1605), was only 17 when he took command. He conquered the whole of northern India. Although the Mughals won their empire by force, Akbar kept it by good government.

▷ The Rajputs were the fiercest opponents of the Mughal conquerors. They were a caste of warriors from north-west India, famous for their bravery and independence. Akbar won their support by a mixture of force and friendship. One of his wives was a Rajput princess.

Muslim rule was not new in northern India, but Akbar won over Hindus by showing them respect. He married a Hindu princess, attended Hindu festivals and employed Hindu officials as well as Muslims. He brought peace and justice to places that had not seen them before.

It is said that Akbar could not read. But he certainly had a vast amount read to him, and during his reign Mughal style and customs fascinated all Indians, as well as foreigners.

Akbar's palace

Akbar built the magnificent ceremonial centre of Fatehpur-Sikri, near his capital, Agra, because it was the birthplace of his son and successor, Jahangir. There he listened to the arguments of Muslims, Hindus, Jesuits and others. He once suggested that a Christian with a Bible and a Muslim with the Koran should step into the fire to see who was burned. They politely refused.

▽ Although the Mughal Empire was largest under Aurangzeb, it was less peaceful, as the Mughal government was breaking down.

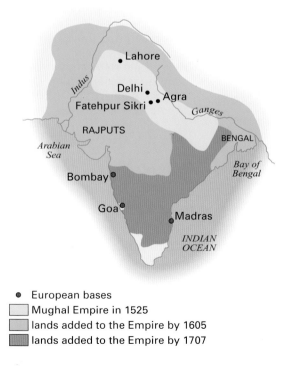

- ● European bases
- ☐ Mughal Empire in 1525
- ☐ lands added to the Empire by 1605
- ☐ lands added to the Empire by 1707

Shah Jahan

Mughal rule after Akbar was more strict. Shah Jahan (1628-53) even ordered Hindu temples to be destroyed, although his order was not obeyed. In the 18th century, Europeans were able to control the seas and parts of the coast because the Mughals did not have a navy. The Mughal Empire continued to grow, but it was no longer so rich. Taxes were so high that peasants left their land, to avoid paying them. The roads, which Akbar's good government had made safe, became the hunting ground of bandits.

▽ The Taj Mahal, the most famous of the many marvellous buildings of the Mughals. It is a tomb built by Shah Jahan for his favourite wife. He is buried there too.

Aurangzeb

Under Aurangzeb (1658-1707) the empire was at its largest. But the costs were high. Aurangzeb was often away fighting, so the country was not governed properly, and rebellions increased. After his death, the Mughal emperors steadily lost their power. In 1738 Nadir Shah captured Delhi and carried off the treasures of the Mughal court. With no strong central government left, the Europeans gradually moved in. By 1765 the greatest power in India was not the Mughal emperor, but the British East India Company. This was a trading company, but in order to increase its own trade and profits it became a ruling power. It took over Bengal in 1757, and by 1815 it controlled most of India, either directly through a governor, or by dominating the local Indian princes.

The Expansion of China

Life in China changed very little over the centuries. In spite of rebellions, civil wars and foreign rule, Chinese civilisation was preserved by a small group of learned men, called mandarins, who ran everyday government.

The Ming dynasty

The Ming took over from the Mongols of the Yuan dynasty in 1368. Under the strong rule of the early Ming emperors, the Chinese Empire was restored to health. Farming improved, thanks to new crops, canals and irrigation works. The Ming even tried to help the hard-worked peasants, against the big landowners. In the towns, industry flourished, especially cloth-making. In the city of Nanking, there were about 50,000 looms for weaving silk. European traders paid in silver for Chinese tea, silk and porcelain, so Chinese merchants grew rich. The population was growing again.

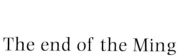

◻ Ming China, 1368
▨ Manchu China at its largest, about 1760
▨ Manchu homeland
--- Great Wall

◁ The Chinese potters under the Ming and Manchu were magnificent artist-craftsmen. This vase was made during the late Ming period. Europeans were astonished by these imported pots, which they called 'china'.

△ The Manchu emperors conquered Mongolia and Tibet, and pushed the Chinese Empire into central Asia.

▷ Mandarins were imperial officials. The colour of the knob on a mandarin's hat showed his rank. Mandarins were also scholars, artists and landowners. They had to pass an exam to become officials.

The end of the Ming

With rising industry and trade, a rich middle class began to develop. But the landowners and upper-class officials still held all the power. They jealously guarded their position against rivals. At the same time, the Ming emperors were losing their early energy. Although they ordered the Great Wall to be rebuilt, it did not prevent raids by the Mongols. Japanese pirates attacked the coast and sailed up the Yangtze River to raid inland cities. The Ming were losing control. After 1582, they left government to greedy and dishonest palace officials. Rebellions broke out among the peasants and in towns. The Manchu, a warlike people from Manchuria, were asked to help restore order. Instead, they set up their own dynasty, the Qing, in 1644.

▷ The Forbidden City, built by the Ming as a home for the emperor and his family. It is a little city inside Beijing, the Ming capital. No one except royalty and officials could enter, on pain of death.

The Qing dynasty

The Manchu emperors of the Qing dynasty did not try to change Chinese customs, though they did make officials wear pigtails (a Manchu custom) as a sign of loyalty. With peace and strong government, the Chinese grew richer. Intelligent Qing emperors encouraged art and learning. Under Kangxi (reigned 1661-1722) great works of literature were produced, including an encyclopedia of about 2,000 volumes.

Chinese civilisation seemed as strong and brilliant as ever. But it was not changing much. Although trade brought China into contact with Europe, which was changing fast, China stood still. By about 1800 the Qing, like the Ming before them, had lost control. Half the country was in revolt against the government. The navy could not leave port for fear of pirates. Europeans controlled Chinese trade. The old empire was doomed, yet somehow it lasted until 1911.

Expeditions overseas

From 1405 to 1433 Admiral Zheng Ho led great expeditions overseas, sailing as far as East Africa. His 60 ships, called junks, were larger and safer than European ships. He sailed to buy luxuries for the imperial court, and to collect taxes from Chinese colonies. Later, foreign voyages were forbidden, and any merchant caught trading abroad was executed.

Foot-binding

Small feet were a sign of good birth. In upper-class families, the feet of some young girls were tightly bound with strips of cloth to stop them growing. It also made them unable to walk properly.

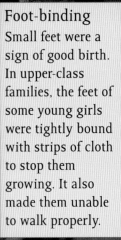

Tokugawa Japan

From 1615 to 1854, Japan's rulers kept their country apart from the world. Foreigners were not allowed in, and Japanese were not allowed out. But after 1854, Japan began to change fast, and by 1900 it was the greatest power in Asia.

Shutting out the world

Under the rule of the Tokugawa shoguns, Japan was shut off from the world. The only foreigners allowed in were a few Dutch merchants, and they were only allowed on one small island. The Japanese needed them to supply Western products, especially guns. The shoguns did not allow the daimyo, the local lords, to have much power, and they also stopped raids by warriors on foreign coasts and ships. They wanted peace and order. People were supposed to follow the old customs, and stay in the class and occupation they were born into. This was difficult for some people, such as the samurai, who were warriors and so had nothing to do in a country at peace. Japan was one of the richest countries in the world in the 18th century, but it was becoming backward compared with the West, which was changing rapidly.

◁ Planting rice in a rain storm. Although farm land was scarce, Japanese peasant farmers made the most of it. By making terraces, they could grow rice on steep slopes. But they did not own the land, and the profits were made by those who collected rice as a form of tax.

A changing country

The Tokugawa shoguns did not like change, but changes happened anyway. Thanks to better rice farming, the population grew fast. The use of money became common in trade, and a new class of merchants grew up. Because they did not produce anything, merchants were classed below the peasants. All the same, they became richer, and more powerful, than the daimyo.

Japanese arts

Japanese arts flourished. New, colour-printed posters, showing scenes of everyday life and people, were popular. These were a strong influence on Western art in the 19th century. In spite of government opposition, popular forms of theatre such as Kabuki and the Bunraku puppet theatre developed into true art forms in the 17th and 18th centuries. These actors (right) are dressed for the parts of a murderer and his victim in a Kabuki drama.

The end of the shogunate

Although the towns became rich and lively, the peasants in the countryside were still poor. Peasant rebellions broke out more often. The government of the shogun was growing weaker. In 1854, Japan was forced to open its ports to western trade. The daimyo hated the foreigners and turned against the shogun. Others realised that the powerful westerners could not be kept out.

▽ In 1853 a US naval squadron sailed into Tokyo Bay and demanded that Japan open its ports to foreign trade. The shogun unwillingly agreed. Japan's long isolation was over.

△ The Japanese believed in making ordinary things beautiful and artistic. Even tea drinking was a ceremony, held in a special room.

The Rise of Science

People began to understand more about nature and the universe as a result of scientific discoveries in the 17th century. The invention of instruments such as the telescope and the microscope made these advances possible. Galileo's observations proved that the Earth moves around the Sun, and Newton explained why.

Science in the East

Before this time, science in China, India and Islamic countries was more advanced than in Europe. The Chinese were especially good at technology. More than 1,000 years ago they invented the abacus (the first calculator), clocks, rockets, paper and printing. They knew more about medicine than people in other countries.

The Hindus in India were ahead in mathematics. They invented the idea of 0 (zero) and the numbers we use today. In Islam, the caliphs of Baghdad encouraged science, as long as it did not contradict religious teaching. Arab astronomy and geography were the best in the world. The Arabs took their mathematics from the Hindus. They translated and studied the work of ancient Greek scholars, who had been forgotten in Europe.

▷ Scholars in this 16th-century observatory in Constantinople (Istanbul) are using instruments for taking measurements of the stars. At the back are a cross-staff, a quadrant and an astrolabe, all used by travellers to work out where they were from the position of the stars. The study of the stars was important in Islam. It helped the Muslims to work out the direction of Mecca from wherever they were, so they knew in which direction to pray.

▷ When Galileo heard how a Dutchman had invented the telescope in 1608, he immediately made one himself. With it he saw that the surface of the Moon was rough and uneven.

Sensational discoveries

1608 First telescope made by Lippershey.
1628 Harvey shows how blood circulates.
1658 Huygens makes pendulum clock.
1662 First study of statistics.
1673 Leeuwenhoek's microscope can magnify 200 times.
1676 Römer calculates speed of light.
1687 Newton publishes his theory of gravity.

Learning about the universe

Before the 17th century, science was held back by the Christian Church, which punished anyone whose ideas disagreed with its teaching. Copernicus, a Polish monk, wrote a book on astronomy which denied the Church's belief that the Earth was the centre of the universe. He dared not publish it until he was dying, in 1543. Nearly 100 years later, an Italian called Galileo got into trouble for teaching Copernicus's ideas. He knew Copernicus was right because he had looked at the sky using a telescope. He saw that Jupiter has moons that move around it, just as our Moon moves around the Earth. Changes in the appearance of the planets showed that they were circling the Sun. Galileo's telescope solved many mysteries. He showed that the planets seem larger than the stars because they are nearer, and that the Milky Way is not just a sheet of light, but billions of separate stars.

However, Galileo could not explain why some planets move around others. It was an English scientist, Isaac Newton, who discovered the law of gravity which he explained in a book, known as Newton's *Principia* ('principles'), one of the greatest science books ever written. Newton saw that the orbit of the Moon depends on the same force that makes an apple fall to Earth – the force of gravity.

△ When Robert Hooke made his microscope he was able to see a tiny flea clearly enough to make this detailed drawing.

Studying living things

The most sensational discoveries of the Scientific Revolution were in mathematics, physics and astronomy, but people also made important advances in other sciences, especially biology. A book on the human body by a Flemish doctor called Vesalius (1543) described the organs of the body, with brilliant drawings based on his dissections. This helped William Harvey, an Englishman, to understand how the blood circulates through the body (1628). Many discoveries followed Leeuwenhoek's invention of a better microscope. Robert Hooke, an Englishman, was the first to describe the cells of living things.

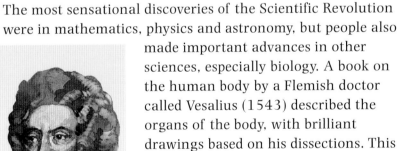

Scientific societies

Universities began to take science seriously. Gresham College, London (1575) had lectures in astronomy. Sir Isaac Newton (right) studied mathematics and science at Cambridge University, England. From 1660 scientific societies or clubs, like the English Royal Society and the French Academy of Science, were founded. By bringing scientists together to discuss their ideas, they encouraged scientific progress.

Louis XIV's Europe

The powers of European kings were at their greatest in the 17th century. The French king Louis XIV was the most powerful king in Europe. Most countries were growing richer, but under the old form of royal government much of those riches were wasted.

Louis XIV's France

The reign of Louis XIV (1643-1715) was the longest in European history. France was a strong country with a large population, good farmland, profitable trade, and an almost unbeatable army. Louis's power had few limits; he made all important decisions himself and did not have to consult a parliament. He wanted to make France the most powerful nation in Europe by expanding her frontiers. As his soldiers invaded land belonging to other countries, European powers including the Dutch, and later the English, made alliances against France in a series of wars.

Although he won some victories in these wars, Louis did not gain much of the land he wanted. The heavy costs of war, and the deaths of men in battle, made France weaker. The king did not improve the lives of people either. The poor paid most of the taxes, and nobles and rich churchmen paid little. The population fell, farmers were paid less for their crops, and thousands of peasants died of starvation.

When Louis XIV lay dying, he told his heir, "Do not copy my love of building or my love of warfare."

▽ Louis XIV's grand and hugely expensive palace of Versailles was the wonder of Europe. Here the 'Sun King', as Louis was called, lived a life of long, boring public ceremonies. He was attended by the nobility of France, who were forced to live at court to keep them out of mischief. It was the custom that the king's subjects should be able to see him, so while Louis ate his dinner, which was cold by the time it reached him, a stream of visitors passed by to stare at him. They paid a small fee.

The English Civil War

Like Louis XIV, Charles I (reigned 1625-49) believed God had chosen him to rule his country. But the English parliament wanted more control over how the king governed, and tried to control him by not allowing him to raise taxes. He needed Parliament's consent to do this. Charles and Parliament quarrelled and the result was civil war (1642-46). The armies of Parliament ('Roundheads') defeated the armies of the king ('Cavaliers'). When Charles plotted with his Scottish subjects to regain the throne, he was executed as a traitor to his people (above). For a few years, England was a republic, but in 1653

Oliver Cromwell, parliament's leading general, took over the government. He was called 'Lord Protector', and ruled much like a king. After Cromwell died, Charles's son was asked back to be king, and crowned Charles II in 1660.

The European nations

In Austria, Portugal and Spain, the powers of the monarch were almost unlimited. However, Spain was no longer the greatest European power. The Spanish king Charles II (1664-1700) wanted to keep the Spanish Empire together, so he left the Spanish crown in his will to a grandson of Louis XIV. Louis's enemies did not want France to control the Spanish Empire, and in the War of the Spanish Succession (1702-14) they defeated the great French army.

The independent states in the Netherlands formed a group of republics, led by Holland. Their leader, called the stadtholder, was a monarch of a kind, but he shared power equally with the States General (parliament). In northern Europe, the Swedish Vasa kings had won an empire centred on the Baltic Sea, but Russia, under its powerful tsar, was the great and growing power in this region.

▽ Ordinary people suffered greatly in the English Civil War and in the wars in mainland Europe. Soldiers were often unpaid, and had to live on what they could steal.

European Trading Empires

The struggle for trade and colonies carried European wars onto other continents and brought many peoples under European control.

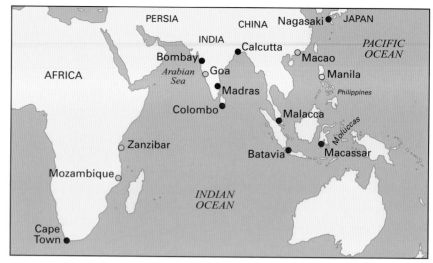

The Dutch

The newly independent Dutch republic was a small state in the early 17th century, but it was rich and confident. Dutch wealth was based on shipping and trade. The giant Dutch merchant fleet carried most of Europe's overseas trade, and the Dutch were among the first to believe that trade was worth fighting for. They built up their trade and business empire, mainly at the expense of the Portuguese. The soldiers of the Dutch East India Company drove the Portuguese out of many trading posts in the East Indies and West Africa.

But the Dutch were soon challenged by England, a more powerful sea-going power. The English controlled the English Channel, through which the Dutch trading ships had to sail. In its attempt to break the Dutch hold on Europe's overseas trade, England fought three wars at sea between 1652 and 1674. In 1689 the Dutch prince William of Orange, became king of England, and the two rival countries united against Louis XIV's France.

places controlled
by Europeans
- Dutch
- English
- Spanish
- Portuguese

East India Companies

The trading empires of the Dutch, English, French and others were won mainly by private business companies. Merchants, or stockholders, provided the money for these companies, but they needed government support. The Dutch and English East India Companies each had a monopoly granted by its government, which meant that no other company from their country was allowed to compete with it. They were very aggressive, and used force against their foreign trading rivals. Similar companies traded in other parts of the world. In America, the Massachusetts Bay Company financed the settlement of Massachusetts in 1630. The goods that the Europeans wanted were things they could not get at home, such as silk and porcelain, tea, coffee and spices. The American colonies produced tobacco and cotton.

Trading colonies

The Dutch East India Company founded Batavia (now Jakarta) as a rival to the Portuguese port of Malacca in 1619. It became the capital of the Dutch East Indies. The Dutch company was more powerful than any rivals in the 17th century. It captured Malacca in 1641, and secured a monopoly of trade with Japan.

In 1652 the Dutch set up a base near the Cape of Good Hope, to provide rest and supplies for ships bound for Batavia. It was a beautiful, fertile land, with few people. After 1685 the Cape attracted settlers from the Netherlands, as well as Huguenots driven out of France by Louis XIV. This was the first successful European colony in Africa.

▽ An Indian prince entertains officials of the British East India Company. Although the British became rulers of India, that was not why they went there. They wanted to make money, not run the government.

Christian missionaries

Besides traders, adventurers and soldiers, among the first Europeans on other continents were Roman Catholic missionaries. In Spanish America, Franciscans and Jesuits tried to protect native Americans against the greed of the conquerors, though they also helped to destroy their non-Christian customs. The greatest missionaries were Francis Xavier in Japan and Matteo Ricci, who brought Christianity to China. He tried to make Christianity fit in with Chinese customs. He was a man of great learning, who wrote books in Chinese and lived like a Chinese mandarin himself, and he was greatly respected in Beijing, where he lived (1601-10). But his own Church rejected his policy of changing Christian ideas to suit Chinese traditions. The picture shows Father Ricci standing before a Christian altar with his first Chinese convert.

The first British Empire

The European wars of the 18th century were fought both in mainland Europe and worldwide. The main rivals, Britain and France, both wanted to increase their trade and were building overseas empires. Each of them had a strong navy to make this possible. When the Seven Years' War ended in 1763, British victories on land and sea had driven France out of Canada and India.

The Rise of Russia

In the 18th century a great new power appeared on the European scene: Russia. The biggest country in the world, the land ruled by the Russian tsars stretched for over 12,000 km, from the Baltic Sea to the Pacific Ocean. But much of that land was cold and barren, and its people were poor and uneducated.

▷ The expansion of Russia. The huge Russian empire grew from the small grand duchy of Moscow, which by 1533 had thrown off Mongol rule, defeated rival princes and gained much of modern Russia.

Northern Europe

Control of the Baltic Sea was at the centre of affairs in northern Europe. The region was rich in trade and resources. All western Europe depended on the Baltic for timber, rope, and other naval stores. Denmark grew wealthy in the 16th century from the customs duties it collected by controlling the entrance to the Baltic.

In the 17th century Sweden became the leading power. Gustavus Adolphus, the most successful general of the Thirty Years War (1618-48), made Sweden a powerful force in Europe. But the Swedes found that success produces enemies, and their power began to fail. They had some success against their enemies in the Great Northern War (1700-21), under Charles XII, but were defeated by the Russians at the Battle of Poltava (1709). The balance of power in the region was turning away from Scandinavia, in favour of larger nations on the continental mainland – Russia and Prussia.

Russia looks west

The Grand Dukes of Moscow increased their land by conquering the Muslim territories to the east, and in 1547 Grand Duke Ivan IV took the title of tsar (emperor). Russian civilisation was strongly influenced by Byzantium, especially in religion, and the tsars saw themselves as successors to the Byzantine emperors. The defeat of Sweden in the Great Northern War extended Russia's territory to the coast of the Baltic, making Russia the greatest power in northern Europe.

Peter the Great (Peter I, reigned 1682-1725), the 'father' of modern Russia, was determined to bring his backward country up to date with western Europe. His methods were tough, sometimes cruel, but effective. He controlled troublesome groups like the boyars, who had once ruled Russia for their own selfish benefit, and replaced them with his own officials. He brought Western experts to St Petersburg as teachers, and travelled through Europe himself, picking up new ideas. He even worked in Dutch and English dockyards, disguised as 'Peter Mikhailov'.

▷ Peter built a magnificent new capital, St Petersburg, on the Baltic as his 'window on the West'. It gave Russia an important Baltic port, which put the ports of Western Europe within easy reach. Peter ordered the building of this Winter Palace, which was completed under Catherine the Great. Today it is part of a famous museum, the Hermitage.

the Russian Empire in 1533
lands gained by 1725
lands gained by 1796

Catherine the Great

Russian territory and influence continued to
grow. Catherine the Great, a German princess
who succeeded her husband, Peter III, as empress
(1762-96), dreamed of a new Russian Orthodox
Christian empire. She increased the empire through
wars against the Turks, and joined with Austria and
Prussia to divide up Poland. Like Peter, she tried to
'westernise' Russia. A rebellion of peasants and
others in 1773 made her realise that change was
needed, but her reforms only helped nobles and
townspeople, not the peasants.

Serfs

*Most Russians were poor
peasants or serfs (right),
who were almost slaves.
They had few rights,
owned no land, never went
to school, and often died
of hunger. Desperation
often forced them into
rebellion against the
landowners. The
value of an estate
in Russia was measured not by its area but by
the number of serfs it contained. The reforms
of Peter and Catherine gave more rights to
the nobles but did not help the serfs, on whose
labour they depended.*

▽ Although Peter tried to
make Russians look west,
towards Europe, he also
encouraged Russia's
expansion south-east,
towards the Black Sea and
Caspian Sea, and east. He
supported the Cossacks,
adventurous outlaw bands
who conquered Siberia.
He organised the
exploring expeditions
which later reached the
Pacific and Alaska.

Europe in the 18th century

The wars of rival royal powers in Europe continued during the 18th century. Some of the 'players' were new. Russia and Prussia now had large parts. But their ambitions were the same – to increase their power and influence.

The rise of Prussia

The Habsburg emperors of Austria (Holy Roman Emperors) had failed to unite Germany. At the end of the Thirty Years War (1648) Germany remained divided into many small states, with different kinds of government and different religions, Catholic and Protestant. One of these states, Brandenburg, was ruled by an able royal family, the Hohenzollens. They inherited the duchy of Prussia in eastern Germany, and in 1701 formed the kingdom of Prussia. Hardworking peasants turned the plains into a rich farming region. The Prussian nobles, the Junkers, formed a powerful military class, and the large Prussian army was the best in Europe. Protestant Prussia became a rival to Catholic Austria as the leading German power.

▽ Wolfgang Amadeus Mozart (1756-91) began performing at concerts when he was five. He was one of the great German-speaking composers who appeared in the late 18th century. Others were Haydn and Beethoven.

Frederick the Great

With a full treasury and a large army, Frederick the Great of Prussia (Frederick II, 1740-86) was in a strong position. In 1740 he seized the rich Austrian province of Silesia. A brilliant general, he still held it after eight years of war. The struggle was renewed in the Seven Years War (1756-63), in which Austria had powerful allies – France and Russia. Prussia's only ally was Britain, which sent money but few soldiers.

Frederick was a lover of music and a friend of philosophers. He was one of a new, more modern kind of ruler in the 18th century, like Catherine the Great of Russia and the Austrian emperor Joseph II. They believed that intelligent reasoning, which had solved so many scientific problems, could also solve problems of government. They were active reformers who brought many benefits to their subjects, but, although they made some sensible changes in law, education, business affairs, and in government, they never gave up any of their royal powers.

Main European wars 1689-1789
1689-97 War of the 'Grand Alliance'
          against France
1700-21 Great Northern War
1702-13 War of the Spanish Succession
1740-48 War of the Austrian Succession
1756-63 Seven Years War

Coffee houses

Coffee, imported from the Middle East, was a popular drink in Europe from the 17th century. Coffee houses in cities (right) provided a meeting place for businessmen and professional people. They could also read the new daily newspapers there. The famous insurance business, Lloyds of London, began with a group of merchants and ship-owners meeting in Lloyd's Coffee House.

Winners and losers

In the 18th century, France was still the greatest European power, and still the leader in style and fashion, but it no longer dominated the continent. Overseas, it lost many of its settlements and trading posts to its rival, Britain, which by 1763 ruled a large world empire. In central Europe, Habsburg Austria still seemed stronger than Prussia, but it was under threat from Russia's push towards south-east Europe. The Habsburg Empire, unlike Prussia, was made up of a mixture of people, different religions and different races (there were more Slavs than Germans). The loss of Silesia to Prussia was the first sign that Austria was in danger of losing its position as the leading power in Germany.

◁ Austrians and Prussians fight during the Seven Years War. Although Prussia suffered in the war, by 1770 it was powerful again. Besides keeping Silesia, in 1772 Frederick gained part of Poland.

▽ Craftsmanship reached a peak in 18th-century Europe. This desk was made for the king of France, the leading country in style and fashion.

The division of Poland

While Russia and Prussia were growing, another old European nation, Poland, disappeared. The Polish monarchy was not hereditary. Polish kings were elected, which meant that other countries were always interfering to get their favourite candidate on the throne. The Polish nobles controlled the election but, like the Russian nobles, they were interested in making themselves rich, not in the good of the nation. The rest of the Poles were powerless peasants. These weaknesses allowed Poland's three powerful neighbours, Russia, Prussia and Austria, to divide the country between them. Russia took about half, the others took the rest. By 1795, Poland ceased to exist.

The North American Colonies

The first English colony in North America was founded in Virginia in 1607. By 1750 there were 13 British colonies lining the east coast of America. Although each colony was different, in 1776 they united to form a new nation, the United States of America.

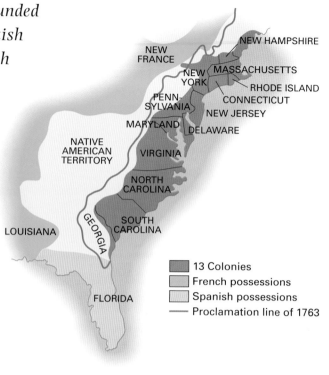

The thirteen colonies

The native population in this region was small and scattered. There was space for all, and relations between colonists and Native Americans started well. The early years were hard, and many colonists died. In Massachusetts more would have died if Algonquin farmers had not helped them grow American crops. But the two groups never mixed. Thousands of Native Americans died of European diseases, and, as the colonies grew, distrust and violence increased. The peaceful Quakers of Pennsylvania treated their neighbours honourably. But some other colonists showed no respect for native rights.

There were hundreds of small nations of Native Americans. Apart from the Iroquois League, which controlled northern New York State, they seldom acted together. But in 1675, a chief called Metacom united some Massachusetts tribes and attacked colonial settlements. Although other Native Americans came to their aid, colonists attacked innocent villages in revenge.

△ This shows the 13 British colonies in 1756. Most people lived very close to the coast. The Proclamation line was meant to stop them moving west into Native American territory.

▷ Towns like this one in the northern colonies grew fast in the 18th century. By 1770 Philadelphia (the largest) was bigger than most European cities. Because so much of the country was wooded, most houses were built of wood.

From Maine to Georgia

The colonies were started at different times and for different reasons. Some were business companies, hoping for profits through trade. Many of the colonists were religious refugees. The early leaders of Massachusetts were Puritans, with strict religious beliefs. The southern colonies became quite different. There, landowners were rich, thanks to crops such as tobacco and sugar, grown on large plantations worked by slaves. The colonies, especially the northern colonies later called New England, developed without much interference from England. Most had an assembly of elected representatives. There were royal governors, but the assemblies had some power because they controlled taxes.

Although most came from the British Isles, settlers also arrived from other European countries. New York was Dutch before the British took it. Germans, Swiss, Scandinavians and others settled in Pennsylvania. The British and French fought over land in Canada, and in the south.

◁ In this painting William Penn, an English Quaker leader, makes a treaty with the Delaware nation and pays for its lands (1682). His policy gave the colonists of Pennsylvania a long-lasting peace with the Native Americans.

New foods

The animals and plants of the New World (the Americas) were different from those of the Old World. The crops from the colonies in North and South America improved the diet of Europeans with new kinds of food. Potatoes were the most important, then maize (sweet corn). Tomatoes, green peppers and turkeys were welcome luxuries.

Trade and industry

Britain expected its colonies to provide cheap raw materials for British industries, and then to buy British goods. They were not expected to have their own industries, or to trade with other countries. The southern colonies supplied crops that needed a warm climate, such as tobacco, rice and sugar (a big crop in the West Indies). The northern colonies had poorer soil and a colder climate, but supplied fish and furs. They also developed industries of their own, such as shipbuilding. They even found ways to trade with other countries.

Harvard University

The first successful university was founded in 1636 in Cambridge, Massachusetts. The town was named after Cambridge, England, where many Puritan ministers had trained. The university was named after one of these ministers, John Harvard, who left his money and library to the university.

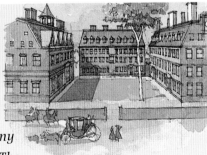

The Slave Trade

European traders found few spices and little gold when they first arrived in West Africa. But they soon discovered another, very valuable product – people. Between the 17th and 19th centuries about 20 million people were captured in Africa, carried across the Atlantic, and sold as slaves to colonists in the Americas.

▽ The 'triangular' trade. Sometimes the prisoners on a slave ship rebelled. But they had almost no chance of escaping. In the West Indies, some did escape. A few became pirates.

Cheap labour

The first African slaves were sold in Portugal as early as 1434, and by 1700 the slave trade was a big international business. European colonists in the Caribbean and other warm regions in the New World needed large numbers of workers for their sugar and cotton plantations. They paid high prices for African slaves, who were good workers – and did not have to be paid.

route of trading ships

Slavery

Slavery has existed in most countries since ancient times. Trade in slaves, run mainly by Muslims, existed in East and other parts of Africa too, but the slave trade to the Americas was particularly cruel. People were uprooted and shipped like cattle to another continent, with no hope of freedom. Families were broken up, and slaves were often overworked and cruelly treated on the plantations. Many owners thought blacks were not fully human, which made slavery seem less evil. In West Africa, large regions were ruined by the raids of slavers from the coast.

△ A diagram showing how a slave ship was filled with its 'cargo'. Not an inch was wasted.

The triangular trade

Huge profits could be made in the slave trade. The ships started out from European Atlantic ports, such as Liverpool in England or Bordeaux in France, carrying cheap guns, strong drink and other goods. They sold these to people on the West African coast, who used the guns to round up helpless villagers from farther inland. The captives were sold to the European traders, and shipped across the Atlantic to be sold again, at a large profit, at auctions in the colonies. The ships then took on cargoes of sugar or other produce from the colonies, which they carried back to Europe. With luck, they made a profit on all three parts of this 'triangular' trade.

Toussaint l'Ouverture

In 1791 the slaves in Haiti, led by Toussaint l'Ouverture (right), rebelled against their vicious French masters. The French promised to end slavery, and Toussaint, now governor, fought for the French against Spanish and British invaders. Later the French sent an army to restore French rule. They captured Toussaint, who died in France, but the French were defeated and Haiti became independent in 1804.

The abolition of slavery

As time went by, more and more Europeans were disgusted by slavery and the cruelties of the slave trade. Britain, the chief trading nation, made the trade illegal in 1807, But there was still a big demand for slaves in the plantations of the American South, the West Indies and Brazil, so the trade went on. Slavery continued in the Southern states until the Civil War (1861-65), and in Brazil until 1888. In some countries slavery was still legal up to the 1960s.

◁ Slaves, dealers and European traders on a slave ship off West Africa. A woman is being branded with an owner's mark.

The Early Modern World

In this period, all the different parts of the world came into contact for the first time. But people were not drawn together more closely. They were divided by different ideas and customs, and especially by different religions. The

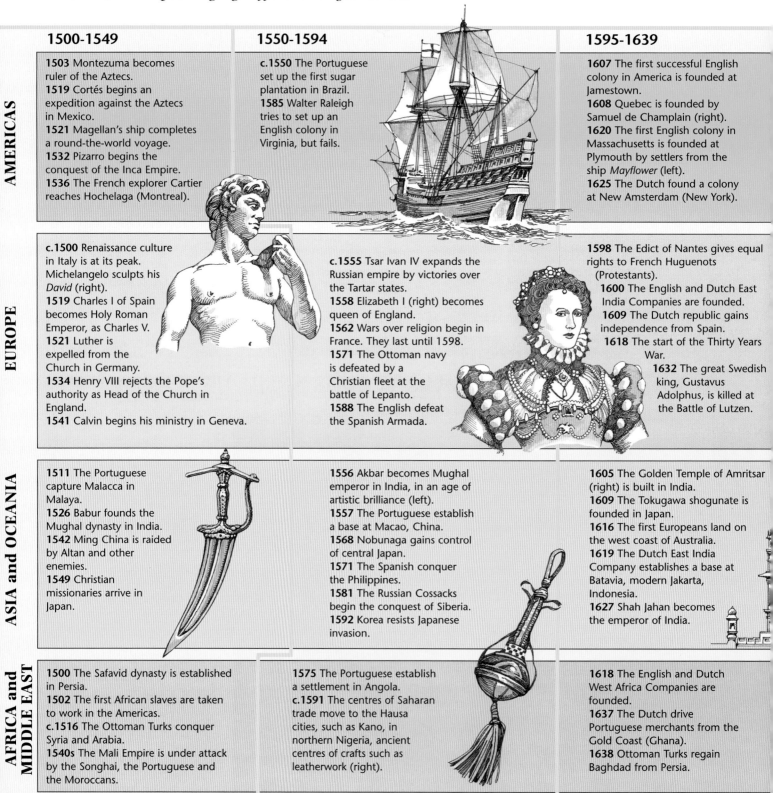

AMERICAS

1500-1549
1503 Montezuma becomes ruler of the Aztecs.
1519 Cortés begins an expedition against the Aztecs in Mexico.
1521 Magellan's ship completes a round-the-world voyage.
1532 Pizarro begins the conquest of the Inca Empire.
1536 The French explorer Cartier reaches Hochelaga (Montreal).

1550-1594
c.1550 The Portuguese set up the first sugar plantation in Brazil.
1585 Walter Raleigh tries to set up an English colony in Virginia, but fails.

1595-1639
1607 The first successful English colony in America is founded at Jamestown.
1608 Quebec is founded by Samuel de Champlain (right).
1620 The first English colony in Massachusetts is founded at Plymouth by settlers from the ship *Mayflower* (left).
1625 The Dutch found a colony at New Amsterdam (New York).

EUROPE

1500-1549
c.1500 Renaissance culture in Italy is at its peak. Michelangelo sculpts his *David* (right).
1519 Charles I of Spain becomes Holy Roman Emperor, as Charles V.
1521 Luther is expelled from the Church in Germany.
1534 Henry VIII rejects the Pope's authority as Head of the Church in England.
1541 Calvin begins his ministry in Geneva.

1550-1594
c.1555 Tsar Ivan IV expands the Russian empire by victories over the Tartar states.
1558 Elizabeth I (right) becomes queen of England.
1562 Wars over religion begin in France. They last until 1598.
1571 The Ottoman navy is defeated by a Christian fleet at the battle of Lepanto.
1588 The English defeat the Spanish Armada.

1595-1639
1598 The Edict of Nantes gives equal rights to French Huguenots (Protestants).
1600 The English and Dutch East India Companies are founded.
1609 The Dutch republic gains independence from Spain.
1618 The start of the Thirty Years War.
1632 The great Swedish king, Gustavus Adolphus, is killed at the Battle of Lutzen.

ASIA and OCEANIA

1500-1549
1511 The Portuguese capture Malacca in Malaya.
1526 Babur founds the Mughal dynasty in India.
1542 Ming China is raided by Altan and other enemies.
1549 Christian missionaries arrive in Japan.

1550-1594
1556 Akbar becomes Mughal emperor in India, in an age of artistic brilliance (left).
1557 The Portuguese establish a base at Macao, China.
1568 Nobunaga gains control of central Japan.
1571 The Spanish conquer the Philippines.
1581 The Russian Cossacks begin the conquest of Siberia.
1592 Korea resists Japanese invasion.

1595-1639
1605 The Golden Temple of Amritsar (right) is built in India.
1609 The Tokugawa shogunate is founded in Japan.
1616 The first Europeans land on the west coast of Australia.
1619 The Dutch East India Company establishes a base at Batavia, modern Jakarta, Indonesia.
1627 Shah Jahan becomes the emperor of India.

AFRICA and MIDDLE EAST

1500-1549
1500 The Safavid dynasty is established in Persia.
1502 The first African slaves are taken to work in the Americas.
c.1516 The Ottoman Turks conquer Syria and Arabia.
1540s The Mali Empire is under attack by the Songhai, the Portuguese and the Moroccans.

1550-1594
1575 The Portuguese establish a settlement in Angola.
c.1591 The centres of Saharan trade move to the Hausa cities, such as Kano, in northern Nigeria, ancient centres of crafts such as leatherwork (right).

1595-1639
1618 The English and Dutch West Africa Companies are founded.
1637 The Dutch drive Portuguese merchants from the Gold Coast (Ghana).
1638 Ottoman Turks regain Baghdad from Persia.

aggressive behaviour of Europeans, whose ships and armies travelled all over the world, caused serious disturbances in other continents, especially in the Americas. It had less effect, at first, on the great empires of Asia.

1640-1684

1654 The Dutch are driven from Brazil.
1664 The English obtain New York from the Dutch.
1684 La Salle sails down the Mississippi and claims the region, called Louisiana, for France.

1642 Civil war breaks out in England, between the king, Charles I, and parliament.
1649 King Charles I of England is executed.
1654 Russia gains control of the Ukraine.
1658 The peace of Roskilde between Sweden and Denmark marks the high point of the Swedish Empire.
1683 The Ottoman Turks besiege Vienna.

1644 The Qing (Manchu) dynasty is founded in China.
1645 Tasman reaches New Zealand.
c.1653 The Taj Mahal is built at Agra in India.
1661 Millions die in India after two years of drought.

c.1650 The slave trade begins to spread inland from the coastal regions of West Africa.
1652 Cape Colony is founded by the Dutch East India Company, as a base for supplying their trade with the East Indies.

1685-1729

1713 European settlers drive the Tuscarora and other Native Americans from the Carolinas.
1726 Nathaniel Bacon leads a rebellion against the governor of British Virginia, in an effort to drive Native Americans out of the colony.

1699 The Habsburgs regain Hungary from the Ottoman Turks.
1700 The Great Northern War breaks out, between Sweden and its neighbours, including Russia.
1703 St Petersburg is founded as the new Russian capital.
1704 Blenheim Palace (left) is the queen's reward to the British Duke of Marlborough for his victory against France, in the War of the Spanish Succession.
1707 England and Scotland are united by the Act of Union.

1690 Calcutta is founded by the British in Bengal, India.
c.1695 China establishes control over Mongolia.
c.1700 The Hindu Mahratta state in India revives under its peshwas (hereditary chief ministers).
1720 China gains control of Tibet.

c.1690 Asante power, rich in gold (this eagle, left, is an example), rises in West Africa.
c.1700 The Oyo kingdom of the Yoruba is the dominant state in the region of Nigeria.
c.1700 Lunda states form an empire including southern Congo and much of Angola and Zambia.
1705 Algerian tribes reject Ottoman rule and win independence under the Dey of Algiers.

1730-1774

1741 Ships from a Russian expedition led by Vitus Bering, a Dane, sail from Siberia across the Bering Strait to Alaska.
1759 The British take Quebec and conquer New France (French Canada).
c.1770 The Iroquois League of Native American peoples begins to break up. The Iroquois made this shoe (right).

1740 Prussia seizes Silesia in the War of the Austrian Succession.
1751 The first volumes of Diderot's *Encyclopedia* are published in France.
1756 The Seven Years War begins, with Prussia and Britain against Austria, France, Russia and others.
c.1769 James Watt invents a better steam engine.
1774 The treaty of Kuchuk Kainarji leads to growing Russian influence in the European provinces of the Ottoman Empire.

1736 Qianlong (left) becomes emperor of China.
c.1750 The Chinese empire expands to include Tibet.
1757 Alaungpaya re-establishes the kingdom of Myanmar.
1757 Victory at Plassey in north-east India leads to British control of Bengal.
1771 The British Captain Cook explores the coast of New South Wales.

1736 Nadir Shah destroys the Safavid dynasty in Persia.
1747 Afghan chiefs elect Ahmed Shah Durani as king of Afghanistan and he creates a powerful state.

Who's Who

Abbas the Great (1558-1629), shah of Persia from 1586. The greatest of the Safavid rulers, he created a professional army and greatly increased Persian territory, driving out the Uzbeks and winning land from the Ottoman Turks. He encouraged the arts and trade, granting rights to Dutch and English merchants.

Akbar the Great (1542-1605), Mughal emperor of India from 1556. After conquering most of India, he set out to make it a strong and united empire, in which Muslims and Hindus were equal. He even tried to introduce a new religion that combined Hindu and Muslim beliefs.

Champlain, Samuel de (1567-1635), French explorer. His journeys in Canada took him up the St Lawrence River to Lake Huron, and south to Cape Cod. He saw Canada as a place for settlement, not just making money from furs. He founded Quebec in 1608 and encouraged settlers in 'New France'.

Columbus, Christopher (?1451-1506), navigator, born in Genoa, Italy. Hired by Spain to find a sea route to the Far East in 1492, he reached the West Indies. In three more voyages, he explored Caribbean islands and the South American coast. In 1500 he was arrested. He died poor and neglected.

Cromwell, Oliver (1599-1658), English army general and ruler. A country squire and member of parliament, he became the most successful general on parliament's side in the English Civil War. When quarrels between different groups made republican government impossible, Cromwell became ruler as 'Lord Protector' (1653-58).

Erasmus (Geert Geerts, 1466-1536), Dutch scholar. He was a leader of the Renaissance in northern Europe and a friend of many European scholars. Like Luther, he wanted reforms in the Church, but he opposed the founding of new, Protestant Churches.

Frederick the Great (1712-86), king of Prussia from 1740. The best general of his time, his wars increased Prussian territory and its standing in Europe, while his government reforms strengthened the kingdom. He was also a good musician,

a friend of French philosophers, and the author of many books on history.

Galileo Galilei (1564-1642), Italian scientist. The greatest scientist of his time, he was born in Pisa and used its leaning tower to prove that light and heavy objects fall at the same speed. He discovered the principle of the pendulum, and made a telescope to study the Moon. His ideas angered the Church which tried to stop his studies.

Ivan IV (1530-84), tsar of Russia from 1533. He strengthened royal government, fought many wars to increase his lands, and supported the Cossack conquest of Siberia. After 1560 he became savage, slaughtering the wealthy boyars, killing his son in a rage, so earning his nickname, 'The Terrible'.

Kangxi (1654-1722), emperor of China from 1661. He strengthened the Qing (Manchu) dynasty, crushing rebellion in the south and defeating the last Ming forces, and gained control of Tibet. He encouraged scholars and artists, and accepted Christian missionaries for their knowledge of science.

Leonardo da Vinci (1452-1519), Italian artist, engineer and scientist. A great genius of the Renaissance, he worked mainly for the rulers of Florence, Milan and France, designing weapons, machines and buildings, as well as painting. His portrait of a lady, known as the *Mona Lisa*, is perhaps the world's most famous painting.

Louis XIV (1638-1715), king of France from 1643, the longest reign in European history. He took over the government after the death of his first minister Cardinal Mazarin in 1661. Powerful and ambitious, he dominated European affairs, but while his court was hugely rich, poor people became poorer, and the last of his wars ended in defeat.

Luther, Martin (1483-1546), priest and teacher. He began the Reformation in Germany. He was condemned by the Pope and the Holy Roman Emperor, but protected by the ruler of Saxony. In the 1520s he organised the German Protestant Church.

Newton, Sir Isaac (1642-1727), English mathematician. The outstanding genius of the 'scientific revolution', he explained how the universe works according to the law of gravity. Among many discoveries, he showed that white light is made up of rays that make different colours when passed through a prism.

Peter the Great (1672-1725), tsar of Russia from 1682. Determined, energetic, ruthless, Peter set out to modernise Russia and make it a great power by copying more advanced countries like France. His reforms covered education, religion and every part of government, and his wars increased Russian territory to the east and west.

Philip II (1527-98), king of Spain from 1556. He also ruled much of Italy, the Netherlands, and the Spanish Empire in America. Hardworking and honest, he was a keen defender of Roman Catholicism. But he failed to end the Dutch revolt, his Armada against England was a disaster, and his policies weakened Spain.

Richelieu, Cardinal (1585-1642), French statesman. As first minister of Louis XIII, he directed the government for 20 years, increasing royal power and weakening the Protestant Huguenots. But in the Thirty Years War he sided with the Protestant states against the Habsburgs and made France the strongest power in Europe.

Shakespeare, William (1564-1616), English playwright and poet. He acted and wrote for a company that owned the Globe Theatre, in London. He wrote about 36 plays including tragedies (like *Hamlet*), and comedies (like *Twelfth Night*) which are still performed all over the world.

Suleiman the Magnificent (reigned 1520-66), Ottoman Turkish sultan. The Ottoman Empire was at its greatest in his reign. He won new lands in the Middle East, Europe and North Africa, gaining the whole Arab world. At home, he built splendid buildings, reformed the law and made taxes more fair.

THE
MODERN
WORLD

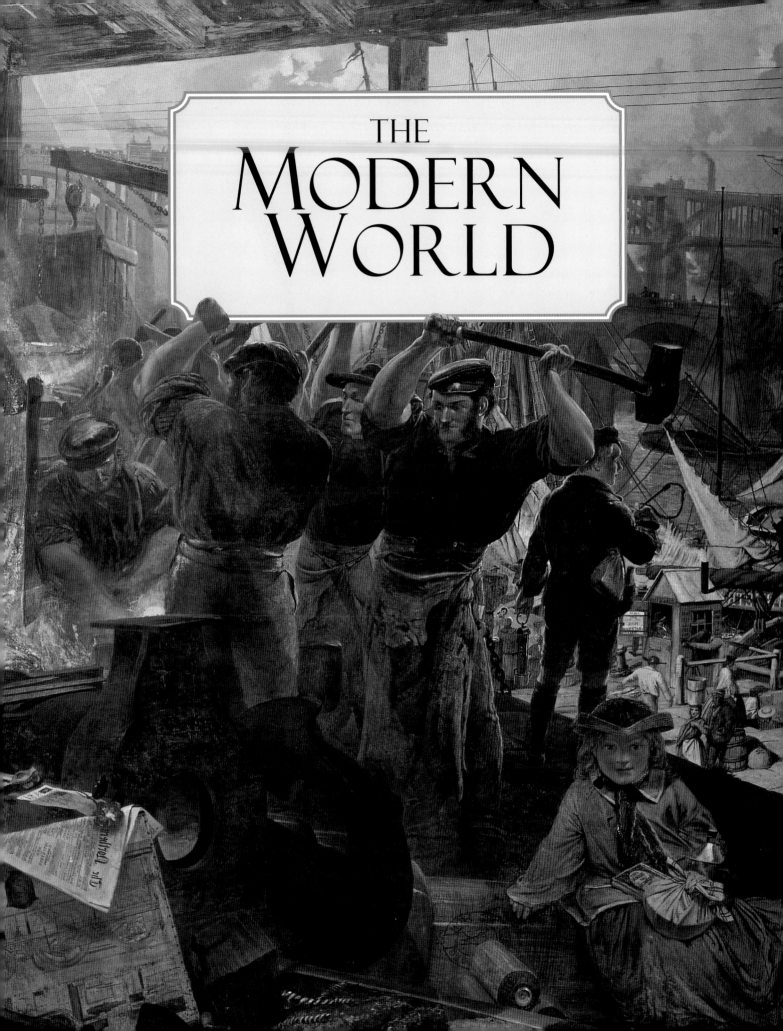

American Independence

In 1776 the British colonies in North America declared their independence from Great Britain. In the war that followed, the colonists defeated the British forces and joined together as the United States of America.

Revolution

After 1763, Britain tried to bring the colonies under closer control. When the British parliament imposed new taxes, the colonists objected because they had no representatives there. Anti-British feeling was strongest in Massachusetts, where British restrictions on trade hit hardest. After the Boston Tea Party of 1773 (below), the government punished Massachusetts with new penalties. Anger rose. Massachusetts was also the centre of revolutionary ideas. Tom Paine's *Common Sense* (1776) was eagerly read. He wanted a democratic republic, an end to slavery and equal rights for women. In Boston in 1775 revolutionaries were collecting guns. When British soldiers tried to seize them, shots were fired. The American Revolution had begun.

◁ A minuteman. The minutemen were groups of part-time soldiers, who fought against the British. They gained their name because they said they could be ready for action at a minute's notice.

▽ The Boston Tea Party. In a protest against the British East India Company's control of the tea trade, a gang of Bostonians, disguised as Mohawks (Native Americans), threw the Company's tea into the harbour in 1773.

War

Although the 13 colonies were very different, and many people there were loyal to Britain, the colonies agreed to have their own central government, and appointed George Washington as their army commander. The rebels were not trained soldiers, but they knew the country well, unlike the European soldiers. Most of them were also experienced hunters, and they had better guns. After a long, hard struggle the colonists, with valuable help from France, defeated Britain's professional armies, which included soldiers hired in Germany. The last British army was forced to surrender at Yorktown in 1781 when its supplies were blocked by the French fleet. Two years later, Great Britain reluctantly recognised the independent United States of America.

The new nation

Representatives of the 13 colonies, which were now independent states, met to decide on a form of government for the new nation. After long discussions, they agreed on a constitution in 1787. It created a federation, with a federal (central) government, an elected president, and a congress (legislature) of representatives from each state. The federal government controlled national affairs, such as taxation, defence and foreign policy, but each state also had an elected local government to control its own affairs.

△ *George Washington*

The United States of America became the first modern democracy, in which the power of the government depended on the agreement of the people. But who were the people? The constitution said that all people were equal, yet slaves remained slaves, with no rights. Native Americans were also ignored, and no women could vote. Even so, it was a great advance on other Western governments, which were still controlled by small groups of rich men.

The Declaration of Independence

The Declaration of Independence, of 4 July 1776, explained why the Continental Congress had voted for independence from Britain. It was mainly written by Thomas Jefferson, a future president. It claimed that 'all men are created equal' and have the right to 'Life, Liberty and the pursuit of Happiness'. Its main purpose was to persuade people that independence was the right choice.

The French Revolution

A violent upheaval in France beginning in 1789 destroyed the old royal government and aristocracy, and created a republic. Although the monarchy was later restored, the French Revolution showed that governments in Europe now needed the agreement of the people.

The old regime

In the 1770s France was still the greatest country in Europe. The French king still lived in grand style, but the royal government was out of touch with its subjects and, worse, it was bankrupt. The expensive wars of the past hundred years were partly to blame, and so was the system of taxation, in which the rich paid nothing and the growing middle class, which produced most of the nation's wealth, paid most. In the 1780s, bad harvests brought higher food prices, but lower wages. There was famine in Paris. People were in an angry mood.

The National Assembly

In this crisis, the royal government called a meeting of the Estates General in 1789. This contained representatives of the Three Estates – nobles, clergy and the middle classes (the Third Estate), who had not met for 164 years! When they met, the Third Estate took over and declared themselves a National Assembly. Ignoring the royal government, the National Assembly completely reformed France. A new constitution ended the special rights of the nobles and clergy, and declared all men to be equal in the eyes of the law. Church lands were taken over for the nation. All censorship ended. When the king tried to stop the meetings of the Third Estate by locking them out of their chamber, the members refused to obey and met instead in the royal tennis court. There was great excitement in France. In the name of 'liberty, equality and brotherhood', a completely new society was created. France changed more in two years than it had in two centuries.

△ The *Corvée*, a duty that forced peasants to work on the roads for no pay, was one of the many causes for anger at the royal government.

△ On 14 July 1789 a crowd stormed the Bastille, a royal fortress in Paris, an act that marks the beginning of the French Revolution. July 14 is now a French national holiday.

▽ A doctor named Guillotine invented a new machine for executing people. It was gruesome, but it was very quick. Thousands died by the guillotine during the Terror.

'The Terror'

Excitement soon began to get out of hand. Mobs in the country burned the castles of the nobility. Aristocrats fled abroad. In 1793 a more extreme government, led by Robespierre, gained power and launched a reign of terror against 'enemies of the Revolution'. Over 2,000 people, including the king and queen, were executed by the guillotine, a machine for chopping off heads. No one was safe – not even Robespierre, as events turned out, because he was overthrown and executed in 1794.

The rest of Europe looked on in horror. Other governments were terrified that the revolution might spread. War broke out between France and Austria, joined by Prussia and later Britain. The government called up ordinary citizens to fight, the first 'people's army'. Inspired by revolutionary patriotism, they defeated the professional soldiers of France's enemies.

In Paris, different governments came and went. They were less savage than Robespierre's, but inefficient. Strong leadership was needed and, ten years after the outbreak of the Revolution, a young general, Napoleon Bonaparte, seized power. The Revolution was over, but Europe would never be the same.

Napoleon's Europe

Napoleon gained power in France after the last government of the French Revolution was overthrown. For 15 years he dominated Europe as no one person had done since the emperors of Ancient Rome. His conquests helped to spread the French Revolution's ideas about freedom and equal rights for everyone to other countries.

General and emperor

Napoleon Bonaparte was a brilliant young general in Revolutionary France when he came to power in 1799. France was then the enemy of all other states, whose rulers feared the republican ideas of the Revolution. In a series of campaigns, he defeated all the great continental powers – Austria, Prussia and Russia – and became master of Europe.

Napoleon was a skilful politician and diplomat. But as well as his own energy and ability Napoleon's real strength was the new citizen-army of France. He chose to fight his enemies in the open, avoiding the long and exhausting sieges of earlier wars. The French armies proved unbeatable on the battlefield. All the great powers were forced to make peace at one time or another, but the peace never lasted long because Napoleon's ambitions went on growing.

△ Napoleon's conquests brought huge changes to Europe. The Holy Roman Empire ceased to exist, after 1,000 years. Many small, independent German states disappeared. The French Empire became gigantic, and new 'puppet' states were created, some with Napoleon's relations on the throne.

Europe in 1812
- French Empire
- ruled by Napoleon's relations
- dependencies of France

▽ Napoleon at the battle of Austerlitz, 1805. For 14 years, he was never defeated on land.

▽ One of the practical reforms after the Revolution was the metric system. It was introduced in 1795. The original metre was a platinum bar, kept in Paris.

Napoleon's Europe

Crowned emperor in 1804, Napoleon had the powers of a dictator, and sometimes behaved like one. For example, he ended freedom of speech and sometimes imprisoned opponents without trial. But he also believed in the ideas of the Revolution, for example that men should be rewarded because of their achievements, rather than because of their noble birth. One improvement was his new, fairer law system, called the Napoleonic Code. This came to be used in South America and Japan as well as Europe.

Napoleon wanted to be not just a great military leader, but a great ruler of a peaceful empire. Under him, the whole system of government and education in France was reformed and brought under efficient, central control. In the long run these reforms were more important than his victories in battle. Napoleon's influence is still strong in France today.

△ Napoleon was a small man with enough fizz and energy for 100 men. His soldiers loved him, and the French people put up with constant war for the sake of glory.

France and Britain

Britain was Napoleon's most dangerous opponent. Napoleon was unbeatable on land, but Britain was protected by the sea. He tried to close all European ports to British trade, and the British navy replied by blockading French ports. He planned an invasion, and even collected barges in the Channel ports, but the British naval victory at Trafalgar (1805) made invasion impossible. While supporting Napoleon's enemies in Europe with money, Britain sent an army under the Duke of Wellington to help rebels against French rule in Spain and Portugal. There was a long, tough fight which held down some of Napoleon's forces. By 1813 Wellington had advanced into southern France.

Defeat

Napoleon's own ambition finally defeated him. In 1812 he invaded Russia, which was a huge and dangerous operation. He reached Moscow, but the Russians burned their own city, and the French pulled out. It was an extra-cold winter. Half a million Frenchmen died during the long retreat.

The disaster encouraged Napoleon's enemies to combine against him. He was defeated at Leipzig, his enemies invaded France, and he was sent into exile on a Mediterranean island (1814). A year later, he returned to Paris and regained control. He reigned 100 days, before his final defeat by Wellington at Waterloo.

The Pacific Lands

Australasia was the last continent to be settled by humans. It was also the last to be reached by European explorers. As in America, the Europeans soon took over.

The first immigrants

The islands of the Pacific were settled by people from south-east Asia. The ancestors of the Aborigines arrived in Australia over 50,000 years ago, probably on rafts. The ancestors of the Polynesians, including the Maoris of New Zealand, came later, between 2,000 and 4,000 years ago. They travelled thousands of kilometres in sailing canoes. How they found the Pacific islands is a mystery.

▽ We do not know exactly what the boats which the Polynesians used on their first Pacific voyages looked like, but they may have been like this modern version.

European explorers

Portuguese and Dutch sailors landed on the coasts of Australia and New Zealand in the 17th century, usually by mistake. The British and French began to send expeditions to explore the region only in the 18th century. The greatest of these explorers was a British captain, James Cook. During his voyage of 1768-71 he sailed all around New Zealand and along eastern Australia, claiming it for Britain. Geographers believed there must be a giant southern continent in the south to balance the huge mass of Europe and Asia in the north. Cook proved that this did not exist.

▽ Captain Cook (below) spent six months carefully mapping the coasts of New Zealand. Then he sailed along the east coast of Australia inside the Great Barrier Reef – a dangerous voyage for a sailing ship.

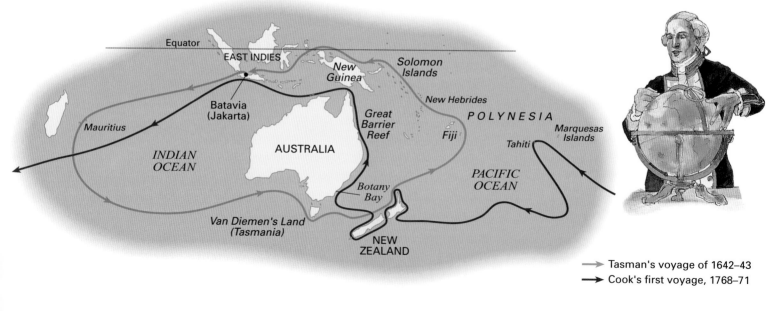

Equator
EAST INDIES
New Guinea
Solomon Islands
New Hebrides
POLYNESIA
Batavia (Jakarta)
Great Barrier Reef
Fiji
Marquesas Islands
Mauritius
Tahiti
INDIAN OCEAN
AUSTRALIA
PACIFIC OCEAN
Botany Bay
Van Diemen's Land (Tasmania)
NEW ZEALAND

→ Tasman's voyage of 1642–43
→ Cook's first voyage, 1768–71

Australia

The Aborigines were a Stone Age people, who lived in large groups where everyone was related. They had no metals, and lived by hunting and gathering food. Men hunted using spears and boomerangs made of wood. They believed that human beings are part of nature, in the same way as trees, rocks and animals. Because they were often on the move, they had no proper houses and few clothes or belongings.

△ This fish was painted on rock by Aborigine artists at Obirr Rock. It almost looks like an X-ray of a fish.

New Zealand

The Maoris were more advanced in technology. They lived in fortified villages, growing crops, making clothes, and waging wars. Their main weapons were heavy wooden clubs, until the Europeans brought in guns, which made Maori wars far more deadly.

The Maoris loved dancing, feasts and ceremonies. They used feathers as decoration and, like other Polynesians, they practised tattooing. The skin was pricked, then vegetable dye was rubbed into the pricks, forming beautiful patterns.

△ Wooden forts protected Maori villages. Like all Polynesians, the Maoris were expert wood carvers and decorated their houses with complicated designs. Their clothes were woven by women in the village. Using a large swing was a popular pastime.

Convicts and colonists

The first British settlers in Australia were convicts, sent into exile at Botany Bay, and their guards. Other colonists followed, hoping for a new life. Though life was hard, they made a living catching whales. Raising sheep and cattle brought more profits, but this also took up the Aborigines' land and almost destroyed the old way of life. The Dutch explorer, Abel Janszoon Tasman, reached New Zealand in 1642 and was driven off by the Maoris. Later European sailors found a better welcome, but the first colonists did not arrive from Britain until after 1800.

The Industrial Revolution

Between 1800 and 1900 life in Western countries changed more, and more quickly, than ever before. The biggest change was from a world of villages and farms to one of cities and factories, where machines produced goods much faster than the old methods. This was a revolution as important as the French Revolution.

The world's workshop

From about 1780 to 1860, the leading industrial power was Great Britain, which was also the world's biggest trading country. In 1850 more than one-quarter of the world's manufactures came from British factories, and nearly half the world's coal from British mines. By 1900, Germany and the USA had caught up.

Life before the Industrial Revolution

In about 1750 most people still lived in the countryside. They produced most of their own food and made their own clothes. Goods were made in workshops by country craftsmen, as they had been for centuries. There were no factories, and the machines in use, such as looms for weaving cloth, had not changed much for centuries. They were still powered by human muscle. Goods were transported either by pack horses and wagons on country tracks, or by boats along rivers and on the growing number of canals.

Manpower and money

The Industrial Revolution was possible because by the mid-18th century there was enough money to set up factories and enough people to work in them. Capital – money for investment – was needed to build the factories, and banks could provide it thanks to the profits made in trade. In spite of wars, trade had been growing since the 16th century, especially in countries such as Britain and France. At the same time there were more men, women and children available to work in the new factories because the population was growing fast. More people needed more food, and this was provided by improvements in farming. Fewer people died young thanks to advances in health and medicine, which helped prevent diseases like plague.

Machines and factories

The first industry to be 'revolutionised' was the cotton industry in Britain. In the old system, cloth was made by spinners and weavers, who often worked in their own cottages. When the spinning jenny was invented, it made the task of spinning 100 times faster. That encouraged other people to invent machines to speed up the weaving process and the harvesting of raw cotton. In this way, one new invention led to others, and progress in one industry led to progress in others.

The new machines were huge and needed a lot of power. They had to be kept in one building – a factory. The workers had to come to the factory, where they were supervised and everyone worked the same hours. In the factory, jobs became more specialised. Each worker performed one small job in the manufacturing process.

▷ Farming in the 18th century became more 'scientific'. New crops, new types of fertiliser, and new inventions such as the seed drill helped increase production. This huge sheep resulted from experiments in animal breeding.

Power for the factories

Before the Industrial Revolution, simple machines were powered by watermills or windmills. The earliest factories were built beside rivers partly because they needed water power to drive their machines. But the power that made the Industrial Revolution work came from the steam engine. Steam engines of a sort had existed for many years. They were large, clumsy and inefficient, but useful for pumping water out of mines. In about 1770 a Scottish engineer, James Watt, produced a far better steam engine. Versions of Watt's engine powered the machines of the new factories.

△ One of the first steam machines was called 'the Miner's Friend', because it was used to pump water out of mines. Steam engines were too low powered and clumsy for most other jobs, until James Watt's improvements.

Fuel for the engines

Engines need fuel, and the fuel used by steam engines was coal. In coal mining, new machines were not so important. The main job was still done by men chopping away the coal face with pick axes. But now the number of coal miners increased from a few thousand to several million, as many new, deeper mines opened. Coal was also needed for the new type of blast furnaces in the iron industry, which became the most important heavy industry of the century.

◁ Until the 18th century, iron could only be made in small amounts. In the Industrial Revolution, it became the chief raw material of 'heavy' industry thanks to improvements in technology. James Nasmyth, a Scottish engineer like Watt, made many of them, including (left) his steam hammer (1839), for forging huge iron objects.

Advances in Transport

The Industrial Revolution depended on better and quicker ways of transporting raw materials and finished goods. Among the many ways that transport improved, the most important was the building of railways.

▽ The Pont Cysyllte Aqueduct (1805) in Wales. New engineering skills allowed canals to be carried across valleys on aqueducts and through mountains in tunnels.

Roads and canals

For thousands of years, the fastest way to travel was on a horse. Goods were carried by wagons or pack horses, but the roads were poor. Bigger loads, when possible, went by boat. New industries needed better transport. New roads and bridges were built and, more important, waterways were improved by making rivers fit for horse-drawn barges and by building canals.

Railways

Canals carried big loads at low cost, but they were slow. The answer to the transport problem in industrial countries was the railway. Wooden railways with trucks pulled by horses already existed in mines. Public railways linking towns and cities were made possible by the invention of reliable iron rails and by the locomotive – the mobile steam engine.

People in every country saw how important railways were for industrial development. The iron rails crossed Europe, North America and, soon, the rest of the world. At first, railways were often built by British companies. In 1870, about one mile in twenty of the world's railways, from Australia to Argentina, had been built by the British contractor Thomas Brassey. Other countries soon caught up. Railways were especially important in large countries such as the USA. Mines could be opened and factories started in places that had no water transport.

▽ More railways – about 200,000 miles of them – were built in the USA from 1865 to 1915 than anywhere else. When the Union Pacific line was completed in 1869, it became possible to travel from the Atlantic to the Pacific coast by train.

Ships

Transport by sea was already much more efficient than transport by land, and many years passed before iron steamships took over from sail. For a long voyage with a large cargo, sailing ships were best. Paddle steamers were seen on rivers in the 1820s. But at sea, steamers were a rare sight until after 1840, when the screw propeller was invented. Even then they still had sails as well as an engine. In steamships, cargo space had to be used to store coal for the engines, and on very long voyages steam ships had to stop to refuel.

The Suez Canal between the Mediterranean and the Red Sea opened in 1869. It reduced the sailing distance from Europe to the Far East by 8,000 km, which gave steamships a big advantage.

△ The USS *Savannah* crossed the Atlantic in 1819, using her steam engine for a few hours only. The real breakthrough was the *Great Britain*, the first large iron ship, the largest ship in the world, with a screw propeller. She crossed in 1845.

Communications

New inventions, made possible by scientific discoveries, also speeded up communication between people. The first good telegraph system, a method of sending messages electrically by wire, was started by an American, Samuel F. B. Morse. It used the dot-dash code that he invented. The telephone (above), invented about 1875, was even better than the telegraph, allowing people in different cities to talk directly to each other.

Industrial Society

The Industrial Revolution made some people rich. It also created a new kind of society, with huge new problems. Because it had happened fast, there were no laws or organisations to deal with these problems.

Factories and slums

To a traveller in Europe about 1850, country districts showed little sign of change. But in the industrial cities, everything was new and strange. Thousands of people worked in factories that were noisy, dirty and dangerous. Work was boring, hours were long – 12 hours a day or more – and wages were low. The coal mines were even worse. Miners often worked by candlelight, which could cause explosions. They had no helmets, and they were lowered down the mineshaft, perhaps 300m deep, on ropes.

The industrial workers lived in crowded houses. Sometimes a whole family had to share one room. The houses were built as quickly and cheaply as possible, without proper drains, running water or even fresh air. For the poor there were no parks, no schools, no entertainment, no holidays with pay, no sickness benefit, no unemployment pay. Of course, craftsmen and farm workers had none of these things either. What was new and shocking in industrial slums was the size of the problem.

△ Factory smoke over a steel-making town in Pennsylvania, USA, in about 1900. Industrial cities grew from country towns or villages in a few years. The noise, smoke, dirt and slums struck outsiders with horror.

◁ Children did not have to go to school. Poor children went to work at an early age, sometimes five or six. Dangerous machines, like this mechanical loom, were unguarded and accidents were common.

Rich and poor

In the end, industrialisation made almost everyone better off. But at first it made a few people rich, while others were so poor they did not have enough to eat. The purpose of industrial society was to make profits. Employers believed that to make their profits as large as possible, workers' wages should be as low as possible. A few wise people saw that this was not even true, such as the reformer Robert Owen. He set up a factory in Scotland with decent conditions and good homes. Unfortunately, few bosses copied him. A capitalist with money to invest looked around for some profitable business. He seldom invested in projects such as better housing, which were really needed, because they would not make him a big profit.

Working people had no power and in most European countries were forbidden to form trade unions to try to improve wages and conditions. But some people remembered the power of the city crowd during the French Revolution. In Lyons, weavers and other workers rebelled in 1831, in 1834 and again in 1849.

▷ Machine breaking. The new machines made many skilled workers unemployed. In some parts, gangs of angry people attacked the machines, and sometimes the factory bosses too.

Emigration

In the 19th century the population grew faster than ever. In 1800 Europe had about 180 million people, but by 1900 there were about 400 million, mostly living in cities. The real increase was even larger, but many Europeans emigrated, like these Italian families on the first stage of their journey to Canada. Besides North America, they went to Australia and other countries, whose populations grew even faster. Millions of people fled Ireland to escape starvation in 1845-46 when the potato crop failed.

Government action

The problems of industrial society were so great, they could only be solved by new laws. Governments were slow to act, but after about 1820 they passed laws to improve housing and working conditions. Factory inspectors enforced the rules. Working time was reduced, child labour stopped, and trade unions were allowed. Local governments collected rubbish, built sewers and supplied clean water. Cleaner cities brought better health. Outbreaks of cholera, which had killed thousands, ended. In Prussia, laws were passed in the 1880s to help the old and sick. By 1900, living standards were rising.

Reform and Revolt

The ideas of the French Revolution and the growth of a new middle class in industrialised countries led to demands for more democratic government. In most countries, the struggle for power was violent.

Europe after Napoleon

In 1815, the leaders of Europe met at the Congress of Vienna to sort out Europe's affairs after the defeat of Napoleon. As far as possible, they tried to restore the old Europe, where governments were controlled by kings and nobles. This could not last. Two great forces opposed the old system. The first was nationalism, the idea that states should be independent nations, not part of a foreign empire. Most people who believed in nationalism also believed in liberalism, the second great force for change in 19th-century Europe.

1848 – the year of revolutions

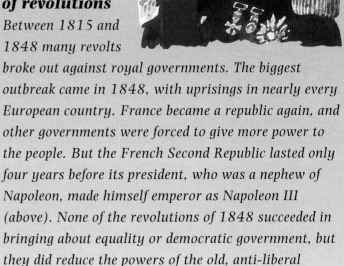

Between 1815 and 1848 many revolts broke out against royal governments. The biggest outbreak came in 1848, with uprisings in nearly every European country. France became a republic again, and other governments were forced to give more power to the people. But the French Second Republic lasted only four years before its president, who was a nephew of Napoleon, made himself emperor as Napoleon III (above). None of the revolutions of 1848 succeeded in bringing about equality or democratic government, but they did reduce the powers of the old, anti-liberal governments over their citizens. Although Europe had no more 'years of revolution' after 1848, liberal reforms came slowly. In 1900 there were still only two republics in Europe – Switzerland and the French Third Republic (founded after Napoleon III's defeat in 1870).

▽ Some protests in 1848 were peaceful. There was no violence in Britain, for example. Here, German workers present a petition demanding liberal reforms to the local government. In German states, one common demand was for a united country.

Liberalism

Liberalism means freedom. In politics, it meant more freedom for ordinary people to take part in government. With that went other freedoms, such as freedom to say what you believed without fear of arrest, or to follow any religion you chose. Liberalism was strong among the new middle class and skilled tradesmen. Liberals also wanted less government control. This idea made it difficult for governments to deal with the problems caused by the Industrial Revolution, especially the poor living conditions of industrial workers.

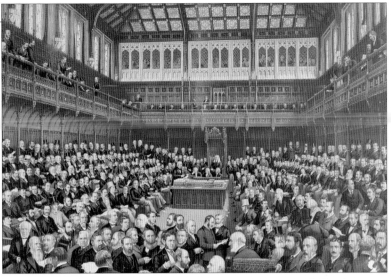

△ The British House of Commons in 1888. Parliament had been the most powerful part of government since the 17th century, but it was still controlled by rich landowners until the Reform Acts.

Peaceful reform

Liberal reformers looked to Great Britain as an example. Britain had a long tradition of parliamentary government. Power was held not by the monarch, but by parliament. Britain was the most liberal of the larger powers. However, before 1832 very few Britons had the right to vote in elections to parliament. A huge city like Manchester had no members of parliament, while some small villages had two. The Reform Act (1832) made voting more fair, and later reform acts (1867 and 1884) gave more men the vote.

Socialism

Socialism was a growing force in 19th-century Europe. Socialists wanted to give power to working people by taking away the wealth and property of the small number of people at the top. In a socialist state, everyone would be equal. All property would be owned by the state on behalf of the people. All profits from business would go to the state, for the good of the people. Some socialists, including Karl Marx, believed that this kind of state could be won only by a violent revolution of the working class against the middle and upper classes. Marx's *Communist Manifesto* was published in 1848, but had little effect until later. Other socialists believed in peaceful reform, by legal, democratic means. Socialists opposed liberalism just as strongly as they opposed royal governments.

Education

The new, industrial working class was weak not just because they could not vote, but because they were uneducated (most socialist leaders, like Marx, were middle-class by birth). By 1900, this was changing. Many European governments had come to realise that everyone should be educated. No longer was education left to the Church. Each country had a national system of education. Primary education (up to age 12 or 14) was usually free, and every girl and boy had to go to school. Secondary and higher education also expanded, because industrial countries needed more skilled people. Many new universities and technical colleges were founded. But these advances were slower in eastern Europe. More than half the people of Russia in 1917 could not read or write.

△ With education for all, everyone could read the news for themselves and form their own opinions.

Australia and New Zealand

In the 19th century, nearly all the islands in the Pacific were under European rule. The largest land masses, Australia and New Zealand, attracted many European settlers. As in North America, these settlers founded new nations.

GOVERNOR DAVEY'S PROCLAMATION TO THE ABORIGINES 1816.

▷ This Australian poster of 1816, in picture language, promised that whites would be hanged for killing 'blacks' as well as blacks for killing whites. But white settlers often committed violence without being punished. Some hunted the Aborigines like animals, and almost destroyed the ancient way of life before they even understood it.

Australia

New South Wales began to do well and attract colonists when sheep pastures were found to the west of Sydney. More colonies were started privately around the coasts of Australia. For the sake of law and order, the British government soon took them over. But they remained separate colonies, with their own governments, and even different widths of railway line. These colonies became states and joined together as a nation only in 1901.

Australia is bigger than the whole of Europe, not counting Russia, and for many years the colonists did not travel far from the coast. When they began to explore the centre, they found mostly hot, harsh desert. The explorers Burke and Wills were the first to travel across Australia, from south to north (1861). Only one member of their expedition got home alive. No one tried to start new settlements in central Australia. But things changed when gold was discovered in the 1850s. Mining towns sprang up, thousands of prospectors arrived from North America, China and Britain, hoping to get rich, The population began to grow at a much faster rate.

New Zealand

The first European settlements in New Zealand were camps made by the crews of whaling ships and traders from Australia. British missionaries and colonists followed. Reports of cruelty against the native people, the Maori, resulted in the British government taking over. This encouraged more British settlers to come, but did not prevent wars over land. In the Treaty of Waitangi (1840), Maori leaders agreed to accept British rule in return for a promise that their rights would be protected. This promise was not kept. The discovery of gold later in the century and the good farming land attracted still more settlers, mostly from Britain.

◁ In spite of the British government's promises, settlers in New Zealand's North Island took over lands that belonged to Maori tribes. The result was a series of wars in 1860-72, in which the Maori were eventually defeated. They lost their independence and much of their land.

▽ European colonies in south-east Asia and the Pacific at the end of the 19th century.

Exports

Australia and New Zealand traded farming products, such as wool and meat. Their main market was Britain, which also supplied the goods they needed to import. Britain was far away, and only goods that would not perish could be exported. In 1880 a new technology changed that: refrigeration. As frozen meat could be exported, sheep farmers could export mutton as well as wool; also beef, butter and cheese. By 1890 Australia had one sixth of the world's sheep.

New nations

Both Australia and New Zealand remained closely tied to Britain. Their national income came chiefly from trade with Britain, and they had few links with nearer neighbours such as China and Japan. Although both gained their own, independent governments, they remained loyal members of the British Empire. Most newer immigrants were British, and the Australian government refused to admit non-Europeans until 1945.

Europeans in the Pacific

Besides the British, the French were also active in the Pacific. They claimed many groups of small islands, and took over Vietnam and Cambodia on the Asian mainland. Most of modern Indonesia was officially Dutch, although the Dutch never explored it all. The 7,000 islands of the Philippines, part of the Spanish empire since the 16th century, were taken over by the USA in 1898.

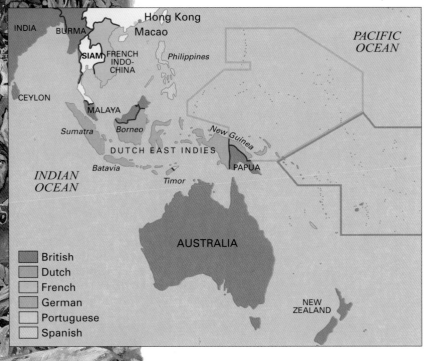

INDIA
BURMA
Hong Kong
Macao
SIAM
FRENCH INDO-CHINA
Philippines
PACIFIC OCEAN
CEYLON
MALAYA
Sumatra
Borneo
New Guinea
DUTCH EAST INDIES
Batavia
Timor
PAPUA
INDIAN OCEAN
AUSTRALIA
NEW ZEALAND

British
Dutch
French
German
Portuguese
Spanish

The American Civil War

The American Civil War began when the Southern states tried to leave the Union, which the federal government refused to accept. The defeat of the South, after four years of fighting and one million deaths, resulted in the end of slavery and a stronger union under Northern control.

North vs. South

The union of American states had been created to fight the British, and was never strong. The sharpest division was between the farming South, which depended on cotton produced by slaves, and the industrial North, where slavery was illegal. Some Northerners believed slavery should be abolished in the South too. The different views on slavery caused serious conflict as the country expanded westward. In the new territory of Kansas, fighting broke out between supporters and opponents of slavery. In politics, tempers were high. The Democratic Party, which depended on support in North and South, split in two, for and against slavery, each with its own candidate for president. As a result, the 1860 election was won by Abraham Lincoln, candidate of the Republicans, a new party of Northerners which was strongly against slavery in the South.

Many Southerners believed that the Republicans would end slavery, taking away their workforce, and feared the blacks would attack them. Before Lincoln had entered the White House, the Southern states officially withdrew from the Union and founded the Confederate States of America. When the Confederates attacked a federal fort at Fort Sumter, South Carolina, in April 1861, the Civil War began.

Confederate States
Union States
territories not yet states

△ The Northern (Union) and Southern (Confederate) states. The war was important for other countries too. For example, most of the cotton used in European factories came from the South. When the war stopped cotton imports, thousands of workers lost their jobs.

War

The Union had big advantages over the Confederates: more men, more money, most of the industry and railways. They also had control of the navy, which prevented the Confederates getting help from abroad. But the Confederates had great fighting spirit and, at first, better generals. Besides, they only had to defend the South, while the Union had to invade and conquer it. As a result, the war lasted four years, before the Confederates were forced to surrender.

◁ Although the Confederacy had no navy, it had two or three warships. Most famous was the *Alabama*, a sailing ship with a steam engine. Her career lasted two years, and she captured or destroyed about 70 Union merchant ships. In June 1864 she fought her final duel with a Union frigate in the English Channel, and was sunk.

◁ At the Battle of Chattanooga in November 1863, Union forces led by General Grant defeated the Confederates in a decisive confrontation. The Union could now use Chattanooga, in Tennesee, as a base for General Sherman's invasion of Georgia.

Events of the Civil War

1861 February: Jefferson Davis is elected president of the Confederacy.
April: Confederates attack Fort Sumter.
July: Confederate victory at Bull Run.

1862 August: Confederates under General Lee invade the North.
October: Lee's advance is checked.

1863 January: Lincoln proclaims the freedom of slaves.
July: Union victory at Gettysburg.
November: Lincoln delivers his Gettysburg Address in praise of unity and democracy.

1864 Union army under Sherman invades Georgia and burns Atlanta.

1865 Confederate commander Robert E. Lee surrenders to General Ulysses S. Grant at Appomatox.

The end of slavery

Some slaves escaped to the North, some were Union spies, and some joined the army. In 1862 President Lincoln's Emancipation Proclamation declared an end to slavery, causing celebrations among the slaves (below). About 4 million slaves became legally free, but they had no money and no property, and still depended on their former owners. Even in many northern states, blacks were not allowed to vote in elections until after 1870. A long struggle for equality lay ahead.

India and the British

During the 19th century the Indian subcontinent was controlled by the British. After a rebellion against British rule, a movement for independence developed. At the same time, a division was growing between Hindus and Muslims.

India and the East India Company

During the 18th century, the British East India Company began to take over government, at first in Bengal. By 1850 it ruled more than half of India, and indirectly controlled the rest. The Company had completely changed its nature from a trading company to a government.

The British built roads and railways, schools and hospitals. They introduced new systems of law. But they employed no Indians in the higher ranks of government, or in the army. They remained a ruling class, and lived apart from the Indians. English became the official language, and European missionaries preached Christianity. The government treated British trade as more important than Indian industries. It caused offence to many Indians by its efforts to 'modernise', which meant Westernise, the country, because its reforms often took no account of Indian customs.

◁ Two British officers are entertained by an Indian prince's household, in about 1800. Later, the British were less willing to follow Indian customs. India contained over 500 princely states. Although the princes remained in power, they could do little without British approval.

▽ Some grand buildings were built in British India, in a style that mixed European and Indian styles. This looks as if it might be a prince's palace, but it is the railway station in Bombay.

The Revolt of 1857

In 1857 some Indian soldiers mutinied because new army practices offended their religious beliefs. Rebellion spread across much of northern India, and both sides committed acts of horrible cruelty. This was more than just an army mutiny, although it never became a true national rebellion. It was crushed in the end, largely by loyal Indian troops. The British were a tiny minority, and could not have stopped the revolt otherwise.

'Empire'

The 1857 rebellion ended the rule of the East India Company. The British government took over India, and Queen Victoria was given the title 'Empress of India'. The rebellion also sharply divided British and Indians. The British now felt the Indians could not be trusted. Many Indians began to dream of independence, and were angry at the widespread poverty and at British discrimination against them. Although the British gave way to some demands, and brought more Indians into government, they still did very little to improve industry. They wanted Indians to buy British goods, not produce their own. Cheap, factory-made cottons from Britain had already ruined the Indian cotton industry, which was still based on country workshops.

In 1885 Indian nationalists formed the Indian National Congress. At first it demanded moderate changes, such as more Indians in senior posts in government and teaching. But some members wanted full independence. The nationalists supported Britain in the First World War (1914-18), mainly because Britain promised them self-rule. But after 1918, the government failed to carry out its promise, and nationalist opposition increased.

▽ Members of the first Congress meeting in Bombay in 1885. Their first aim was to make India a Dominion of the British Empire, like Australia. Later, they decided on full independence.

Asians and Europeans

During the 19th century the influence of Europe and the USA spread throughout the world. Some countries, such as China, tried to resist this, while others, such as Japan, adopted Western methods and ideas.

▽ For centuries, Europeans were amazed by the civilisation of China. But in the 19th century, China seemed backward. It still had beautiful arts and crafts, but it was helpless before the power and energy of the industrial West.

Rebellion in China

The Chinese Empire was bigger than Europe, but the Qing government was weak and losing control. During the Taiping Rebellion, from 1850 to 1864, rebels controlled most of central China. The country was in chaos. In the north, millions died of famine. But the imperial court blocked all efforts by Chinese officials to reform the government.

China and the West

The rebels gained extra support from the government's feeble dealings with the West. Once, China had been ahead of Europe in many ways. Now, it was far behind. But the Chinese still believed that other nations were 'barbarians'. For thousands of years the Chinese had considered their civilisation superior. Immigrants, like the Qing themselves, soon became 'Chinese'.

But the Europeans were different. They bought tea from China and, in exchange, tried to force the Chinese to buy goods from them. One thing the Chinese people were ready to buy was opium, a drug forbidden by their government. British efforts to sell opium, which was grown in Bengal, led to two 'opium wars' (1839-42 and 1856-60). China was easily defeated. Beijing was looted by French and British troops, and China was forced to open its ports to Western trade. Many cities came under Western control. Hong Kong became a British colony, Russia seized land in the north, and France took over Indo-China (Vietnam, Laos and Cambodia).

The Boxer Rebellion

The 'Righteous Fists' or Boxers, as Westerners called them, were a secret society united by hatred of Western influence. Their rebellion in 1900 was not against the Chinese government, but against the foreigners who seemed to be taking over China. The Boxers killed Christian Chinese, as well as Western missionaries, and attacked the embassies of Western governments in Beijing. Their rebellion was crushed by European, not Chinese, forces.

The Republic

It looked as though the whole of China would be carved up among the Western powers. But in 1911, the Chinese reformers won at last. The last emperor was deposed, and a republic was created under Sun Zhong Shan (Sun Yat-sen), leader of the Guomindang or Nationalist party.

Japan's emperor restored

After the USA had forced Japan to open trade with the West in 1858, the ruling Tokugawa were overthrown and the Meiji emperor was restored to power. The new Japanese leaders were determined to make Japan rich and powerful, and the way they did it was by learning the lessons of the West. Government, laws, and schools were completely changed as Japan followed Western examples.

▽ The Russo-Japanese War showed that an Asian country could be a great power. At the battle of Tsushima (1905), a huge Russian fleet was destroyed by Japan's up-to-date warships.

▽ Some Japanese welcomed Western ideas. This lady has a western husband and western clothes.

Japan and the West

The Japanese government did all it could to encourage industry and trade. It built a national railway network to improve travel between the mountainous Japanese islands. The special rights of the old warrior class, the samurai, were ended. Instead, a modern people's army was created.

By 1900 Japan was the equal of the West as an industrial country. But Japanese leaders also intended to make their country an imperial power. In 1894-95 Japan fought a successful war against China, gaining Taiwan. In another war in 1904-5, Japan fought Russia in Korea and in China's northern province of Manchuria. It seemed impossible that a small Asian country could beat a huge European power, but Japan won every important battle.

Nationalism

A powerful force in the 19th century was the idea that nations – groups of people who spoke the same language – should rule their own country. Some of the old empires, made up of many nations, were breaking up. New nation-states grew from the pieces.

▷ Garibaldi captured the Kingdom of the Two Sicilies with about 1,000 of his famous 'Redshirts'. (He had led them in a war in Uruguay, and they brought their red shirts to Europe with them.) They were helped by many local risings.

New European nations

One of the first new nations in Europe was Belgium. This independent kingdom was formed when the Belgians rebelled against their ruler, the king of Holland, in 1830. The Catholic Belgians were divided from the Protestant Dutch by religion, as well as by language differences.

Religion was also the main cause of the Greeks' fight against the Ottoman Turks. Greece won independence in 1830, and was the first of the Balkan countries to break away from Turkish rule. The Ottoman Empire was now weak. It continued to exist only because rival European powers supported it, to stop each other taking over the Turks' European provinces. This rivalry caused the Crimean War (1852-54), when Britain and France fought against Russia. But although new nations were being created, not all nationalist revolts were successful.

△ The Greeks kept their national customs and culture, even under Turkish rule.

Italy

After 1848, the *Risorgimento*, or 'rebirth', of Italy was led by the kingdom of Sardinia, in north-west Italy. It was directed by a skilful statesman, Count Cavour, and supported by France. Meanwhile, in the south, a rebellion began against the conservative rulers of the Kingdom of the Two Sicilies. The leader of this revolt was a patriotic adventurer, Giuseppe Garibaldi. He had also fought for freedom in South America and was an inspiring figure. The northern and southern movements combined to create a united Italy in 1862. The king of Sardinia became king of Italy. But Rome was still ruled by the Pope. He refused to give up the city, but he had no army to defend it. In 1870 the new government took Rome, which became the capital.

Dates of Independence in Latin America	
1811 Colombia	1821 Mexico
Ecuador	Peru
Venezeula	1822 Brazil
Paraguay	1823 Central
1814 Uruguay	America
1816 Argentina	1825 Bolivia
1818 Chile	

Latin America

Beginning with Haiti in 1804, most Latin American countries gained independence before 1830. In South America, the rebels against Spanish rule were usually Creoles, middle-class people of European descent. Their greatest leader was Símon Bolívar (left), who created 'Gran Colombia'. It was later split into separate states, ending the dream of making the old Spanish province of New Granada into one large nation. However, after Brazil gained independence from Portugal, it remained one country, a state larger than the USA. In Mexico, peasants and poor people took part in the fight for independence, as well as Creoles.

A united Germany

The main German-speaking states were Protestant Prussia, in the north, and Catholic Austria (the old Habsburg empire) in the south. Which one would unite the German nation? Guided by the great statesman, Bismarck, Prussia proved the stronger. Bismarck brought about a war with Austria, and Prussia won in four weeks. Prussia's influence now increased in the Catholic south, as well as the Protestant north. The Austrian Empire, with its many non-German peoples, was weakened by nationalist revolts, especially in Italy and Hungary. The Hungarians gained their own government in 1867.

The power of Prussia alarmed the French. In 1870, again through Bismarck's schemes, war broke out with France. In six weeks, France was defeated and in despair at the loss of its northern provinces, Alsace and Lorraine. On a tide of German nationalist excitement, a German empire was declared. The king of Prussia became emperor of Germany, with the trusty Bismarck as his chancellor. A great new national state had been created, larger and stronger than France or even Britain.

▽ Steel works at Essen, Germany, 1910. The division of Germany delayed trade and industrial development. After 1871 it caught up fast. By 1900 it had passed Britain as the leading industrial state in Europe.

The Scramble for Africa

While small nations in Europe were fighting against the empires that ruled them, Europeans were taking over on other continents. By 1914, 80 percent of the world was ruled by 'Westerners' – Europeans or their descendants.

Europeans in Africa

In 1880 Europeans controlled little of Africa, except South Africa. In the next 20 years almost the whole continent came under European rule. The 'scramble' for colonies began when King Leopold of the Belgians gained the Congo, as a huge estate for himself. Then Germany, a new nation with no colonies, grabbed territories in four different parts. In the north, the weakness of the Ottoman Empire allowed France to move into North Africa and Britain into Egypt. A European conference in Berlin (1885) recognised Leopold's right to the Congo and encouraged rivals, especially Britain and France, to divide up the continent.

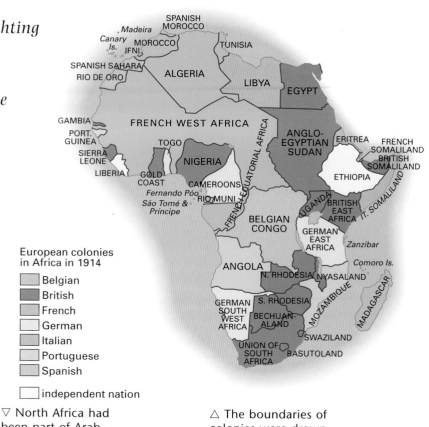

European colonies in Africa in 1914

- ☐ Belgian
- ☐ British
- ☐ French
- ☐ German
- ☐ Italian
- ☐ Portuguese
- ☐ Spanish

- ☐ independent nation

▽ North Africa had been part of Arab-Islamic civilisation for centuries. After the French conquest, many French people settled in Algeria. This would cause trouble in the future.

△ The boundaries of colonies were drawn by statesmen in Europe, who knew almost nothing about the peoples living in the regions they were dividing up.

Colonies in Africa

Most European governments did not really want new colonies in unknown lands. So why did they take them? Businessmen hoped for new opportunities. Missionaries longed to spread Christianity. Governments were afraid of a rival power gaining a position from which it could threaten their trade. Also, a nation that saw its neighbours winning foreign empires felt that they should do the same. Few colonists considered the wishes of the people they came to rule. Many believed that by bringing them Western civilisation, including Christianity, they were doing the Africans a favour.

South Africa

The British took over the Dutch colony at the Cape of Good Hope in 1814, to protect the sea route to India. British settlers began to arrive. The Afrikaners, descendants of the early Dutch settlers, disliked British control. Beginning in 1836, many left the Cape to get away from it. They set up home in Natal, in spite of clashes with the Zulu, a warlike people who later defeated British professional soldiers in a few battles. When the British took over Natal, the Afrikaners moved on again. In Transvaal they still could not escape the British and other foreigners, who flooded in when gold and diamonds were discovered there.

The South African War

Disagreements between the British and Afrikaners finally led to the South African War of 1899. For a few thousand farmers to take on the mighty British Empire seemed crazy, but the Afrikaners held out for three years before finally giving up the unequal fight. The peace treaty (1902) recognised British rule, and led to a union of all the South African territories, including Cape Colony, in 1910. The Union of South Africa then joined Canada, Australia and New Zealand as Dominions governing themselves in the British Empire.

▽ Beginning in 1836, thousands of Afrikaner families, travelling in ox wagons, took part in the Great Trek from the Cape to the north-west. They crossed the Drakensberg Mountains in search of fresh grazing land and freedom from the British.

Ashanti

Ashanti was a small but powerful kingdom in West Africa. Its symbol was a Golden Stool (below). Quarrels with the British over trade led to war. Ashanti won the first war, in 1824, but when it again attacked British trading posts it was defeated. In 1901 the British took over the Ashanti kingdom, to strengthen their position in West Africa against the French.

The Growth of the USA

In the second half of the 19th century all Western countries grew richer and stronger at an amazing rate. The country that grew fastest was the USA. By 1900 it was the richest country in the world.

The American West

The West filled up with settlers, and the population increased rapidly. The Homestead Act (1862) gave pioneer families 160 acres of land free if they lived on it for five years.

Cities grew even faster. Cities like Cincinnati grew up on the profits of the meat industry. Herds of cattle now grazed on the plains where once the bison had roamed. A new kind of wheat was developed for the prairie soil, and farmers produced so much grain that world prices fell sharply.

▷ The Statue of Liberty, 46 metres high, was erected in New York harbour in 1885. It was designed by a French sculptor and was a gift from the French to the people of the USA. This great landmark became the first sight of New York for poor immigrants from Europe.

The Indian wars

As millions of farmers and mining prospectors swarmed across the American West, the Native Americans were either killed or crowded into reservations. Wars against the Sioux, Cheyenne and other peoples, which lasted from 1864 to 1886, finally destroyed their way of life. One of the greatest leaders in the Indian wars was Sitting Bull (left), a chief of the Sioux. He took part in the battle of Little Bighorn (1876), where US cavalry, commanded by General Custer, were defeated.

California

In the 1840s California belonged to Mexico, although a few hundred US citizens lived there. In 1848, after the US-Mexican war, California passed to the USA. In the same year, a settler in California discovered gold. The population doubled in a few months, as thousands of people hurried to join in the gold rush. The gold did not last long, but by the 1860s California was doing well from farming, especially fruit, which (after 1869) could be carried across the continent by rail.

The railway

The 'Iron Horse', as people called the railway engine, seemed an amazing machine. Some people believed it would help to unite America, after the Civil War, by joining north and south, east and west. By 1860, the USA had nearly half of all the railways in the world, and lines had reached the growing towns of the Middle West. A link to the Pacific Ocean was completed in 1869. About 20,000 men worked on it, laying 1,775 miles of track in three years.

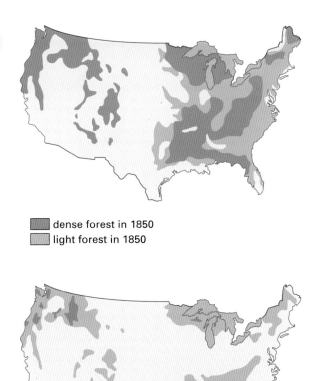

■ dense forest in 1850
▨ light forest in 1850

■ dense forest in 1926
▨ light forest in 1926

△ When the first colonists arrived, half the country was covered with forest. Today, only small patches are left.

Industry

After the Civil War the US government encouraged business and industry, and ambitious men travelled the continent looking for ways to make money. In spite of its problems, the country was in a hopeful mood. Factories and mines developed, helped by the railways which opened up new regions. Vast new industries, such as steel and oil, rose in town and country. These industries provided many jobs, although most people working in them were poorly paid. The big trade unions were formed in the 1880s to campaign for the rights of industrial workers, and wages started to rise.

The people who owned the new industries became millionaires. Their wealth gave them great influence. Some tycoons misused this power and bribed judges and politicians for favours. The big corporations controlled the market and set prices. Small businesses could not compete with them, and were soon taken over or forced to close. It was not until the 1900s that the US government took action, passing laws to control business and make sure prices were fair.

△ Andrew Carnegie (1835-1919) was born into a poor Scottish family, that emigrated to the USA when he was 13. He built a huge steel business, and was so rich he was able to give $350 million to charity.

The Poor

Although clever and ruthless men could make a fortune quickly, many other people were not well off. The blacks may have been free, but they were denied many basic rights. The Native Americans were crowded into special 'reservations' on the poorest land. They were controlled by the US government, which had to supply them with food, because they could no longer hunt. Many poor European immigrants, such as Irish and Italians, who entered the country in millions, struggled to live in city slums.

Science

Human beings came to understand far more about the Earth, nature and themselves in the 19th century. Scientific discoveries led to new industries and, for many people, a longer and healthier life.

Life on Earth

Most Christians in 1800 believed God had created the Earth a few thousand years earlier and little had changed since. Already, some people thought differently. The growth of sciences like biology and geology showed that the Earth was very old and had changed many times. The seas and continents had changed shape and, as fossils proved, different kinds of animals and plants existed in past ages. These discoveries gave rise to the theory of evolution, that all living things change, over millions of years.

▷ Advances in engineering and new materials produced new kinds of buildings. Brooklyn Bridge in New York was an early suspension bridge (opened in 1883). Its deck, 486 metres long, is suspended between towers. The skyscrapers were built later.

Scientists and inventors

This was an exciting and hopeful time. It seemed that all human problems would one day be solved by education and science. Even crime and poverty might disappear, thanks to greater knowledge and better education. In 1800 many modern sciences hardly existed. Schools and universities had few science classes. Many scientific discoveries were made by men and women who were not professional scientists. Inventions were made by craftsmen, not by experts in white coats. The first pedal bicycle was made by a Scottish blacksmith in his forge. Daguerre, the pioneer of photography, was a painter of scenery.

Technology

By 1900 enormous changes had taken place in industrial societies. Transport had gone from the horse and carriage to the train and the motor car. The first aeroplanes were a few years away. New kinds of buildings had appeared, made from new materials. The French engineer Gustave Eiffel built iron bridges across deep valleys before astonishing the world with his famous Tower in Paris (1889). Lighting had changed from candles to electric lamps.

1791 While dissecting a frog's leg, Luigi Galvani notices that an electric spark makes it twitch. This leads to the discovery of electric current.

1800 Alessandro Volta makes the first electric cell battery.

1823 Mathematician Charles Babbage designs what he calls an 'analytical engine', forerunner of the computer.

1826 Joseph Niépce and Louis Daguerre get together to make an early type of photograph.

1831-36 Charles Darwin (right) studies animals in South America, and develops his ideas of how evolution works by natural selection.

1831 Michael Faraday explains how a magnet can produce electricity, leading to the electrical generator.

1842 US surgeon Crawford Long uses ether as an anaesthetic, to put his patient to sleep.

1844 Samuel F. B. Morse sends the first message by telegraph on a wire between Washington and Baltimore, USA.

1856 Henry Bessemer's converter allows steel to be made cheaply and in large amounts.

1859 Darwin finally publishes his book about evolution, *On the Origin of Species*.

Medicine

By 1900 people lived longer, and fewer people died while they were still young. The greatest advance in medicine was made by a French chemist, Louis Pasteur, who was trying to find out why wine sometimes went bad. He discovered that tiny organisms were to blame. Later, he proved that such organisms – germs – cause disease. It then became possible to inoculate people against many infectious diseases.

About 1865 a British surgeon, Joseph Lister, read about Pasteur's theory of germs. He guessed that germs might also cause infection in surgery, and developed the first antiseptics. Having an operation became less dangerous. It also became less painful, now that anaesthetics were in use.

▷ One of the first operations using an anaesthetic, ether, to put the patient to sleep. (This is a reconstruction, posed by actors.)

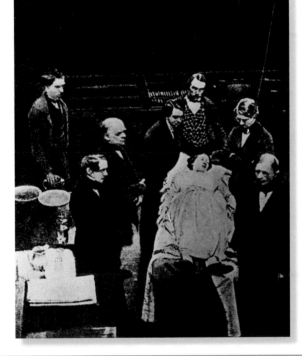

Health and hygiene

Hospitals also improved because of better nursing. Florence Nightingale set up the first modern school of nursing in 1860, and insisted that sick people needed clean beds and good food as well as well-trained nurses. The work of Pasteur and others showed that the greatest cause of disease and bad health is dirt, where germs breed. The industrial cities had no clean water, no sewers, and no street cleaning. Infectious diseases spread quickly. One outbreak of cholera in Britain in 1848 killed 130,000 people. The cities had to be cleaned up. Gradually, water supplies improved and new drains and sewers were built. One result was that cholera disappeared.

1860 French chemist Louis Pasteur shows that diseases are caused by bacteria.

1876 Alexander Graham Bell invents the telephone in the US and makes the first call, to his assistant in another room: "Mr. Watson, come here, I want you."

1876 US inventor Thomas Edison (below) makes a phonograph, forerunner of the record player.

1885 German engineer Karl Benz makes one of the first petrol (gasoline)-driven motor cars (right).

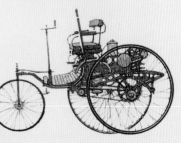

1895 Guglielmo Marconi sends the first 'wireless' message across a garden - the beginning of radio. In 1901 he sends a signal across the Atlantic.

1895 The Lumière brothers in France show one of the first forms of motion picture (right).

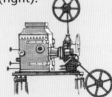

1895 German physicist Wilhelm von Röntgen discovers X-rays.

The Modern World

The modern world began with two kinds of revolution. Political revolutions in North America and France were based on the idea that governments should rule with the agreement of their people. In America, the result was a republic. France returned to royal

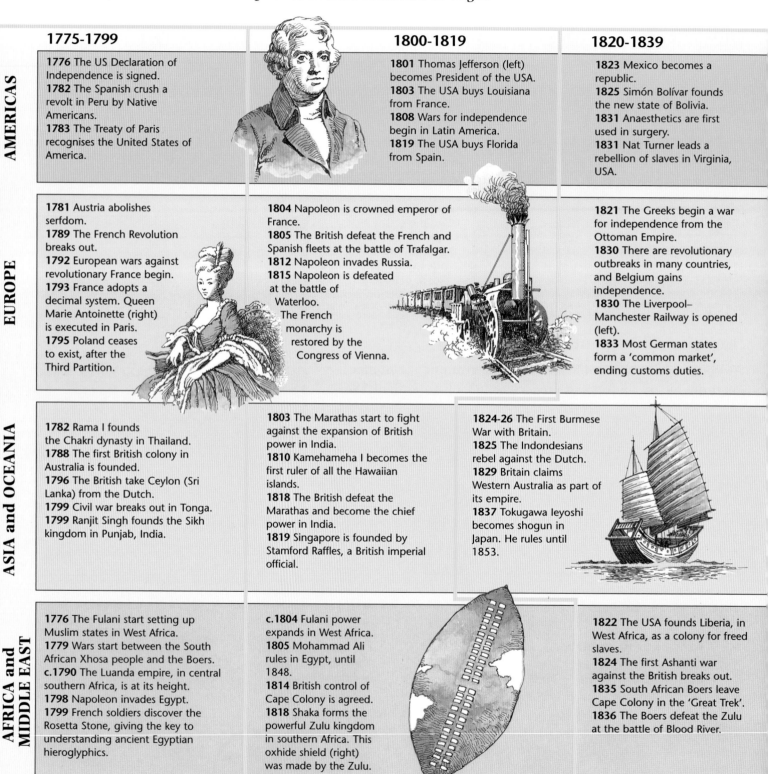

AMERICAS

1775-1799
1776 The US Declaration of Independence is signed.
1782 The Spanish crush a revolt in Peru by Native Americans.
1783 The Treaty of Paris recognises the United States of America.

1800-1819
1801 Thomas Jefferson (left) becomes President of the USA.
1803 The USA buys Louisiana from France.
1808 Wars for independence begin in Latin America.
1819 The USA buys Florida from Spain.

1820-1839
1823 Mexico becomes a republic.
1825 Simón Bolívar founds the new state of Bolivia.
1831 Anaesthetics are first used in surgery.
1831 Nat Turner leads a rebellion of slaves in Virginia, USA.

EUROPE

1781 Austria abolishes serfdom.
1789 The French Revolution breaks out.
1792 European wars against revolutionary France begin.
1793 France adopts a decimal system. Queen Marie Antoinette (right) is executed in Paris.
1795 Poland ceases to exist, after the Third Partition.

1804 Napoleon is crowned emperor of France.
1805 The British defeat the French and Spanish fleets at the battle of Trafalgar.
1812 Napoleon invades Russia.
1815 Napoleon is defeated at the battle of Waterloo. The French monarchy is restored by the Congress of Vienna.

1821 The Greeks begin a war for independence from the Ottoman Empire.
1830 There are revolutionary outbreaks in many countries, and Belgium gains independence.
1830 The Liverpool–Manchester Railway is opened (left).
1833 Most German states form a 'common market', ending customs duties.

ASIA and OCEANIA

1782 Rama I founds the Chakri dynasty in Thailand.
1788 The first British colony in Australia is founded.
1796 The British take Ceylon (Sri Lanka) from the Dutch.
1799 Civil war breaks out in Tonga.
1799 Ranjit Singh founds the Sikh kingdom in Punjab, India.

1803 The Marathas start to fight against the expansion of British power in India.
1810 Kamehameha I becomes the first ruler of all the Hawaiian islands.
1818 The British defeat the Marathas and become the chief power in India.
1819 Singapore is founded by Stamford Raffles, a British imperial official.

1824-26 The First Burmese War with Britain.
1825 The Indondesians rebel against the Dutch.
1829 Britain claims Western Australia as part of its empire.
1837 Tokugawa Ieyoshi becomes shogun in Japan. He rules until 1853.

AFRICA and MIDDLE EAST

1776 The Fulani start setting up Muslim states in West Africa.
1779 Wars start between the South African Xhosa people and the Boers.
c.1790 The Luanda empire, in central southern Africa, is at its height.
1798 Napoleon invades Egypt.
1799 French soldiers discover the Rosetta Stone, giving the key to understanding ancient Egyptian hieroglyphics.

c.1804 Fulani power expands in West Africa.
1805 Mohammad Ali rules in Egypt, until 1848.
1814 British control of Cape Colony is agreed.
1818 Shaka forms the powerful Zulu kingdom in southern Africa. This oxhide shield (right) was made by the Zulu.

1822 The USA founds Liberia, in West Africa, as a colony for freed slaves.
1824 The first Ashanti war against the British breaks out.
1835 South African Boers leave Cape Colony in the 'Great Trek'.
1836 The Boers defeat the Zulu at the battle of Blood River.

142

government, but the idea of equal rights for all remained. Just as important was the Industrial Revolution, which changed the lives of millions and created great wealth for some. Both revolutions happened mainly in the West. In 1899 most of Asia and Africa existed under European control.

1840-1859

1840 Upper and Lower Canada are united. They are given self-government in 1841.
1848 The USA gains Texas, New Mexico and California from Mexico.
1848 Gold is discovered in California.
1859 The first US oil well is set up, in Pennsylvania.

1840 Britain introduces the use of postage stamps.
1845 Severe famine affects Ireland.
1848 The 'Year of Revolutions', outbreaks throughout mainland Europe.
1852 The French Second Republic falls.
1854 The Crimean War breaks out.
1857 The Irish Republican Brotherhood is founded to fight for Irish independence from Britain.
1859 Darwin's *Origin of Species* is published in England.

1840 Britain takes over New Zealand with the Treaty of Waitingi.
1842 In the first 'Opium War', Britain takes Hong Kong from China.
c.1845 The British take over the major states in northern India.
1851 The Taiping Rebellion against the Qing breaks out in China.
1854 The USA forces Japan to open its ports to international trade.
1857 Indians rebel against British rule.
1858 China is forced to grant extra rights to foreign nations in the second 'Opium War'.

1843 The British take control of Natal as a colony.
1848 Algeria is declared part of France.
1853-56 Livingstone crosses Africa and reaches the Victoria Falls (right).

1860-1879

1861 The American Civil War breaks out.
1867 The USA buys Alaska from Russia.
1867 Canada becomes a British dominion, with self-government.
1869 The first railway is built across North America.
1876 Alexander Graham Bell invents the telephone.

1861 Italy is united and independent.
1861 Serfdom ends in Russia.
1864 Prussia takes Schleswig-Holstein from Denmark.
1866 Austria is defeated in a war with Prussia.
1867 Hungary gains self-government under the Austrian emperor.
1870 France is defeated in a war with Prussia.
1871 The king of Prussia becomes emperor of Germany.
1871 The French Third Republic begins.
1871 The Revolutionary Commune in Paris is crushed by troops.
1878 The Congress of Berlin establishes some Balkan countries as independent of the Ottoman Empire.

1861 Women gain the right to vote in Australia.
1863 France takes over Indo-China, in south-east Asia.
1865 King Kojong introduces reforms in Korea.
1865 In New Zealand the seat of government moves from Auckland to Wellington.
1868 Rama V comes to the throne in Thailand. He reigns until 1910 and makes many reforms.

1869 The Suez Canal is opened, linking the Red Sea with the Mediterranean.
1870s Samori Turé (right) builds a large trading empire in the upper Niger region.
1879 The Zulus fight the British.
1879 The British gain control of Afghanistan.

1880-1899

1876 At Little Bighorn, Montana, the Sioux defeat US troops led by Lieutenant Colonel Custer. A Sioux bow and arrows (left).
1886 The 'Indian Wars' against Native Americans, end in the USA.

1885 German Karl Benz is the first to sell motor cars.
1889 The Eiffel Tower (right) is built in Paris.
1890 Luxembourg becomes independent from the Netherlands.

1885 The Indian National Congress is founded.
1893 In New Zealand women gain the right to vote.
1894 Korea becomes independent in the war between Japan and China.
1898 The USA gains Puerto Rico and the Philippines in a war against Spain.

1881-98 Most of Africa comes under European colonial rule.
1881 The French take over Tunisia.
1882 The British take over Egypt.
1885 The Congo becomes the personal property of the king of Belgium.
1886 The discovery of gold in the Transvaal leads to the foundation of Johannesburg.
1899 The South African War breaks out, with the Boers fighting the British.

Who's Who

Bolívar, Simón
(1783-1830), South
American leader, called
'the Liberator'. He took
command of Venezuela's
forces when it declared
independence from Spain
in 1711 and eventually
drove the Spanish out. He
was chosen president of Colombia,
Venezuela and Ecuador, and also freed Peru
and Bolivia (named after him).

Bismarck, Otto von (1815-98), German
statesman. From 1862 he led the Prussian
government. His policy was to increase the
power of Prussia, and reduce Austrian
influence in Germany. Several quick and
victorious wars led up to the defeat of France
(1870-71) and the creation of a German
empire with Bismarck as chancellor.

Cavour, Count Camillo di (1810-61),
Italian statesman. A brilliant diplomat, in
the 1850s he made Sardinia, the only
independent Italian state, a force in
European affairs. In 1860, he became the
leader of northern Italy in the fight for
Italian unity and independence, which was
won, with the help of Garibaldi in the south,
in 1861.

Darwin, Charles (1809-82), British
biologist. At 22 he was appointed as the only
scientist on the 'Beagle', a small ship making
a five-year voyage of research, mainly in
South American waters. His experiences
gave him his idea of how evolution works by
'natural selection', which shook up not only
science but the whole world.

Garibaldi, Giuseppe (1807-82), Italian
nationalist and freedom fighter. He fled to
South America to escape execution after
fighting against the Austrian rulers of
Italy, but returned to lead guerrillas in the
unsuccessful revolution of 1848. In 1860
he led 1,000 volunteers against Bourbon
rule in Sicily and freed southern Italy.

Lee, Robert E. (1807-70),
commander-in-chief of the forces of
the Confederacy (the South) in the US Civil
War. He did not like slavery, nor did he want
to divide the Union in two, but he was a loyal
southerner. He was the best general on
either side, but the Union had more men and
more money, and Lee was finally defeated.
Lincoln, Abraham (1809-65),

US president. He was a lawyer from a small
town, a wonderful speaker and a
magnificent leader, who was elected
president for the new Republican party in
1860. He led the Union during the Civil War
and ended slavery. Re-elected in 1864, he
was assassinated by a Southern sympathiser.

Marx, Karl (1818-83), German
philosopher, founder of revolutionary
socialism. In 1848, with his partner
Friedrich Engels, he wrote *The Communist
Manifesto*, calling for a revolution by the
working class. To escape arrest he then
settled in London. 'Marxism' came to have
huge, international influence, not only
among communists.

Morse, Samuel (1791-1872), US inventor.
In the 1830s he had the idea of an electric
telegraph, passing messages instantly by
wire, and in 1843 he created the first US
telegraph, from Washington to Baltimore.
He is remembered especially for the
Morse code, a system of signalling
with dots and dashes.

Napoleon (1769-1821), French
emperor, born Napoleon
Bonaparte. The outstanding
general of the 1790s, he became
ruler of France, and was crowned emperor
in 1805. The last of the great conquerors,
he overran continental Europe before his
failed invasion of Russia (1812). Besides
great slaughter, Napoleon also brought
Revolutionary ideas of freedom to the
peoples of Europe. He died in exile.

Napoleon III (1808-73). Nephew of
Napoleon I, he was elected president after
the 1848 Revolution. In 1851 he rejected
the French republican constitution
and became emperor. His rule was
liberal, and he supported
movements for freedom in other
countries, but crushing defeat by
Prussia in 1870-71 ended his
empire.

Nightingale, Florence
(1820-1910), founder
of the modern profession of nursing. She
made her name reorganising a hospital for
wounded soldiers during the Crimean War.
Her improvements resulted in far fewer
deaths from wounds. At home again in
England, she started a school for nursing in
London.

Pasteur, Louis (1822-95), French chemist,
the founder of microbiology. He discovered
that diseases are caused by germs, or
bacteria. One result was 'pasteurisation', in
which germs in milk are killed by heat.
Pasteur's germ theory made people realise
the importance of hygiene, and saved
millions of lives.

Sun Zhong Chan (or Sun Yat-sen,
1866-1925), Chinese nationalist leader. A
doctor of medicine, he became leader of the
Kuomintang or Nationalists. After the
emperor was deposed (1911), he was
president of the Chinese Republic, but never
led all China, which was only united after
Sun's death.

Washington, Geoge (1732-99),
US statesman. He was a
landowner in Virginia who
fought in the colonial wars
against the French, and was
chosen to become commander
of the American colonial
forces fighting against
British rule in 1775. After
winning the war, he was
elected as the first US
president (1789-97).

Watt, James (1736-1819), British
inventor. While repairing an early steam
engine, he saw how it could be greatly
improved, especially by having a separate
condenser for the steam.
His engine of 1769, with many later
improvements, was the engine that drove
the machines of the Industrial Revolution.

Victoria (1819-1901), queen of England.
Her other titles included Empress of India,
and she reigned (1837-1901) during the
greatest period of the British Empire. She
had little real power, but was a great symbol
of national unity, whose reign is still the
longest in English history.

Voltaire (1694-1778),
French writer. He was a
leading philosopher and
had radical views about
religion and politics. His
views often brought him
into conflict with the
government and the
Church. As well as writing satirical
books, such as *Candide*, Voltaire was involved
in creating the first French encyclopedia.

THE 20TH CENTURY WORLD

The World in 1900

By 1900 the rich countries of the West controlled world affairs. It was a time of peace, but the world was less safe than it seemed. World business went through sharp ups and downs, and in Europe the rival powers formed two hostile groups.

The state of the World

The biggest change since 1800 was the rise of industry, which had made the Western nations rich and powerful. People could travel almost anywhere in the world in a much shorter time, and radio would soon make it possible to pass messages around the world in a few minutes. Yet for poorer people, even those ruled by European states, life had hardly changed at all. In Europe itself, nations remained as divided as ever, and their conflicts would soon plunge the world into war.

The Mexican Revolution

In 1910, the Mexican dictator Porfirio Diaz was driven out after 30 years in power. The Revolution lasted ten years. The biggest quarrel was over land. It was nearly all owned by a few landowners, but others wanted a share. Leaders rose and fell. They included landowners and generals as well as Pancho Villa, who led the cowboys. Emiliano Zapata led the peasants, who farmed the land but owned none of it. From 1920, Mexico was united under a new form of government.

▽ In 1900, to the well-off people visiting the World Exhibition in Paris, the world seemed peaceful and prosperous. They looked forward to a life of peace and comfort. But the 20th century had unpleasant shocks in store.

△ International sport became possible when rules for games such as football (soccer) were agreed. Unlike team games, the athletics events at the first modern Olympic Games in 1896 were much the same as in ancient Greece. This picture is from the 1912 Games.

The power of money

Europe's domination of the world economy rested on the power and wealth of Great Britain. The British navy controlled the seas and guarded shipping routes. London was the world centre of banking and business. The railways of South America were built with British money (and often by British engineers). France, Britain and other rich European states often financed industrial development in other countries, including the USA. French companies financed much of Russia's industrial development.

Only a few people – mainly the middle classes in Western countries – enjoyed the benefits of Europe's economic success. A peasant who became a factory worker was more likely to become unemployed in the 'booms' and 'slumps' that made some firms rich and others bankrupt. Most 19th-century governments believed that they should not interfere in business. Free competition between firms was supposed to keep prices down. This did not always work, especially as companies got together to form business 'empires'.

The confident West

Europeans' success in creating wealth and power made them believe they were superior to non-Europeans. Their way of life seemed far in advance of other continents. Some people believed that education could pass these advantages on to other nations. Others believed that European civilisation was heading for a breakdown.

▽ Nearly every European country had free primary schools for all children by 1914.

Tension in Europe

By 1900 Germany had overtaken Great Britain as Europe's largest industrial power. Its neighbours, France and Russia, feared the new German Empire and formed an alliance, which Britain joined later. Germany, in turn, felt threatened by that alliance but had its own partners in Austria and Italy. Besides having a well-equipped army, Germany began building a navy to challenge the British, and wanted more colonies in Africa. There were several tense international incidents, when the two rival alliances came close to war.

The most dangerous region was the Balkans – the small countries of south-east Europe which were breaking free from the Ottoman Empire. Serbia and Bulgaria especially were competing against each other for land and power. Austria and Russia both wanted influence in the region too. Two Balkan wars in 1912-13 ended with Serbia as the most powerful Balkan state. This situation alarmed Austria because, by ethnic background and religion, the Serbs were linked to Russia.

The First World War

The First World War was the first general war in Europe for 100 years. It was fought with the new weapons and explosives of modern industry, by armies made up of every young man fit enough to fight. More than 8 million soldiers were killed.

Allied Powers
Central Powers
neutral country
— Western Front in 1918
— Eastern Front in 1918

△ Europe during the First World War. Countries had formed alliances for defence, as a safety measure. A small incident set off war between them.

Murder in Sarajevo

In June 1914 the heir to the Austrian throne was assassinated in Sarajevo, Bosnia, by a Serb terrorist. The Austrians blamed the Serbian government and declared war. Russia came to the support of Serbia, Germany supported Austria and also attacked France, Russia's ally. Britain, with its empire, came to the support of France.

A world war

Other countries were drawn in. Italy joined the Allies (Britain and France) and fought the Austrians in southern Europe. Russia stopped fighting after its revolution in 1917, but the USA joined the Allies. So did Australia, New Zealand and Japan, while Turkey joined Germany and Austria. Although the heaviest fighting was in Europe, there was some fighting against the Turks. The Arabs, with British support, rebelled against their Turkish rulers in the Middle East.

German submarines attacked ships of other nations, including harmless passenger ships. This brought the USA into the war. There was only one great naval battle between the mighty British and German fleets, at Jutland (1916). By 1918, the European nations were worn out. German civilians were starving, and there were mutinies in the French army. In November, revolution broke out in Germany and at the same time, the fleet mutinied. Germany surrendered.

The trenches

At first, people thought the war would be short. Instead, the fighting became bogged down. The soldiers faced each other from defensive trenches. The killing power of machine guns and explosive shells made attack almost impossible, and generals could not break out of this pattern. They tried poison gas, but it could only be used when the wind was in the right direction. Later in the war, they tried tanks.

The home front

Earlier wars had been mostly fought by professional armies, while life at home continued much as usual. But the First World War involved civilians as well as soldiers. Because nearly all young men were called up to fight, women took on their jobs – especially in the factories making weapons, on farms and in transport. They proved just as good as men, sometimes better. They seldom complained or got drunk. The cause of women's rights took a giant leap forward.

◁ Women doing skilled work in an aircraft factory in 1917. This was the first war in which aircraft played an important part.

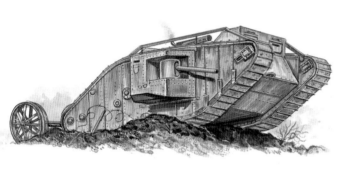

△ Early tanks often broke down, and not many had been built. But military planners saw that they might be the answer to the horrible stalemate of trench warfare.

◁ Apart from rats, mud, shells and poison gas, soldiers were protected if they stayed in their trenches. But when they went 'over the top' to make an attack, they were easily killed. In 1915 about 2 million British and French soldiers were killed in the battles of the Somme. The biggest advance made in any attack was only three miles.

Winners and losers

Over 15 million people died in the war. Germany was in chaos. France was not much better. The Allies were deep in debt, mainly to the USA. The Versailles peace treaty (1919) created new states such as Czechoslovakia and Yugoslavia, and set up the League of Nations to settle international quarrels. The League placed provinces of the defeated Turkish Empire under French or British rule, with a promise of future independence. The peacemakers blamed Germany for the war, and ordered the new German republic to pay huge sums for the damage caused. That made it hard for Germany to recover. The biggest 'winner' was the USA, where war caused rapid industrial growth. By 1919 the USA was clearly the most powerful nation in the world.

The Irish Rebellion

At Easter 1916, Irish republicans rebelled against British rule. The British quickly crushed the Easter Rising, but afterwards, nationalist feelings in Ireland grew stronger. The republican party, Sinn Fein, won many seats in elections and formed an underground government. In 1921, after three years of violence, Britain agreed to a separate government for Ireland, except for six, mainly Protestant counties in the north, which refused to join the Catholic Irish Free State.

The Russian Revolution

In 1917 the people of Russia rebelled against their ruler, the tsar, in a revolution. The result was a completely new system of government, called communism. It was supposed to give power to ordinary working people, but instead just a few men controlled the country by fear.

The coming of revolution

In 1900 Russia was a backward country compared with western Europe. It was something like France before the French Revolution. The peasants were no longer serfs, but their life was still poor and primitive. They had no say in the government. The government was neither efficient nor honest. The tsar, who was supposed to be all-powerful, seemed weak. In the cities, strikes and riots were frequent. Educated people believed that big reforms were necessary in Russia.

In 1905, Russia's shameful defeat in a war with Japan provoked rebellion. The tsar promised to set up a more democratic government, but this did not happen. In 1917, with Russians suffering in the First World War, rebellion broke out again. This time the tsar was deposed and a republic was declared. Six months later, in a second revolution, the Bolsheviks took over the government. Russia was renamed the Union of Soviet Socialist Republics (the USSR), often referred to as the Soviet Union.

The Bolsheviks

The Bolsheviks, led by Vladimir Ilich Lenin (left), were followers of Karl Marx, the founder of communism. They believed in a working-class revolution, with all property owned by the state ('nationalised'). There would be no more rich and poor, no masters and servants: everyone would be equal. The Bolsheviks were a small group but they were well organised. They controlled the workers' councils, called soviets, in the big cities. This gave them the power to take over the government.

▷ November 1917: Bolshevik 'Red Guards' stormed the Winter Palace in St Petersburg. The government surrendered, but the fighting came later.

Civil war

After the Revolution, the Bolsheviks made peace with Germany. But there was no peace inside the Soviet Union. Anti-Bolshevik forces, with help from abroad, fought for three years against the 'Red Army' organised by Lenin's associate, Trotsky.

The Bolsheviks expected communist revolutions to break out all over Europe but, except for a small one in Germany, they did not. However, communist parties did exist in other countries. As allies of the Soviet government, they worked for an international revolution.

▷ A defendant (left) stands before the prosecutors at a state trial in 1931. Innocent people confessed to 'crimes against the state' in order to save their families from punishment.

△ The government used art for propaganda for the workers' state. This May Day poster shows workers marching over symbols for wealth, and the tsar and his government.

Russia under Stalin

After the death of Lenin, Joseph Stalin, as secretary of the Communist Party, increased the power of the Party and banned all other parties. By 1930 he was more powerful than the tsar had been. He built up a huge, efficient secret police, and his rule was based on fear. He treated all his opponents as traitors. He ordered millions of people to be killed, or sent to prison camps in Siberia.

Stalin reorganised the USSR as a communist country. In agriculture, independent farms were forced into large 'collectives' run very badly by Party officials. Millions died of starvation. Stalin was determined to make the USSR a great industrial power that could challenge the USA. Industry did increase but, as in farming, the state grew more powerful while the workers were no better off. Under Stalin, only Party officials lived well.

Between the World Wars

The war caused more problems than it solved. After 1918, Europe was a more dangerous place than before. Democratic governments failed to solve people's problems. Some people turned to communism, represented by Soviet Russia, and others to an extreme form of nationalism.

The 1920s

Living standards rose in the West in the 1920s, the age of jazz, nightclubs and cinema. The American 'Model T' Ford was the first mass-produced car, which ordinary families could afford. More women went out to work. Few of them were lawyers or doctors, but many were wage-earners. Before 1914, working women were mostly servants. Their new jobs brought greater independence as well as higher pay. Although there were fewer servants, machines such as vacuum cleaners and gas or electric cookers made household tasks easier.

△ In the 1920s people wanted to forget the war. They set out to have a good time. Women especially felt a new sense of freedom. The war had made them more independent.

▽ The Great Depression ended the fun. Respectable Americans lost their jobs, their savings and their property. They had to live in shanty towns like this one in Seattle, Washington.

The Great Depression

The capitalist system always had booms and slumps. The worst slump ever began in 1929, with a sharp fall in the value of shares on the New York stock market. The effects spread quickly. Banks and businesses collapsed. People who had been rich suddenly had nothing. The Great Depression affected non-industrial countries too, as the market for their exports almost disappeared. Communists believed that the whole capitalist system was collapsing, as Marx had said it would. But by the mid-1930s, business was beginning to recover.

△ The Fascist leader Mussolini thought of himself as a kind of modern Roman emperor. Fascists believed in power and the glory of the nation. They cared little for ordinary human rights.

Fascism

In countries such as Italy and Germany, the war and the terms of the peace treaty (1919) caused grave problems. Democratic governments seemed unable to solve them, and many people were attracted to extreme nationalist parties. In Italy the Fascist party led by Mussolini gained power in 1922, after a threatening march on Rome. Mussolini ended democracy and made himself a dictator. He promised to make Italy a great power, and set out to create an empire in Africa, conquering Ethiopia.

The Nazis

Adolf Hitler was the head of the National Socialists (Nazis) in Germany. Like Mussolini, he won votes because he promised to solve the country's terrible problems. Then he abolished parliament and made himself a dictator, supported by brutal secret police. The Nazis crushed, or even murdered, all who opposed them, including many communists. They were also racists of an extreme kind. They hated Jews, gypsies, Slavs and all others who they said belonged to an 'inferior race'. Hitler aimed to create a new German empire. He set out to make the country powerful, by building up the army, navy and air force, although that was forbidden by the peace treaty of 1919.

Fascism in the Far East

Other countries, such as Spain and Argentina, came under some form of fascist rule in the 1930s. In Japan, many army officers held fascist ideas, and many ordinary Japanese believed that their economic problems could only be solved by force. The government was weak, and violence was growing. Three prime ministers were murdered between

The Spanish Civil War

Spain became a republic in 1931, but the country was badly split between different groups. The government made some reforms, then cancelled them. There were protests, riots and revolts. The government was losing control, and an army rebellion set off three years of civil war (1936-39). Socialists, communists and other left-wing groups supported the government. The Church, landowners and the army supported the rebels, who also received aid from Hitler and Mussolini. General Franco's victory began a fascist dictatorship which lasted until his death in 1975.

1918 and 1932. Military men gained influence in government. In 1931 the army took over Chinese Manchuria, and further aggression led to war with China. Japan also made agreements with fascist Germany and Italy. When war broke out in Europe in 1939, Japan seized the chance to invade French and British colonies in south-east Asia.

The Arts and Entertainment

From the late 19th century great changes took place in the arts, music and literature, mainly in the West. At the same time, new forms of entertainment were invented for ordinary people, who were now better educated, better paid and had more time for hobbies and amusements.

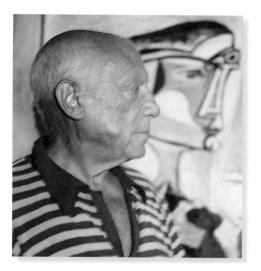

△ Pablo Picasso (1881-1973), the most famous painter of the 20th century. Some people said his art was ugly and unrealistic. But artists were not trying to paint realistic pictures.

Painting and sculpture

Around 1900 many groups of artists broke away from the European style of art, which had not changed much since the Renaissance. If you wanted a picture of something, you could take a photograph! So artists experimented with new ways of seeing. One development was abstract art, which contained shapes and colours but nothing that can be seen in nature.

Architecture

From the 1920s 'modern' architects, like other artists, wanted to break away from the old styles of building. They believed that a building should not be decorative, but should look like what it was, even if it were a slaughter-house. They were able to use new kinds of material, such as concrete, glass and steel, and new engineering techniques. They designed some interesting buildings, quite different from any earlier style. Many cheaper buildings which were influenced by the modern style were not successful, especially those built after the Second World War. By the 1990s, the best new buildings were less severe in appearance.

◁ In cities around the world, huge buildings in new styles and materials appeared among older, more decorative ones. This is in Kuala Lumpur, Malaysia.

Literature and books

The wish to experiment affected all the arts. Experimental novelists stopped telling stories and tried to get inside the mind and feelings of their characters. Others experimented with language itself. A famous example is James Joyce's *Finnegan's Wake* (1939).

At the same time, better education and more spare time created millions of new readers who wanted simpler stories. J. K. Rowling's Harry Potter novels appealed to adults and children alike. In spite of other forms of entertainment, more and more books of all sorts were published during the 20th century.

Music

In music, American jazz became very popular in the 1920s, along with dance music. In the West, young people, like their parents, had more money. That opened new opportunities for business, especially in the entertainment industry. It was helped by advances in sound recording – long-playing records (1948), stereo sound, magnetic-tape cassettes and compact discs (1983). These advances gave rise to trends such as pop music, which appealed directly to the young but was often disliked by older people. Pop music grew into an industry from the 1950s, thanks to advances in sound recording and (later) video, and to more money in teenagers' pockets. After the Beatles leading pop stars, like top sports people and fashion designers, were as rich and famous as the great Hollywood film stars.

△ The Beatles were four boys from Liverpool, England, who became the most successful pop group of the 1960s. Young people bought their records in millions.

Broadcasting

Radio broadcasting spread across the world in the 1920s, providing entertainment at home. Television was invented in the 1930s but did not get going in most countries until the 1950s, delayed by the Second World War. By 1980 nearly every home had a TV. Further advances in technology provided video recorders, and a wider choice of radio and TV channels, broadcast through cables and by satellite, as well as aerials. By 2000 a new method, digital broadcasting, offered more TV channels and opened other opportunities. Homes had many new machines and instruments - for cooking and housework, as well as for entertainment.

Cinema

Moving pictures were invented about 1890. Although films had no sound until 1928, cinema was the chief entertainment for working people between the world wars, along with spectator sports. Hollywood films showed a richer, more glamorous world, and the cinemas themselves were more like palaces. More recently, the Indian film industry, based in Bombay ('Bollywood'), produced more films than any other country.

Germany and the Second World War

Hitler rebuilt a powerful Germany in the 1930s, but his efforts to enlarge the borders of his new German empire led to a new world war, only 20 years after the peace settlement agreed at Versailles in 1919.

◁ German schoolchildren carrying Nazi banners welcome Hitler to the Sudetenland. In September 1938 Britain and France agreed that this part of Czechoslovakia should be given to Germany.

Hitler and Europe

The Versailles treaty after the First World War was meant to stop Germany becoming powerful again. But Hitler took no notice. In 1936 German troops marched into the Rhineland, which was forbidden by the treaty. In 1938, in a peaceful invasion, Hitler took over Austria, also forbidden. He accused Czechoslovakia and Poland of mistreating their German-speaking citizens, and threatened them with war.

No other great power was willing to stop Hitler. The USA wanted nothing to do with European affairs. Soviet Russia was the enemy of both sides and hoped for war between them. Mussolini's Italy was Hitler's ally. That left only the European democracies, Great Britain and France. They had problems of their own, and their greatest desire was to avoid another war. So, while protesting against Hitler's illegal acts, they took no action against him.

Czechoslovakia and Poland

In September 1938 a summit meeting was held in Munich, to try to prevent an attack on Czechoslovakia. Without consulting the Czechs, the British and French leaders agreed that Germany could have the Czech Sudetenland, where most German-speakers lived. The Sudetenland also contained Czechoslovakia's border defences. Six months later Hitler's troops marched into the Czech capital, Prague, and took over the country without a fight. Britain and France now realised that Hitler could not be trusted. They promised to support Poland, which was also threatened. The world was shocked in August 1939 when Nazi Germany signed an agreement with its arch-enemy, Stalin's Soviet Russia. With no danger of a Russian attack, the Germans could then safely invade Poland. But when the Germans did invade Poland in September 1939, Britain and France declared war.

The conquest of Europe

Britain and France could not help the Poles, who were quickly overrun. Events soon showed that they could not stop the German armies anywhere else. Within a year, the Germans had taken Denmark, Norway, Belgium and the Netherlands. In June 1940 France surrendered and German forces occupied most of France. A French government at Vichy governed the south-east and the French colonies, but it took its orders from the Germans. The whole of Europe was then under control of the Axis (the German-Italian alliance) except for Great Britain, and a few neutral countries including Soviet Russia. The British had an inspiring leader, Winston Churchill. They were supported by their overseas empire and protected by the English Channel. The Germans could not invade unless they first controlled the air. In the Battle of Britain (1940), the first big air battle, the German air force failed to win that control.

Blitzkrieg

The Germans invented a new kind of fighting (Blitzkrieg, 'lightning war'), far more effective than trench warfare. Fast-moving columns of tanks, supported by aircraft, drove deep into the enemy's country. Tanks and aircraft had played only a small part in the First World War.

◁ The German conquest of Europe. Apart from neutral states, Germany invaded every European country except the United Kingdom. They also captured much of North Africa.

--- German boundary in 1939
area under German control in 1942
area under Allied control in 1942
neutral country

◁ German troops marching up the Champs Elysée, the ceremonial avenue of Paris, in 1940. The Germans allowed a French government at Vichy, but it was under German orders.

Invasion of Russia

Hitler's ambition was to win more land in eastern Europe for his German empire. In spite of the German-Soviet agreement of 1939, Hitler saw Soviet Russia, not Britain, as his main enemy. The Russians were not only communists, they were also Slavs – a second-class people according to the Nazis. In 1941 the Germans invaded the Soviet Union. Russia was a much larger country than Germany, but there too the German forces advanced swiftly. They reached St Petersburg and Moscow, before fierce defence and the freezing Russian winter brought them to a stop. Stalin's government was surprised by the invasion and its defences were weak, but the Russians moved many of their arms factories across the Ural Mountains into Siberia, where they would be safe from the Germans.

The Second World War

The Second World War lasted for seven years. From 1941 both the USA and the Soviet Union were fighting with the British Empire. Those two giant countries had so many men and such huge industries that the Allies were bound to win in the end.

▽ To escape German bombs, 1.5 million English children were moved from the most dangerous parts of London and other cities to villages in the countryside.

War at sea

The USA opposed Japanese conquests in Asia in 1937-41. The Japanese expected war with the USA sooner or later, so they launched a surprise attack on the US naval base at Pearl Harbor in Hawaii (December 1941). Germany supported Japan, and the USA entered the war.

Like the German Blitzkrieg in Europe, the USA and Japan fought a new kind of war in the Pacific. Early battles were fought between fleets of aircraft carriers and their warplanes. The Japanese started to retreat after their defeat at the Battle of Midway (1942). In the Atlantic, German submarines and cruisers attacked the Allied merchant fleets bringing supplies from North America to Britain. But US shipyards produced ships three times as fast as the German submarines could sink them.

△ US troops landing in the Pacific. The Japanese fought fiercely to defend every island against the US advance in 1942-45.

War in Europe and North Africa

Until 1942 the Axis powers seemed to be winning the war. Then the tide turned. The Russians trapped a large German army at Stalingrad and forced them to surrender early in 1943. The British had been driven out of Europe in 1940, but fought in North Africa. They defeated a German army at the Battle of Alamein (1942). Next year, the Allies drove the Germans out of North Africa. From there Allied forces invaded Italy and overthrew Mussolini. The Italians surrendered, but German troops occupied Italy and held up the Allied advance.

The main Allied invasion of Europe began in June 1944. It was the biggest invasion in history. Under the command of US General Eisenhower, the Allied forces landed in Normandy and drove the Germans back. They freed France from German rule in August, and invaded Germany. As Allied forces advanced from the west, the Soviet 'Red Army' drove the Germans out of Russia and Poland, and invaded Germany from the east. By April 1945 the Red Army was in Berlin. Hitler shot himself, and the German armies surrendered.

The atom bomb

In 1944-45 US forces continued to advance against the Japanese in the Pacific, while the British reconquered Burma. It was obvious that Japan was losing, but many Japanese soldiers believed that defeat is worse than death, and refused to give up. To prevent thousands of American lives being lost, the US government forced Japan to surrender. They used a frightful new weapon that scientists had recently developed: the atom bomb. Two bombs were dropped, on the cities of Hiroshima and Nagasaki, destroying practically every building and tens of thousands of people in a large area. (Allied bombers had caused greater destruction of German and Japanese cities earlier, but not with a single bomb.)

The concentration camps

Young Jewish prisoners welcome Allied soldiers who have come to free them. In 1942, the Nazis had decided on a 'final solution' to get rid of the Jews. They should be killed. Special camps were built, mainly in Poland, as murder factories. The camp at Auschwitz could deal with 12,000 victims a day. People outside Germany did not believe these horrors of Nazi rule, until the Allied and Soviet armies captured the camps in 1945. Altogether, about 6 million Jews died in Nazi Europe.

European failure

The world war destroyed Nazi rule, although it strengthened Stalin's equally murderous regime. From 1945 Stalin controlled the countries of eastern Europe that the Red Army had reconquered from the Germans.

The horrors of the first half of the 20th century made some people think that European civilisation was dying. Certainly, Europeans no longer ruled the world. After the disasters of the two world wars, they could not claim the right to govern other countries. They could not even control their own affairs. By 1945, it was obvious the two victorious 'superpowers', the Soviet Union and the USA, would decide the future of Europe.

◁ In June 1944 hundreds of ships, protected by thousands of aircraft, carried Allied armies from British ports to the beaches of Normandy. It was the beginning of the final campaign, which ended nearly a year later with Germany's surrender.

The End of European Empires

In 1939 European nations ruled nearly all of Africa and much of Asia. By 1970 most of these colonies had become independent states. In some places the change was peaceful. In others it happened only after savage wars.

Self-rule

Most Europeans admitted when establishing their colonies that they would become independent – one day, perhaps far in the future. In 1919 former Turkish provinces such as Syria and Palestine had been placed under French and British rule, but only to prepare them for independence. Britain had also promised independence to India, but progress was slow. After 1945, the old imperial countries came under more pressure to give up their empires. This pressure came not only from the people they ruled, but also from the two great world powers, the Soviet Union and the USA.

India

The Indian National Congress was founded in 1885 and led the struggle for Indian independence. At first it was a tiny party demanding reforms. In the 1920s it gained more support thanks to the leadership of Gandhi, but many Muslims left Congress to form their own nationalist party, the Muslim League. The British made some reforms, giving Indians a bigger part in government, but in 1942 Congress demanded full independence. By 1945 the new British government was eager to leave. But the division between Hindus and Muslims could not be healed. As a result, British India became independent (1947) as two states, Hindu India and Muslim Pakistan. Terrible violence took place between Hindus and Muslims in some areas, with many thousands slaughtered or driven from their homes. The two countries remained on bad terms and fought three short wars between 1947 and 1971. Pakistan itself was divided into two parts. In 1971 India supported East Pakistan when it broke away to become Bangladesh.

△ Gandhi leads a protest march against a British tax, in 1930. He was as much a holy man as a politician, and wanted to change people's hearts – Hindus, Muslims and British alike. His protests were never violent and he dreamed of a country where all races, religions and castes could live together in peace.

Asia

The Japanese had conquered many European colonies in Asia. Although the Europeans returned in 1945, most colonies gained independence within a few years. In 1948 Britain agreed independence for Burma and Sri Lanka (not conquered by Japan). Indonesia had forced out the Dutch by 1949, and the Philippines became independent of the USA in 1946. In South-East Asia things were more difficult, due partly to communist movements. Malaysia became independent in 1963. France withdrew from Cambodia (1949), Laos (1953) and Vietnam (1954), though civil wars continued.

Black Africa

Nearly the whole of Africa was under colonial control until the 1960s. Many colonies remained on friendly terms with their former rulers. But they had special difficulties. Some were very poor, with few resources, low standards of education and not enough people skilled in government. Because the colonial rulers had formed colonies without considering the boundaries between different peoples, the new states contained rival groups who did not easily act together. Governments were unstable, and small groups or military dictators came to hold power. These people made themselves rich but made their country still poorer. Nigeria, the largest, contained different nations and religions. It became a federal republic, but quarrels between the different regions led to civil war and dictatorship.

dates of independence
- before 1940
- 1940–1949
- 1950–1959
- 1960–1969
- 1970–1979
- 1980–1989
- after 1989

△ The countries of modern Africa. In 1940 Egypt and Liberia alone were officially independent, although Ethiopia was a colony only from 1936.

White Africans

The cause of independence brought the greatest violence to countries where many white people had settled. In Algeria, nationalists fought a long and savage civil war against the French authorities and the many inhabitants of French descent. The great French war leader and statesman, Charles de Gaulle, returning to power in 1958, saw that the only solution was for France to withdraw. South Africa, an independent republic from 1961, had been a 'white' country since the 16th century. It adopted the policy called apartheid, 'separateness', which placed all power and wealth in the hands of the white minority. Rhodesia, a British colony, was refused independence because the white leadership refused to share power with the black majority. After a long civil war (1965-79) the colonial government admitted defeat, and Rhodesia became the republic of Zimbabwe.

▽ In new states some people grew rich, but most stayed poor. In places such as Lagos, Nigeria, slums grew up next to modern

The United Nations and the Cold War

The United Nations (UN) was founded in 1945 as a place where quarrels between nations could be discussed and war prevented. Its work was made difficult by the enmity of the two 'superpowers', the USA and the Soviet Union, each supported by its allies.

▽ Some of the UN's most important work was done by special departments, or agencies. These included the World Bank, which lends money to poor countries, and UNICEF, which aims to protect and improve the rights, education and health of children worldwide.

The United Nations

The United Nations replaced the old League of Nations. Nearly every nation became a member of its General Assembly. Decisions were made by the Security Council, dominated by the rival superpowers. As the UN depended on its members for support, it had little real power. It could organise a small force to keep the peace in local quarrels around the world, but it had no permanent army. When it did fight a war, as in the 1991 Gulf War, the 'UN Forces' were mainly US.

▷ When the Hungarian people rebelled against Communist control in 1956, Soviet forces invaded and crushed the rebellion. When Alexander Dubcek introduced a freer form of communism in Czechoslovakia in 1968, Soviet tanks moved in again (right), and Dubcek was removed.

members of NATO and the Warsaw Pact in 1960

- NATO countries (also including USA, Canada and Iceland)
- Warsaw Pact countries
- neutral countries

The Cold War

Members of the UN fell into two groups: the Communist or Eastern bloc, led by the Soviet Union, and the capitalist or Western bloc, led by the USA. As more countries, many of them former colonies, joined, a third bloc developed, sometimes known as the Third World.

The USA and the Soviet Union were the strongest powers in 1945. US troops remained in western Europe and US aid poured into Europe to help revive countries ruined by the war. The Soviet Union had gained an 'empire' of dependent states in eastern Europe, including East Germany. These countries had their own communist governments, but took orders from Russia. From the 1947 to the 1970s the world was shaken by a series of crises resulting from the 'Cold War' between the USA and the Soviet Union – and later, Communist China. At times, another world war looked likely.

The Berlin airlift

The division of Germany was one cause of conflict. Although Berlin lay inside communist East Germany, the western half of the city, like West Germany, was occupied by the Western allies. In 1948 their plan to make West Germany independent annoyed the Russians, who retaliated by stopping all traffic between West Germany and West Berlin. The Allies kept West Berlin supplied with food, clothing, even coal, by air alone, flying in 6,000 tonnes a day. The Russians did not try to stop the flights and, after 15 months, reopened the road.

Cuba

Fidel Castro's revolution in Cuba (1956) established a communist government, supported by the Soviet Union, in 'America's backyard'. In 1962, another world crisis erupted when US spy planes discovered Soviet nuclear missiles in Cuba. US president John F. Kennedy demanded their removal. After a few days when nuclear war seemed possible, the Russians agreed.

The European Economic Community

Groups of countries formed their own international associations. Often the reasons were economic – to increase trade and business by ending customs duties and agreeing to common rules. The European Economic Community was formed in 1957 by six Western European countries, later joined by most others. In 1991 it became the European Union and in 1999 it introduced a single currency, the Euro.

The Middle East since 1945

The Middle East has been the world's most troubled region since 1945. The creation of a Jewish state, Israel, in the Arab land of Palestine was the main cause of wars. There have also been other wars. Other countries, especially in the West, were worried by these wars because the Middle East contains the world's main supply of oil.

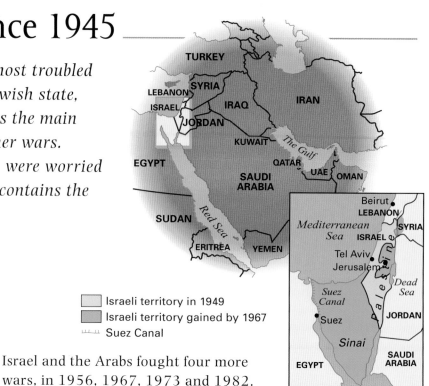

Israeli territory in 1949
Israeli territory gained by 1967
Suez Canal

Arabs and Israelis

Since the early 20th century Jews had settled in Arab Palestine, their biblical homeland. This increased after the Second World War. Although the Arabs protested, in 1947 the United Nations voted to divide Palestine into separate Jewish and Arab provinces. The next year, the Jews declared Israel a republic. Their Arab neighbours at once attacked, but Israel, supported by the USA, won.

Israel and the Arabs fought four more wars, in 1956, 1967, 1973 and 1982. In 1967 Israel captured much Arab land. It kept some of this land, including the Arab part of Palestine called the Occupied Territories.

▽ A Palestinian refugee camp in Lebanon, in 1982.

The Palestinians

After 1947 the Palestinians really had no country. They lived in Israel, the Occupied Territories of Palestine or other Arab nations. Some formed the Palestine Liberation Organisation (the PLO) to fight for an Arab state. After a rebellion by Palestinians in the Occupied Territories,

Israel agreed with Palestinian leader Yasser Arafat (1929-2004) to give Palestinians some control in these areas. Many countries tried to help make a lasting peace but there was still violence on both sides.

Gamal Abdel Nasser
Many of the newly independent Arab states after 1945 were led by strong nationalists. They were often army officers. The greatest was Gamal Abdel Nasser, who gained power in Egypt in 1954. He led Arab opposition against Israel and against Western influence.

Iran

In Iran a religious leader, the Ayatollah Khomeini, came to power after a revolution in 1979. He made Iran a much stricter Muslim country, governed by religious law. After his death (1989) there have been many attempts at modernisation.

◁ Ayatollah Khomeini and his supporters believed that Western civilisation was evil. Under his rule women could not have jobs.

Oil

Oil exports made many Middle Eastern states around the Persian Gulf very rich. The greatest oil producer in the region was Saudi Arabia. Western countries needed that oil, and were therefore interested in Middle Eastern affairs. The USA feared that, if Iraq controlled the Gulf, the oil supply would be stopped.

Iraq – a dangerous neighbour

The military dictator of Iraq, Saddam Hussein, invaded Iran. He was afraid that Khomeini's revolution might spread to Iraq. The Iran-Iraq war lasted eight years (1980-88), and about 1 million people were killed. In 1990 Saddam invaded Kuwait, but the forces of the United Nations, including some Arab states, soon forced him out. In 2003 the leaders of the USA and Britain decided Saddam was still too much of a threat and attacked Iraq, without UN backing. Most people welcomed the overthrow of Saddam, but there was also anger at the invasion. On 13th December 2006 Saddam Hussein was captured by US forces and later executed for crimes against humanity.

△ Saddam Hussein

Asia since 1945

South-east Asia was another troubled part of the world after the Second World War. Besides the two superpowers, China was a powerful force in the region. So was Japan, as it built up its industries after the disasters of the war.

The Korean War

After the Second World War, Korea, freed from Japanese occupation was divided into two – communist North Korea, supported by the Soviet Union, and capitalist South Korea, supported by the USA. In 1950, North Korea invaded the South. A UN force, led by the USA, was sent to defend the South, and Chinese forces fought for the North. A truce was agreed in 1953, leaving Korea divided.

China

In the Chinese republic, nationalists and communists had fought together against the Japanese. But when peace came, their alliance ended and civil war began again. Mao Zedong led the communists to victory and drove the nationalists out of China. With US support, nationalists set up their own state on the island of Taiwan. The Chinese communists had Soviet support, but the two countries later quarrelled and broke off relations after 1960. China's conquest of Tibet (1951), which it insisted was part of the Chinese empire, also caused a short border war with India. The main task of the new regime was to modernise the country. It reorganised farming on the communist pattern (no private land), and started developing industry. Progress was far from smooth. Mao's policies caused distress and chaos, especially the attacks on middle-class people during what was called the Cultural Revolution (1966-69). In the 1980s, after Mao's death, China began to allow private businesses. By the beginning of the 21st century it had become a leading industrial power. There were still questions about how free the Chinese people were, but Beijing was accepted as host for the 2008 Olympic Games.

▽ The world was shocked when Chinese troops killed 1,000 peaceful demonstrators in Tiananmen Square, Beijing, in 1989. The demonstrators, mostly students, were demanding greater democracy. After 1989 the government still kept tight control over the people, but it allowed far more freedom to business and industry.

South-east Asia

Vietnam, like Korea, was divided into a communist North, led by Ho Chi Minh, and a capitalist South, supported by the USA. The USA provided military aid to prevent South Vietnam being taken over by the communists. By the mid-1960s, the USA was fighting a major war against the Vietnamese communists. The war was extremely unpopular with Americans and in 1973 the American forces withdrew. It was the first time the USA had been defeated in war. The communists took over the whole of Vietnam.

△ When North Vietnam conquered the South, thousands of people tried to escape by boat to Hong Kong.

In 1976 Cambodia fell under the control of the Khmer Rouge, an extreme revolutionary movement led by Pol Pot. Millions of ordinary Cambodians died in Pol Pot's reign of terror until a Vietnamese invasion overthrew him in 1979.

▽ Although they had few natural resources, the Japanese were expert in making things. They bought cheap raw materials to make expensive products. In Tokyo, prosperity brought traffic jams.

New Asian states

The new states created from former European colonies suffered some of the problems of other 'developing countries' in Africa and Latin America, including poverty. Most called themselves democracies, but power and wealth remained in the hands of small groups, often dominated by generals. Indonesia (the third largest Asian country after China and India), Pakistan and Myanmar (Burma) were all ruled for long periods by military dictators, who had little respect for human rights. Afghanistan was ruined by endless civil wars that began with Soviet occupation in 1979-89. Other Far Eastern states, such as Malaysia, Singapore, South Korea, even Indonesia, made great progress in industry and business. By the 1980s they challenged the West. But some were troubled by social problems, failing businesses and the threat of revolution.

Japan

The greatest success story in Asia came from Japan. Supported by the USA, Japan became a peaceful, modern and wealthy republic. By the 1980s it was the richest country in the world after the USA. Some other countries followed Japan's example. Hong Kong, a British colony that was returned to China in 1997, was a world centre of business.

Human Rights

Most governments accepted that everyone has rights, such as the freedom to say and believe what they like, although some still ruled by force and fear. At the same time, old divisions of race, class, sex, religion or other differences, though still violent in some countries, became less sharp.

▽ Martin Luther King Jr (1929-68) leading a civil-rights march in Washington, the US capital. He was a Baptist minister from the American South, whose passionate speeches and brave policy of non-violence made him leader of the US civil rights movement. He was murdered, aged 39, by a white racist.

Civil Rights

In the USA, all citizens were supposed to be free and equal. But black people, who made up 15 per cent of the population, suffered from race prejudice. In some Southern states, they were prevented from voting in elections. Black people had separate (and worse) schools, hospitals, even public toilets. In the North there was no official separation, but many lived in all-black slums and could not get good jobs.

The rise of the civil rights movement in the 1950s forced the government to pass new laws to make sure that black people got equal treatment. The greatest civil-rights leader was Martin Luther King Jr. He learned from Gandhi in India that peaceful protest is a less harmful way to bring about change than violent revolution. The new laws did not bring prosperity to all black people or change the black slums in many cities. They did not end racial prejudice, as people always find reasons to hate neighbours who are 'different'. But black people could live and work where they liked, and race relations did improve.

Political freedom

Many other Western countries contained racial minorities which, from about 1960, also won equal rights and opportunities. In Australia and New Zealand, the rights of Aborigines and Maoris were recognised at last. They even regained some of the lands that early white colonists had taken. Multi-racial societies developed in European countries such as Britain and France, which gained many immigrants from former Asian and African colonies. But in countries such as South Africa, although the white rulers were a minority, black and 'coloured' people were third-class citizens.

Women

The civil rights movement strengthened the cause of women's rights. Even in democratic countries, women did not gain the vote until the early 20th century. In other ways they were still far from equal with men. In 1950 it was still difficult for a woman to go to university, to own property, or work in business and professions such as law and medicine. Only the Soviet Union and other communist countries had laws that made women equal with men. The idea that a woman's place is in the home was still common. To win equal rights, women needed not only new laws but new customs, which cannot be changed so easily. Women campaigned against sex discrimination at work and at home, and for the right to equal pay, as they were often paid less than men for the same work.

▷ Building surveyors in Bangladesh. Twenty years previously, no woman could have held such a job.

Rich and poor

Besides black people and women, most minority groups in the West gained fairer treatment after 1950. This was made easier by growing wealth. International industry and business, aided by amazing advances in science and technology, made most people better off. But the growing wealth mainly affected countries in the northern part of the world – North America, Europe and Japan – plus Australia and New Zealand. In the poorer countries of South America and Africa, and many parts of Asia, the standard of living of most people rose only a little, if at all. In 2001 the average income of someone in the USA was over $36,000, but the average for African countries south of the Sahara was less than $500.

Wealth also means health. Poor countries could not afford many doctors, decent houses, and clean water supplies. So people often died young. In 2004, the average life expectancy of a woman born in central Africa was 51 years. In Japan it was over 84 years.

△ Women making baskets. Simple crafts like this were for centuries the only work for many people. By the 21st century the gap between rich and poor was still huge. The world's wealth was still shared unfairly – a great problem for the future.

Science and Health

After 1950 the living standards of most people in the industrial countries improved. That was made possible by advances in technology, science and medicine. But some people feared that such progress could not go on for ever.

Fossil fuel

Industrial peoples need two things from Nature: the raw materials to make things, and the power to drive their machines. In the Industrial Revolution, power came from burning coal. After 1950, oil became the chief industrial fuel. Both coal and oil are fossil fuels, formed in the Earth over millions of years. In the 1970s people feared that supplies of oil would run out in a few years. Their fears ended when new deposits of oil and gas were found, some under the seas. But the need to find new kinds of power continued.

Nuclear power

Nuclear fission, which produced the atom bomb, could also be used to provide power. In the 1950s, many people believed nuclear power would replace fossil fuels. But it had dangers. After an explosion at a nuclear power station in Chernobyl, Ukraine, in 1986, few new ones were built.

Science

More universities produced more scientists. New discoveries and inventions led to astonishing advances in most kinds of science, from astronomy to zoology. The history of the Earth and the universe became clearer. Proof that the surface of the Earth rests on slowly moving 'plates' showed how the oceans and continents had formed. Advances in electronics caused big changes in many human activities, in work and play. In about 1960 lasers were invented to produce a very precise beam of light. They proved useful in many ways, from making pictures in three dimensions (called holographs) to slowing down atoms to make them easier to study. Some scientists believed that lasers might one day be used to control nuclear fusion, which would solve the energy problem.

The success of medical engineers in making tiny surgical tools ...wed doctors to see inside a patient without making a large cut.

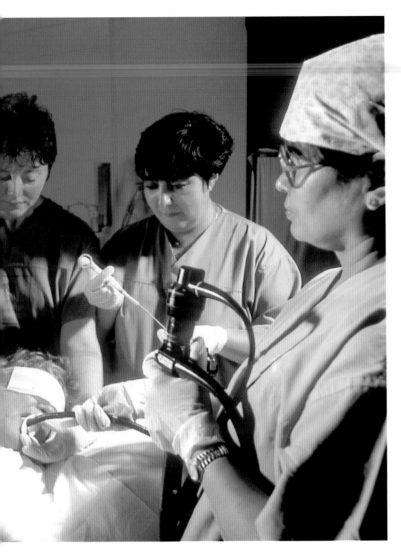

◁ Experiments with the power of the Sun, wind and ocean tides provided 'alternative' energy. This wind farm supplied energy for a small town, but required a large space, damaged wild life and looked ugly.

Medicine

Lasers were also useful in surgery. For instance, surgeons sometimes used their precise beam to 'burn' out a growth like a cancer. Another spectacular advance in surgery was transplanting living organs. In 1967 a South African surgeon, Christiaan Barnard, carried out the first transplant of a human heart.

Expensive surgical operations affected only a few people, but medical researchers also had many successes in fighting infectious disease. Smallpox disappeared by 1979, thanks to the efforts of the World Heath Organization. There were new vaccines that prevented other killer diseases, such as polio (poliomyelitis), and new drugs, such as antibiotics. Newly discovered treatments also made some kinds of cancer less deadly. However, new diseases, such as AIDS and the flu-like SARS virus, also appeared, and some that had been largely conquered, such as TB (tuberculosis), started to increase again.

Genetics

Perhaps the most extraordinary advance was in genetics, the discovery of how the characteristics of a living thing are inherited through its genes. With this knowledge, scientists were able to alter crops, for example, to make them bigger, and also worked on ways to cure or prevent human diseases with genetic engineering. Looking to the future, it might even be possible to change human characteristics. Many people found this frightening.

Dolly the sheep

She looked like an ordinary sheep, but Dolly was 'grown' in a Scottish lab from a single cell of a six-year-old ewe in 1996. Because she had exactly the same genes as that ewe, she was a 'clone', a perfect copy. When Dolly died in 2003 she had reached only half the usual age for a sheep. Both her life and her death raised questions. Could other animals be cloned, and how long would they live? Would the next step be an artificial human being? These experiments with Nature worried many people.

People and the Planet

In the late 20th century people began to worry that human beings were seriously damaging their planet. There were two main problems. The first was the growth in world population. The second was pollution.

Population explosion

Ten thousand years ago, the world contained about 10 million people. By 1650 there were 500 million, by 1930 2 billion, and by 2000 about 6 billion. Not only did the population constantly increase, the rate at which it grew also increased. About three-quarters of the world's population lived in the poorer 'developing' countries, where the rate of growth was highest. The rising population in those countries made it difficult to raise the standard of living, as populations tended to grow as fast or faster than the nation's wealth.

In richer countries, population grew more slowly because many people practised birth control, so families had fewer children. But poor countries could not afford birth-control programmes, and poor families often want lots of children. Some religions taught that birth control is wrong. China, which had the world's largest population, passed a law to stop any married couple having more than one child. But such extreme methods could be used only where the government had absolute power.

▷ The rising population was one of many causes of worldwide worries about the environment. In parts of Africa, good soil was worn out by too much use. In tropical countries, valuable forest was cut down for farmland.

The environment

Serious pollution of the Earth began in the Industrial Revolution, but the effects were not seen for many years. Not until the 1980s did ordinary people begin to fear that the planet was being ruined. Natural resources were being used up at a dangerous rate – not only fossil fuels but forests, fish, even fresh water. Many plants and animals were becoming extinct. Little true wilderness was left on Earth.

Factories and machines poured dangerous gases into the air. In Scandinavia, trees died and lakes were poisoned by 'acid rain', formed when industrial chemicals are dissolved in rain drops. Human waste was pumped into the sea, and oil spilled from giant tankers killed sea life.

▽ In rich countries, people produced more and more rubbish, as everything became highly packaged. In poor countries, people would pick through a rubbish dump, looking for anything to sell, or to eat.

Climate

In the 1980s, most scientists agreed that the Earth's climate was getting warmer. This 'global warming' was blamed on the 'greenhouse effect', caused by industrial gases, such as carbon dioxide from burning oil, that form a kind of blanket around the Earth. In 2001 an increase of as much as 6°C was predicted by the end of the 21st century. That would melt ice in polar regions, bringing huge floods, and could also cause droughts and other extreme weather. Changes were also noticed in the atmosphere. The ozone layer, which protects the Earth from the Sun's harmful ultraviolet rays, was thinner. The main cause was traced to man-made chemicals called chloro-fluorocarbons (CFCs).

▷ Human beings have been cutting down the forests for hundreds of years. By the end of the 20th century around 15 million hectares of rain forest were destroyed every year by timber companies, miners and farmers. Rain forests contain many unknown species of wildlife, and plants that could provide new medicines.

The Rainbow Warrior

The Rainbow Warrior *belonged to the environmental group Greenpeace. It was blown up in New Zealand by French secret agents in 1985 to prevent it interfering in tests of nuclear weapons in the Pacific. Greenpeace, founded in 1971, was one of the liveliest of many international charities working for the environment.*

Conservation

In 1990 most countries agreed to stop using CFCs. In 1992 an international conference on the environment showed that the whole world was worried about pollution and global warming. Governments promised to reduce the harmful effects of their industries, to protect fishing, and reduce fumes from vehicles and factories. But the problems were not easy to solve, because the solutions were expensive. The poor countries did not want to stop industrial development. The rich countries did not want to reduce their standard of living by expensive methods of controlling pollution.

A Small World

By the 21st century the world seemed a small place. People travelled more. News and pictures were broadcast round the world in seconds. Someone with a computer linked to the Internet could exchange information with almost anyone, anywhere.

◁ Dealers in stocks and shares can see how prices are changing in stock markets all over the world at any one moment.

International business

Agreement on customs duties and international associations such as the European Union or OPEC (Oil Producing and Exporting Countries) helped the growth of world trade. Business became international. Large companies had offices, factories and shareholders in many countries. A German car might have parts made in France, Britain and Japan. Large companies bought rival firms in foreign countries. Cities around the world looked more alike. Businessmen in Frankfurt and Tokyo wore the same kind of suits and worked in similar offices. They often spoke the same language, English, which was becoming an international language.

Transport

Air travel became quicker and cheaper as more people spent holidays abroad. Huge improvements in surface transport included a tunnel under the English Channel and a 2,000-metre bridge joining two of Japan's islands. Increasing trade and more car-owning families increased road traffic by millions of vehicles. More leisure time and more money meant people could afford to travel abroad more often, and further. By the new century tourists could visit the most remote places on Earth.

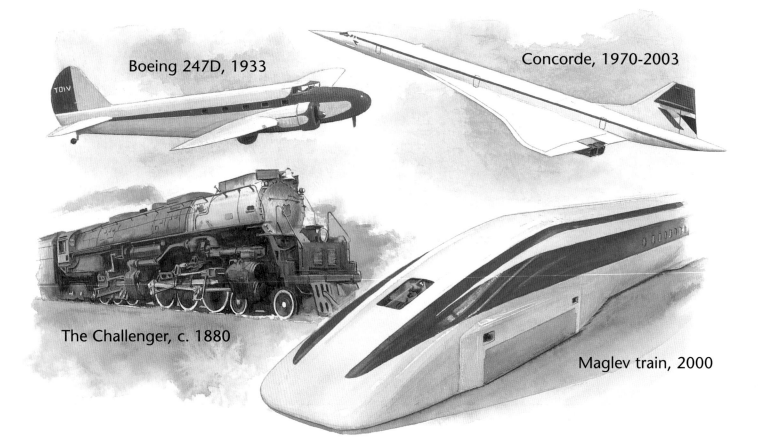

Boeing 247D, 1933

Concorde, 1970-2003

The Challenger, c. 1880

Maglev train, 2000

Space

The space age began in 1961 when a Russian, Yuri Gagarin, circled the Earth in Sputnik I. In 1969 Americans landed on the Moon. In the 1970s the Russians developed the space lab, where several scientists could work in space for months.

The Americans invented the space 'shuttle' (1981), part spacecraft, part airplane, which could be used many times. Unmanned spacecraft explored the planets and beyond. By 2000 hundreds of man-made satellites were circling the Earth. Some were for scientific research, providing new knowledge of the Earth and tracking weather systems. Many were for communications, sending TV and other signals around the world. The American Hubble telescope scanned the universe from Earth orbit.

▷ US astronaut Bruce McCandless tested a Manned Manoeuvering Unit from the Space Shuttle in 1984. This device allows an astronaut to move about freely in space.

△ Computers entered schools and homes, as well as offices, when PCs (personal computers) were developed in the 1970s.

The communications revolution

Of all the technological changes of 1950-2000, the most important were in electronic communications. They affected everyone in the world, bringing some problems as well as great benefits. The first computers were developed to decipher enemy radio messages during the Second World War. They were really just huge calculating machines. The first one, called Colossus, weighed over a tonne but was far less powerful than a modern laptop. In 1971 the invention of the 'microprocessor', needing only one small silicon chip, resulted in smaller, cheaper computers. The personal computer (PC) followed. The computer business itself created many new industries to produce computer equipment. By the 1980s, most businesses and many homes used computers. New developments such as fax, e-mail and the Internet followed, along with video recorders and camcorders, mobile telephones, digital cameras and digital TV.

Into a New Millennium

The main event of the last years of the 20th century was the collapse of the Communist system in Europe, beginning in 1989. In other parts of the world too, governments that had relied on force to keep them in power disappeared. Democracy took a step forward.

The end of the Soviet Union

Communism had dominated the Soviet Union, the world's largest country, since 1917. Since the 1940s the Soviet Union had also controlled more than half of Europe and much of central Asia. In 1985 Mikhail Gorbachev became Soviet leader. He was a bold reformer. He introduced new policies to give people more freedom, and was willing to listen to those who disagreed with him. Political prisoners were set free. Gorbachev also wanted to end the Cold War, which was not too difficult as the US government and its allies also wanted to end it.

However, his decision to reduce the power of the Communist Party had an unforeseen result. It gave the nations in the Soviet Union, and other states of Eastern Europe under communist rule, the chance to get rid of Soviet control and communist governments. The huge Soviet empire suddenly broke up, as countries elected democratic governments. The Communist Party was banned in Russia in 1991, but without the Party system, the government was weak. Crime increased and living standards fell even further below the standards of the West. By the new century wages had improved, but Russia was still involved in a bitter guerrilla war with Chechnya, which wanted full independence.

▷ Nelson Mandela welcomed by his supporters after his release from prison. Between them, he and De Klerk made South Africa a democracy.

▽ East Germans rejoicing at the demolition of the Berlin Wall, in November 1989. The Wall was built in 1961 to stop people escaping to the West. As the communist government of East Germany collapsed, thousands of people left for the West. In 1990 the two Germanies were reunited as one country.

South Africa

With its racist policy of apartheid, South Africa was an outcast among other countries. Some reforms were made before F. W. de Klerk, South Africa's Gorbachev, became president in 1989 and promised to end apartheid. In 1990, the African National Congress, the banned black nationalist party, was legalised and its leader, Nelson Mandela, released from prison after 26 years. South Africa ended the apartheid laws (1991) and held the first fully democratic elections in 1994. The ANC won a majority and Mandela, a popular hero throughout the world, became the first black president of the 'rainbow nation' (people of all colours). Today South Africa faces many problems, from crime to AIDS, but it has come a long way.

Latin America

After gaining independence, most Latin American countries suffered from unstable, unjust governments and crude military dictators, sometimes supported by the USA. Bolivia had 180 rebellions between 1825 and 1952. About 100,000 Guatemalans died by violence between the 1960s and 1980s. But by the 1990s, reforms and democracy brought better times to many countries. Dictators, some of them mass murderers, were overthrown in Argentina (1983), Brazil (1985), Chile, Paraguay and – by US forces – in Panama (1989). Long and murderous civil wars ended in Nicaragua (1990), El Salvador and Guatemala (1992). The countries set up more just and more democratic governments. Huge human problems remained, especially the terrible poverty of the big-city slums.

△ Rigoberta Menchú Tum of Guatemala receives her Nobel Peace Prize in 1992. It was awarded for her campaigning for human rights, especially for indigenous peoples.

The world at the beginning of the 21st century

Looking back over the 20th century, human beings could see that it had been the most violent in their history. It had more wars, with more people killed, and more brutal governments, than any earlier century. But it was also an era of great achievements. Most people, though not all, were better off by 2000, and science and medicine had made amazing advances. Looking forward, there were challenges old and new. Famine and disease had not ended, and there were natural disasters such as the Asian tsunami of 2004. After the World Trade Center was attacked on September 11, 2001, people feared the growing threat of international terrorism and the USA led wars against Afghanistan and Iraq. However, many nations and people had grown more tolerant. Through the UN and other organisations, countries were more willing to help others. More people recognised that every human being has rights. They were learning to live peacefully with others of different ethnic background, class or gender.

The Modern World

Two terrible world wars were fought in the first half of the century.
After 1945, the year of the atomic bomb, world statesmen founded
the United Nations, to prevent another world war. At the same time,
the West began to see that freedom and equality should be for

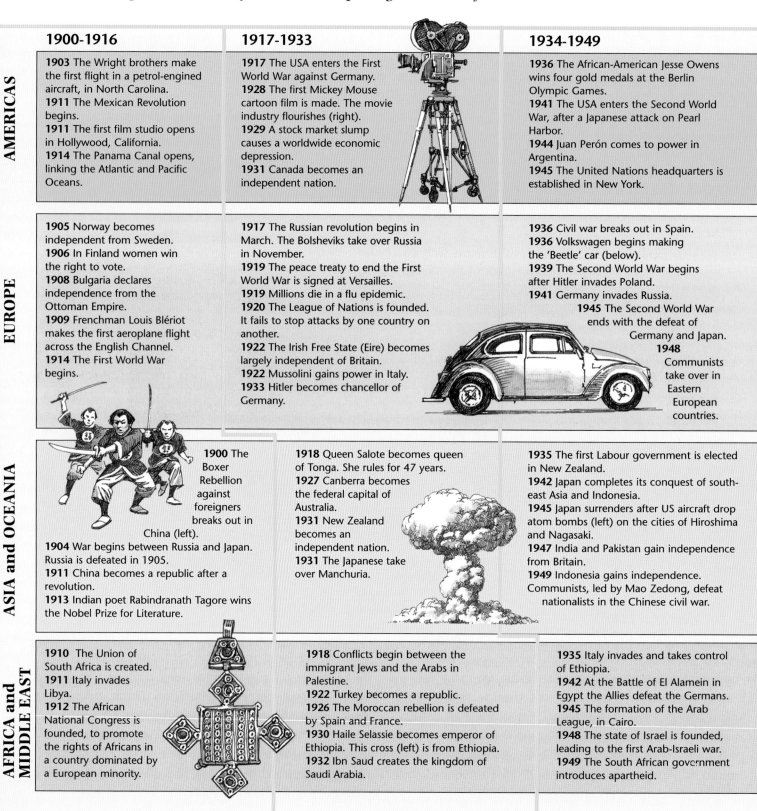

1900-1916

AMERICAS

1903 The Wright brothers make the first flight in a petrol-engined aircraft, in North Carolina.
1911 The Mexican Revolution begins.
1911 The first film studio opens in Hollywood, California.
1914 The Panama Canal opens, linking the Atlantic and Pacific Oceans.

EUROPE

1905 Norway becomes independent from Sweden.
1906 In Finland women win the right to vote.
1908 Bulgaria declares independence from the Ottoman Empire.
1909 Frenchman Louis Blériot makes the first aeroplane flight across the English Channel.
1914 The First World War begins.

ASIA and OCEANIA

1900 The Boxer Rebellion against foreigners breaks out in China (left).
1904 War begins between Russia and Japan. Russia is defeated in 1905.
1911 China becomes a republic after a revolution.
1913 Indian poet Rabindranath Tagore wins the Nobel Prize for Literature.

AFRICA and MIDDLE EAST

1910 The Union of South Africa is created.
1911 Italy invades Libya.
1912 The African National Congress is founded, to promote the rights of Africans in a country dominated by a European minority.

1917-1933

AMERICAS

1917 The USA enters the First World War against Germany.
1928 The first Mickey Mouse cartoon film is made. The movie industry flourishes (right).
1929 A stock market slump causes a worldwide economic depression.
1931 Canada becomes an independent nation.

EUROPE

1917 The Russian revolution begins in March. The Bolsheviks take over Russia in November.
1919 The peace treaty to end the First World War is signed at Versailles.
1919 Millions die in a flu epidemic.
1920 The League of Nations is founded. It fails to stop attacks by one country on another.
1922 The Irish Free State (Eire) becomes largely independent of Britain.
1922 Mussolini gains power in Italy.
1933 Hitler becomes chancellor of Germany.

ASIA and OCEANIA

1918 Queen Salote becomes queen of Tonga. She rules for 47 years.
1927 Canberra becomes the federal capital of Australia.
1931 New Zealand becomes an independent nation.
1931 The Japanese take over Manchuria.

AFRICA and MIDDLE EAST

1918 Conflicts begin between the immigrant Jews and the Arabs in Palestine.
1922 Turkey becomes a republic.
1926 The Moroccan rebellion is defeated by Spain and France.
1930 Haile Selassie becomes emperor of Ethiopia. This cross (left) is from Ethiopia.
1932 Ibn Saud creates the kingdom of Saudi Arabia.

1934-1949

AMERICAS

1936 The African-American Jesse Owens wins four gold medals at the Berlin Olympic Games.
1941 The USA enters the Second World War, after a Japanese attack on Pearl Harbor.
1944 Juan Perón comes to power in Argentina.
1945 The United Nations headquarters is established in New York.

EUROPE

1936 Civil war breaks out in Spain.
1936 Volkswagen begins making the 'Beetle' car (below).
1939 The Second World War begins after Hitler invades Poland.
1941 Germany invades Russia.
1945 The Second World War ends with the defeat of Germany and Japan.
1948 Communists take over in Eastern European countries.

ASIA and OCEANIA

1935 The first Labour government is elected in New Zealand.
1942 Japan completes its conquest of south-east Asia and Indonesia.
1945 Japan surrenders after US aircraft drop atom bombs (left) on the cities of Hiroshima and Nagasaki.
1947 India and Pakistan gain independence from Britain.
1949 Indonesia gains independence. Communists, led by Mao Zedong, defeat nationalists in the Chinese civil war.

AFRICA and MIDDLE EAST

1935 Italy invades and takes control of Ethiopia.
1942 At the Battle of El Alamein in Egypt the Allies defeat the Germans.
1945 The formation of the Arab League, in Cairo.
1948 The state of Israel is founded, leading to the first Arab-Israeli war.
1949 The South African government introduces apartheid.

*everyone, and European empires came to an end. That led also to
greater equality among people of different race, religion and gender.
Of course wars, violence and prejudice continued, but after over 2000
years of conflict the peoples of the world were coming closer together.*

1950-1966	**1967-1982**	**1983-present day**

1955 President Perón is overthrown in Argentina.
1959 Hawaii becomes the 50th state of the USA.
1963 US President John F. Kennedy (right) is assassinated in Texas.
1965 America enters the conflict in Vietnam.

1968 The black civil rights leader Martin Luther King is assassinated.
1969 US astronaut Neil Armstrong becomes the first person on the Moon (right).
1973 President Allende of Chile is overthrown in a military revolt led by Pinochet.
1974 US President Nixon is forced to resign after the 'Watergate' scandal.

1992 An international 'Earth summit' at Rio de Janeiro discusses problems of the environment.
2001 Thousands are killed in the 9/11 terrorist attacks on New York and Washington.
2005 Hurricane Katrina hits New Orleans killing hundreds of people
2008 Fidel Castro hands leadership of Cuba to younger brother Raul Castro

1951 The first nuclear power stations are built.
1956 Soviet tanks crush an anti-communist revolt in Hungary.
1957 The European Community is founded.
1957 Russia launches the first space satellite, Sputnik I.
1961 The Russian Yuri Gagarin becomes the first person to travel in space.

1968 The liberal government in Czechoslovakia is overthrown by Soviet invasion.
1969 The IRA begins fighting for a united Ireland.
1973 Greece becomes a republic.
1975 The monarchy is restored in Spain.
1980 The Polish trade union, Solidarity, is founded (left) and opposes the Soviet-controlled communist government.

1989 Demonstrations force communists from power in East European states.
1991 Wars break out in the Balkans, as Yugoslavia splits into separate states.
1995 A peace agreement ends the civil war in Bosnia.
1999 NATO forces attack the Serbs over their treatment of Albanians in Kosovo.
2000 Vladimir Putin becomes president of Russia.
2004 Ten new member states join the European Union, increasing its population by 75 million.
2005 Pope John II dies aged 87. His successor is Pope Benedict XVI

1950 The Korean War breaks out.
1953 Hillary and Tensing reach the top of Mount Everest (right).
1957 Civil war begins in Vietnam.
1962 A border war breaks out between China and India.
1966 The Cultural Revolution begins in China.

1971 Bangladesh gains independence from Pakistan.
1973 The last US troops leave Vietnam.
1975 Pol Pot gains power in Cambodia, and communists control Laos and Vietnam.
1984 The Indian prime minister Indira Gandhi (above) is assassinated.

1989 Chinese government forces massacre student protesters in Tiananmen Square.
1997 Britain returns Hong Kong to China.
1998 Riots in Indonesia force the country's military leader, Suharto, to resign.
2004 A tsunami, a giant wave, devastates the coasts of countries around the Indian Ocean.
2007 Leader of the Pakistan Peoples Party, Benazir Bhutto, is assassinated.
2008 An earthquake hits China and a tropical cyclone hits Burma, killing thousands of people.

1957 Nkrumah (right) leads Ghana to independence.
1957 France and Britain begin to withdraw from their colonies.
1962 Algeria gains independence from France.
1965 Rhodesia declares its independence from Britain.

1967 Biafra withdraws from the federation of Nigeria, causing civil war.
1975 Angola and Mozambique gain independence from Portugal.
1979 Ayatollah Khomeini gains power in Iran. Soviet forces invade Afghanistan.
1980 The Iraq-Iran war begins.
1982 Israel invades Lebanon.

1984 About 1 million people die of starvation and disease in an Ethiopian famine.
1994 About 1 million die in civil war in Rwanda. Mandela becomes President of South Africa after the first ever multi-racial election.
2003 US-led forces invade Iraq and overthrow Saddam Hussein who is executed in 2006.
2008 President Robert Mugabe rigs election in Zimbabwe. Holds talks with Morgan Tsvangirai.

Who's Who

Castro, Fidel (born 1927), Cuban leader. He led a popular revolution against the Cuban dictator, Batista, in 1958, and turned Cuba into a communist state, supported by the Soviet Union. In spite of US efforts to get rid of him, he stayed in power even after the collapse of the Soviet Union in 1989, but in 2006 ill health led Castro to hand leadership over to Raul Castro.

Churchill, Sir Winston (1874-1965), British statesman. He first entered parliament in 1874 and had an up-and-down career until he became prime minister in 1940. He led Britain throughout the Second World War with great heart and skill, inspiring people with his fighting speeches and planning the strategy that brought victory.

De Gaulle, Charles (1898-1970), French statesman. An army general, he escaped to Britain when France was conquered in 1940, and became the leader of the Free French, uniting all those who opposed the German occupation. He was president of France in 1944-46, and in 1959-69, granting independence to Algeria in 1962.

Franco, General Francisco (1892-1975), Spanish dictator. He was a leader of the revolt that led to the Spanish Civil War. From 1939 he governed Spain as a police state. Though friendly to Hitler, he kept Spain out of the Second World War. Afterwards, his hatred of communism gained him some support from the USA.

Gandhi, Indira (1917-84), prime minister of India. Daughter of Jawaharlal Nehru, she followed him as prime minister in 1966 and dominated Indian affairs for 20 years. She lost power in 1977 and was accused of undemocratic government, but won again in 1980.
Like her namesake, M. K. Gandhi, she was murdered.

Gandhi, Mohandas K. (1869-1948), Indian leader. As a lawyer in South Africa until 1914, he worked bravely against racist laws. In India he became leader of the National Congress and worked for independence from Britain by non-violent protest. His efforts to make peace between Hindus and Muslims led to his murder by a Hindu extremist.

Gorbachev, Mikhail (born 1931), last leader of the Soviet Union. He worked his way up through the Communist Party and was chosen as leader in 1985. His reforms, which were meant to bring peace, freedom and better living, led to the break-up of the Soviet Union and the collapse of the communist system in Europe.

Hitler, Adolf (1889-1945), German dictator. A soldier in 1914-18, he became leader of the National Socialist (Nazi) Party. In prison in 1923 he wrote *Mein Kampf* ('My Struggle'), an attack on Germany's supposed enemies, including Jews. Gaining power in 1933, he made Germany a police state and provoked the Second World War.

King, Martin Luther (1929-68), the greatest US civil-rights leader. As a black minister of the Baptist Church in racist Alabama, he was a founder and later leader of the Southern Christian Leadership Conference, which fought for racial equality by the methods of Gandhi. An inspiring speaker, he was assassinated by a white racist.

Lenin real name V. I. Ulyanov (1870-1924), first leader of the Soviet Union. A Marxist and a rebel, often in prison or exile, he led the Bosheviks in the Russian Revolution (1917), and planned the communist system. His policies were brutal, but the worst atrocities of communist rule happened under his successor, Stalin.

Mandela, Nelson (born 1918), South African statesman. He joined the African National Congress in 1944 and led opposition to the racist policy of apartheid. From 1964 to 1990 he was in prison, but when apartheid ended he was elected the first black South African president (1991). He was admired everywhere for his tolerance.

Mao Zedong (1893-1976), Chinese communist leader. He was one of the founders of the Chinese Communist Party, and led the country after the Revolution (1949). His rule was intolerant, his policies often unwise: his 'Great Leap Forward' (1958) was a leap back. After that his influence later faded, but no one dared to criticise him.

Meir, Golda (1898-1978), prime minister of Israel. Meir was Israel's first woman prime minister and the third woman in the world to hold this office. She met with many world leaders to promote her vision of peace in the Middle East. However, the Yom Kippur War in 1973 cost Israel hundreds of thousands of lives. Meir resigned in 1974.

Mussolini, Benito (1883-1945), Italian fascist leader. A socialist in his youth, he founded the fascist movement in 1919, became prime minister in 1922, and made himself a dictator. An extreme nationalist, he believed in force rather than law. He invaded Ethiopia and, as Hitler's ally, led Italy into war. He was overthrown in 1943.

Nasser, Gamal Abdel (1918-70), Egyptian president. After a military revolt against the King of Egypt, Colonel Nasser became leader. He caused a world crisis by taking over the Suez Canal (1956), and was defeated by Israel in the Six-Day War (1967), but was recognised as the greatest Arab leader in the Middle East.

Rice, Condoleezza (born 1954), United States Secretary of State. Rice was the National Security Advisor to President Bush in 2001 and became the first black woman to serve as Secretary of State in 2005. She pioneered policies which focused on democracy in the greater Middle East.

Roosevelt, Franklin D. (1882-1945), US statesman, the only president to have served more than eight years (1933-45). He is remembered most for his 'New Deal' policies in the 1930s, which tried to end the depression by government action, and for his leadership during the Second World War, in close alliance with Churchill.

Stalin real name Iosiph Dzugashvili (1879-1953), dictator of the Soviet Union. He took part in the Bolshevik Revolution (1917) and succeeded Lenin as leader in 1924. He got rid of all opponents, real or imaginary, caused the death or exile of millions of people, but gained credit from the defeat of Germany (1943-45).

Glossary

absolute ruler A king or other ruler whose power is not limited by laws.

acropolis The ceremonial centre in ancient Greek cities, where the chief temples were built. It usually stood on high ground.

allies Countries, or other groups, who join together for some cause, especially in war.

anaesthetic Drug given to patients to prevent them feeling pain during an operation.

apartheid The system of laws of the government in South Africa from 1948 to 1991. It divided people into racial groups and gave more rights and better services to white people.

aqueduct A bridge which carries water in a canal or channel over a valley.

archaeology The study of the past, especially the prehistoric past, through the evidence of actual remains.

artillery Large guns firing cannon balls or, in later times, explosives.

Asia Minor The region of Asia nearest to Europe, roughly the same as modern Turkey.

assembly line A method of production in factories, when the thing being made passes from one group of workers to another. Each group completes one step in the process.

Axis The alliance of Germany, Italy and, later, Japan during the Second World War.

barbarian The name used by the ancient Greeks to describe all peoples who were not Greek, and by Romans for non-Romans. The word came to mean wild and uncivilised.

basilica A large, rectangular, public building in ancient Rome. Early Christian churches usually took this form, with a central aisle, or walkway.

blitzkreig German for 'lightning war', the speedy form of attack, with tanks and aircraft, that German armies made in the Second World War.

Boers A name (meaning 'farmers') for Afrikaners, South Africans descended from Dutch settlers.

Bolsheviks The revolutionary group in Russia who carried out the revolution of November 1917.

boyars The old class of Russian nobles, from about the 11th century.

broadcasting Sending messages in sound and vision by radio waves, which are picked up by radio and TV receivers.

Bronze Age The ancient time when people had learned to make metal tools and weapons, especially of bronze, but had not yet learned to make iron. This happened at different times in different places.

calendar A system for dividing up the year into seasons, months and days, usually by the movements of the Sun and stars.

caliph The leader of Islam. As successor to Muhammad, the caliph was both ruler and religious head. The title became hereditary, but after 1258 no single caliph was recognised by all Muslims.

calligraphy Beautiful handwriting. It was one of the chief forms of art in ancient Egypt, in the monasteries of Europe, and in China and Japan.

caravan A group of traders, and sometimes other people, travelling in a group for safety. Traders in desert regions always travelled in caravans.

caste One of the strict classes into which people were divided, by birth and occupation, chiefly in India. Everyone was supposed to remain a member of the caste into which he or she was born.

chariot A fast, two-wheeled, horse-drawn cart used in ancient warfare.

city-state A state made up of one city with surrounding country and villages.

civilisation A group of people who have reached a state of development that includes living in cities, organised government, a written language, fine arts and learning.

collectivism A system where a group of people share ownership of the land and the means of production, such as factories.

colony A settlement of people in another country, or a country that is ruled by another one.

communism An extreme form of socialism, in which all power and property belongs to the state, and the state is run by a single party.

conscription A system in which all people able to fight have to serve in the armed forces.

Cossacks Meaning 'adventurers', bands of people, mainly in Russia, who lived in their own groups almost independent of the government.

coup Short for coup d'état. The sudden overthrow of a government, usually by a person or persons who hold some power in the state.

crusade A war waged with the support of the Pope for some Christian cause.

Cultural Revolution The policy of the government of Mao Zedong in communist China, in 1966-68. It was an attempt to continue the spirit of Mao's communist revolution, using gangs of youths called Red Guards, but it ended in violence and economic upheaval.

cuneiform Meaning 'wedge-shaped', the early form of writing in Mesopotamia.

customs duties Taxes on goods coming into a country.

daimyo A member of the warrior nobility in Japan.

democracy A country or form of government where power depends on the votes of the people.

dictator A ruler with absolute power, often gained illegally, for instance by a coup d'état.

discrimination Unfair treatment of a group of people because of their religion, ethnic group, sex, or for some other cause that makes them different from the rest.

dissenters People who disagree with accepted laws or beliefs, especially in religion.

dynasty A ruling family, where the title is passed down from each ruler to his or her heir.

economy The management of the whole wealth of a state (or another type of community), including money, trade, and industry.

emancipation Freedom from some kind of unfair treatment, such as freedom from slavery, or the gaining of a right, such as the right to vote.

empire A state which also controls other peoples or states.

fascism An extreme form of government, under a dictator. Fascism puts the interests of the state before the interests of the citizen, and depends more on force than on law.

federal government The central government in a country made up of a number of states or provinces. The state governments control local matters, and the federal government controls national affairs, such as foreign policy and defence.

Fertile Crescent A region in the Middle East, which was one of the earliest centres of farming. It stretched from the Nile valley, north-east along the eastern Mediterranean and south-east through the valleys of the Tigris and Euphrates rivers.

feudalism The way in which life was run in medieval times, especially in Europe. It depended on a bond between man and master. A man swore to work or fight for his master, in exchange for land.

finance The management of all money matters.

galley A type of ship driven mainly by oars, though some also had sails.

genetic engineering Changing the nature of a living thing by altering its genes, which carry the 'instructions' controlling its character.

gladiator In ancient Rome, a man who fought in an arena to entertain an audience. Gladiators were often prisoners or slaves.

guilds Associations of merchants or craftsmen, which controlled much of the trade and business in medieval European towns.

hegira The flight of the Prophet Muhammad from Mecca to Medina in AD 622, the first year of the Muslim calendar.

hereditary title A title that is passed down in one family, from its holder to his or her heir.

heresy A religious belief that opposes the accepted beliefs of the time.

hominid A creature like a human being, an ancestor of the human race.

Huguenots French Protestants in the 16th and 17th centuries.

Ice Age A period when the Earth's climate was much colder, with much of the northern continents covered by ice. The last Ice Age ended about 10,000 BC.

icon A religious picture or sculpture, especially a picture of a saint in the Orthodox Christian Church.

immigrants People who have settled in a foreign country, often because of

persecution in their own country.

Iron Age The period when humans had learned to use iron, following the Bronze Age.

irrigation Watering of fields by the use of canals or channels.

janissary A professional soldier of the Ottoman Empire.

khan A hereditary king or ruler among the Mongols and other people of east-central Asia.

knight A member of a class below the nobility but above the common people. In medieval Europe, knights were horse-riding warriors who wore armour.

Latin America The countries of Mexico and Central and South America, where Spanish or Portuguese are spoken.

legend A story that is probably based on true events.

liberalism Political opinion in favour of reform and greater freedom.

loom A machine on which yarn, or thread, is woven into cloth.

mamelukes Meaning 'slaves', the royal bodyguards in Egypt who gained power as sultans from 1250 to 1570.

mandarin A powerful Chinese official under the Manchu dynasty.

medieval period The Middle Ages in Europe.

mercenary A professional soldier, willing to fight for anyone who pays him.

merchant A person who lives by buying and selling goods. It usually means someone quite rich, more than a simple trader.

Middle Ages The period in Europe between the end of the Roman Empire and the Renaissance of the 15th century.

Middle East The region of south-west Asia from the Mediterranean to Afghanistan.

militia An armed force. Unlike an army, a militia is a local group of part-time soldiers, who are called up in an emergency, such as a rebellion.

missionary Someone, usually a Christian, who teaches their religion to people of other beliefs.

Modern style A general name for the big changes in style of art, architecture and literature that occurred in the early 20th century.

monastery A community of people (monks) who live according to strict religious rules.

mosaic A picture made up of many small stone cubes of different colours.

mosque A Muslim or place of worship.

mutiny A rebellion by soldiers or sailors.

nationalisation Placing industries (or land, or institutions) under the control of the government. This was usually the policy of socialist governments.

nationalism Support for the idea of the nation, especially in a nation that is ruled by another power.

naval blockade Stopping the trade and shipping of an enemy by preventing his ships entering or leaving port.

Nazis Members of the National Socialist German Workers' party, which gained power under Hitler in 1933.

neanderthal An early type of human being in Europe, another type of homo sapiens, or modern man.

Near East The region around the eastern Mediterranean, sometimes including Egypt and south-east Europe. Like 'Middle East', the name has no exact meaning.

nomads People who have no permanent home, but travel from place to place in different seasons. They raise animals but not crops.

nuclear weapons Powerful weapons whose explosions are caused by the process of nuclear fission or nuclear fusion.

oligarchy Government by a small group of people, usually aristocrats.

one-party state A government where all power belongs to a single party.

papyrus A kind of paper made from reeds, cut into strips and pressed into sheets. It was used by the ancient Egyptians, Greeks and Romans.

parliament A government assembly, made up of people elected by the citizens. In modern democratic countries, parliament is often the body that makes the laws.

patricians The nobles, members of the Senate, in ancient Rome.

patriotism A person's love of his or her country.

peasant The lowest class of country people, usually farm workers. Some peasants owned their own land. Others were serfs.

philosophy The study of the basic truths on which human life and thinking are based.

plantation A large farm or estate, usually in a warm country, that grows one main crop, often for export, and has its own workers.

plebeians The ordinary citizens of ancient Rome.

pollution Damage to the natural environment caused by human activities.

pope The head of the Roman Catholic Church.

porcelain A very fine, hard type of pottery, which light will shine through. It was made in China 1,200 years ago, but in Europe only since the 18th century.

pottery Vases, cups, plates and other vessels made from clay and baked hard.

prehistoric Belonging to a time 'before history', which means before written records were kept.

proclamation An official announcement.

prophet Someone who was believed to speak God's message.

Protestants People who, during the European Reformation, 'protested' against the Roman Catholic Church and formed their own Churches.

pueblo A village community living in a large building built of adobe (clay) or stone in what is now the south-western USA.

Puritans Protestants in the 16th and 17th centuries who wanted a simpler, stricter form of religion.

pyramid A huge, square, stone building whose four sides slope up to a point. In ancient Egypt, they contained the tombs of kings.

refugee Someone who is forced to leave their home or country due to war, or because they are persecuted by their government or neighbours.

regent Someone who rules on behalf of a monarch, when the monarch is unable to rule, often because he or she is too young.

regime A government. It may mean any kind of government, but is often used for a military government or dictatorship.

reliquary A precious box, often made with gold and jewels. It contained a holy relic, such as the bone of a saint.

renaissance Meaning 'rebirth', a time of lively developments in the arts and learning, especially in Europe in the 15th and 16th centuries.

republic A state that has no monarch. A republic is usually a democracy, with a president and a parliament elected by the people.

revolution A violent change, usually of government (as in the French Revolution of 1789), in which ordinary people take part. The name is sometimes given to other kinds of rapid change (such as the Industrial Revolution in the 19th century).

rune stone A large stone slab with writing carved in letters called runes.

samurai A Japanese warrior who belonged to a class like the knights in Europe and followed a strict code of honour and duty.

seal An instrument with a raised design for making a pattern in, for example, a clay tablet.

senate The assembly of patricians in ancient Rome. In many countries today, the senate is one of the two assemblies that make up the legislature.

serf A person in the service of a lord, who 'owns' him or her. Serfs were not quite slaves, as they had some rights.

shogun The military governor, or ruler, of Japan from the 12th to 19th centuries.

shrine A holy place or building, such as the tomb of a saint, which pilgrims visit.

siege An attack on a castle or town defended by stone walls.

socialism A form of government in which all the wealth of a country belongs to the people, not private owners.

statesman A politician or government official of great ability, especially one who has an influence on international affairs.

Stone Age The time before human beings learned to use metals, and made tools from stone.

stupa A Buddhist monument, usually in the shape of a dome, which marks a holy place.

suffrage The right to vote.

sultan A Muslim ruler, especially the ruler of the Ottoman Turkish empire.

superpowers The most powerful states in the world. From 1945 to 1989 they were the USA and the Soviet Union.

technology All the tools, instruments and methods used in industry and other forms of work, which were developed through scientific knowledge.

telegraph A method of sending signals by electric wire. Messages are turned into a code, made by signals of different length.

Third Estate The representatives of ordinary, middle-class people who, with the First and Second Estates (nobles and clergy) made up the Estates General in France before the 1789 Revolution.

Third World A name sometimes given to the poorer countries of the world, in Africa, Asia and Latin America.

trade union An organisation to protect the rights of workers.

treasury A place where money and valuables are kept. The word is used now for the department of government that controls finance.

tsar The title, meaning 'emperor', of the ruler of Russia before the 1917 Revolution.

tyrant A ruler who holds supreme power, above the law. It has become a name for an evil dictator who holds power by force.

vizier An important minister in some Muslim countries. The chief minister of the Ottoman empire was called the grand vizier.

welfare state A state in which the government provides aid for people in need, such as the old, ill, handicapped, retired or unemployed.

yurt A large tent made of felt on a wooden frame, the home of nomads in central Asia, including Mongols.

ziggurat A religious building like a pyramid, but with sides that rise in a series of steps.

Index

E

Eastern bloc 163, 178, 179
Eastern Front *148*
East India Companies 87, 96, *97*, 106, 107, 110, 130–1
East Indies 97
Ecuador 135
Edison, Thomas *141*
education 63, 125, 140, *147*, 154, 170
Egypt 42, 47, 68, 84, 136, 143
    Arab-Israeli conflict 165
    Fatimids 68, 69
Egyptian civilisation *16–17*, 22, 23, 27, 28, 42, 43
Eiffel, Gustave 140
Eiffel Tower (Paris) 140, *143*
Eire *see* Irish Free State
Eisenhower, Dwight D. 158
electricity 140
electronics 170, 175
Elizabeth I, Queen of England 80, *106*
El Salvador 177, 179
e-mail 175
energy supply
    alternative energy *171*
    coal 118, 119, 170
    fossil fuels 119, *143*, 170, 172
    nuclear power 170, 179
    oil *143*, 164, 165, 170, 172
    steam engines 107, *119*
engineering 49
England 80
    Act of Union 107
    Anglo-Saxons *57*
    Civil War *95*, 107
    Norman conquest 60
    Reformation *77*, 80
    unification 57
    Vikings 59
    see also Great Britain
English language 174
environment 172–3, 179
Erasmus 74, 108
Eratosthenes 29
Eric the Red 70
Essen *135*
Ethiopia *55*, 153, 178, 179
Etruscans 30
Euclid 29
Euripedes 27
Europe
    Christianity 56–7, 60–1, *76–7*
    colonies *see* colonies
    eighteenth century 100–1
    exploration *72–3*
    feudalism 60–1, *62*, 64, 65
    French Revolutionary Wars 142
    independent nations 80–1, 94–5, 134–5
    Medieval 60–3
    Napoleonic *114*, 115, 142
    nation states 56–7

    Renaissance *74–5*, 106
    twentieth century 147
    year of revolutions 124, 143
    see also individual countries
European Economic Community (EEC) 163, 179
European Union (EU) 163, 174, 179
evolution, theory of 140
exploration 69, *72–3*, 89, 106, 116, 143

F

factories 118–19, 120, *122–3*
Faraday, Michael 140
farming 12–13, 16, 40, 42
    Agricultural Revolution *118*
    collective farms 151
    feudalism *62*
    genetic engineering *171*
Faroe Islands 59
fascism 152, 153
Fatehpur-Sikri *86*
Fatimids 68, 69
Ferdinand of Aragon 69, *80*
Fertile Crescent 12, 13
feudalism 60, *62*, 64, 65
films *see* cinema
Finland 178
fishing 11, *16*, 42
Florida *102*, 142
food
    farming 12–13
    hunter-gatherers 11
    Medieval Europe 62
football 146
foot-binding 89
Forbidden City (Beijing) *88–9*
Ford, Henry 180
Ford `Model T' 152
forests *see* deforestation
fossil fuels 118, 119, *143*, 170, 172
France 80, 94, 101
    atomic weapons *173*
    corvée *112*
    Huguenots *77*, 97
    Italian Wars 69
    Napoleonic 114–15, 124, 142
    Paris Commune 143
    Second Republic 124, 143
    Terror *113*
    Third Republic 124, 143
    Vichy government 157
    Wars of Religion *77*, 106
    World War I 148, 149
    World War II 156–9
    see also French Empire; French Revolution
Franciscans 97
Franco, Francisco 153, 180
Franco-Prussian War 135
Franks *56*, 68
Frederick II (the Great), King of Prussia

100, 108
French Empire 73, 79, 97, 101, *102*, 103, 105, 107, 114–15, 127, 132, 136, 143, 160, 161, 179
French Revolution *112–13*, 114, 115, 123, 142
French Revolutionary Wars 142
Fulani 142

G

Gagarin, Yuri 175, 179
Galileo Galilei *92–3*, 108
Galvani, Luigi 140
Gandhi, Indira *179*, 180
Gandhi, Mohandas K. (Mahatma) *160*, 168, *180*
Gandhi, Rajiv 179
Garibaldi, Giuseppe *134–5*, 144
Gaul 31, 35, 43
genetics *171*
Genghis Khan 66, 67, 69, 70
geography 92
geology 140
geometry 29
Germany 81, 100–1, *124*, 142, 147
    colonies 147
    communism 151
    industrialisation 118, *135*, 147
    Nazis 153
    Reformation *76*
    second empire 135
    unification 135, 176
    West and East 163, 176
    World War I 148–9, 153
    World War II 156–9
Ghana (Gold Coast) 106, 179
Ghana (empire) *54*, 68, 69
gladiators *31*
glass *23*, 33, 62, *69*, 154
gold 15, *17*, 55
Golden Horde, Khanate of the 67
Gorbachev, Mikhail 176, 179, 180
Goths *34–5*, 43
Gran Colombia 135
Grand Alliance, War of the 101
Grant, Ulysses S. 129
Great Britain
    empire *see* British Empire
    House of Commons *125*
    Industrial Revolution 118, *119*
    Napoleonic Wars 115, 142
    Reform Acts 125
    Roman invasion 31, 32, 33
    wealth and power 147
    World War I 147
    World War II 156–9
    see also England; Scotland
Great Depression *152*, 178
Great Empire 127
Great Northern War 98, 101, 107
Great Schism 69

Acknowledgements

Design by Sally Boothroyd
Picture research by Caroline Wood

The publisher would like to thank the following for illustrations:

Julian Baker; p66t
Richard Berridge; p10t,
Gerry Ball; p75b
Chris Brown; Back cover flap t, p12c, p12b, p21l, p30, p39b, p41tr, p49cr, p54-55b, p59b, p64-65, p74-75t, p77t,
p90-91, p95b, p100, p112c, p113r, p117c, p122bl, p123cr, p126b, p132t, p138tr, p155b,
Peter Bull; p149cl,
Tim Clarey; 31br, p44, p70, p93, p94t, p108, p111t, p112t, p124t, p135t, p144,
p153tl, p165br, p177cr, p180
Mike Codd; p11tr
Peter Connolly; p24tr, p24-25b, p26b, p28, p30t, p32-33b, p58b
Gino D'Achille; Cover flaps b, p2, p68-69, p83b, p84b, 99t, 99b, p106-107, p119tr, p120b, p121br, p127t,
p131t, p134t, p140-141b, p142-143, p149t, p153tr, p157t, p163t, p171b, p173b, p178-179
Gino D'Achille and Robbie Polley; p42-43
Richard Hook; p16-17b, p40-41b
Barbara Lofthouse; p52b, p76t, p80t
Alan Marks; p116br
Steve Noon; Back cover bl, p14-15b, p22b, p23b, p88b, p89t, p92b, p102b, p128b, p128tr,
p134bl, p137bl, p158t, p167t, p174b,
Olive Pearson; all maps
Robbie Polley; p60b, p61t, p103br
Martin Sanders; p35t, p51b, p73t, p84t, p110t, p169tr
Oxford illustrators; backcover tr

The publishers would like to thank the following for permission to use photographs:

Front cover: tl NASA; trBM; cl/r Dorling Kindersley; b "British Library, London, UK"
Back cover: tl "Ashmolean Museum, Oxford"
p9 BAL"Louvre, Paris, France,Giraudon"; p11c BM; p13b ET; p14t BM; p15t BM; p15bc BM; p17tl Boltin Picture Library; p17c MH, BM; p18-19b Bildarchiv Preussischer Kulturbesitz, Klaus Goken; p19ct MH, BM; p19b BM; p20bl Telegraph Colour Library, Mauro Carraro; p21r AKG,"Delhi National Museum,Jean-Louis Nou"; p22-23 c AKG, Heraklion Archaeological Museum; p23tr MH, BM; p25tr MH, BM; p26t MH, BM; p27t ET; p27c AKG,"Musée du Louvre, Paris. Erich Lessing"; p29bc AKG, "The Archaeological Museum, Istanbul,Erich Lessing"; p29cr AKG,"Liebighaus, Frankfurt,Erich Lessing"; p31t AKG; p32t ET,"Staatliche Glypothek, Munich"; p33t Magnum, Dennis Stock; p34l ET; p35br MH, BM; p36b AKG,"Byzantine Museum, Athens,Erich Lessing"; p36r ET; p37t AKG; p38t MH,"Musée Guimet,Paris"; p38b AKG, Jean-Louis Nou; p39t AKG, Erich Lessing; p40t AKG,"National Archaeological Museum,Guatemala,Erich Lessing"; p40bl ET, Museum of Mankind; p45 BAL, Bibliothèque Nationale; p46l Robert Harding, E.Simanor; p47bl Christie's Images; p47cr ET; p48t Werner Forman Archive, Courtesy Sotheby's London; p48b Werner Forman Archive, Beijing Museum; p50r Robert Harding, Gavin Hellier; p51t Werner Forman Archive, Kongo Nogakudo; p52l AKG photo, Jean-Louis Nou; p53tr ET, V&A; p54c MH, BM; p55t Magnum, Bruno Barbey; p55br Comstock, Georg Gerster; p56l AKG; p56-57 Photo Editions COMBIER-Macon; p57t"Ashmolean Museum, Oxford"; p57cr ET, "Bibliothèque Nationale, Paris"; p58tr ET; p61br ET; p62t"By permission of The British Library Ms.Stowe 17, f.89v."; p62b BAL,"British Library, London, UK"; p63t ET; p63b"By permissioin of The British Library Ms Roy 10.E.iv, f.65v "; p64tr BAL,"Fitzwilliam Museum, University of Cambridge, UK"; p65t BAL,"Vetrallaf Cathedral, Italy"; p66b BAL, Private Collection; p67 BAL,"Bibliothèque Nationale, Paris, France"; p71 MH, V&A; p72 Museum of The Royal Pharmaceutical Society of Great Britain; p73br ET; p74bl MH; p75bl The Royal Collection Her Majesty Queen Elizabeth II; p75tr BAL,"Private Collection,The Stapleton Collection"; p76b BAL,"Bibliothèque de Protestantisme,France"; p77r ET, Museum of Fine Arts Lausanne; p78b ET, Private Collection; p79t ET,"The Archaeological Museum of Lima,Peru"; p79bl Mary Evans Picture Library; p80cl BAL,"Thyssen-Bornemisza Collection,Madrid,Spain"; p80br National Trust Photographic Library, Matthew Antrobus; p81t AKG; p82 BAL,"Museo Correr, Venice,Italy"; p83tr BAL,"Louvre,Paris,France"; p85t ET, British Library Add 7880; p85r Sonia Halliday Photographs; p86br BAL,"V&A, London, UK"; p86bl BAL,"V&A,London,UK"; p87b Magnum, George Rodger; p88c"Ashmolean Museum, Oxford", ; p89b Magnum, Marc Riboud; p90bl ET,"Oriental Art Museum, Genoa"; p91tr MH,"V&A,London"; p91br ET, British Museum; p92t ET; p93c Science & Society Picture Library, Science Museum; p94b BAL,"Chateau de Versailles, France,Giraudon"; p95tr Execution of Charles I by an unknown artist reproduced by permission of The Earl of Rosebery (on loan to the Scottish National Portrait Gallery); p96-97 Photo MH, V&A; p97r ET; p98-99 Robert Harding, E.Rooney; p100-101 AKG,"Heeresgeschichtliches Museum,Vienna(detail)"; p101t AKG, Cameraphoto; p101b BAL,"Chateau de Versailles,France"; p103 t"Abby Aldrich Rockefeller Folk Art Center, Williamsburg, VA"; p104-105 BAL,"Wilberforce House Museum, Hull, Humberside, UK "; p105tr BAL,"Bibliothèque Nationale,Giraudon"; p109 BAL,"Wallington Hall,Northumberland,UK"; p110b BAL, Private Collection; p111b BAL,"Library of Congress, Washington D.C., USA"; p113tl AKG; p114-115 ET, Musée de Grosbois du Chateau; p115tl Archives Nationales,"Centre Historique des Archives Nationales,Atelier de Photographie,Paris.AE/I/23(no 10 et 12/1)"; p115tr ET,"Musée de L'Armee, Paris"; p116t Bishop Museum; p117t Robert Harding, Robert Francis; p118b ET, Lincoln Museum & Art Galleries(detail); p119bl Science & Society Picture Library, Science Museum; p120t Collections, Ed Gabriel; p121t ET, National Maritime Museum; p122-123t Corbis, Library of Congress; p123bl ET, Domenica del Corriere; p124b AKG,"Kunstmuseum, Dusseldorf"; p125t BAL, Towner Art Gallery; p125cr BAL,"Private Collection,The Stapleton Collection"; p126tr BAL,"National Library of Australia,Canberra,Australia"; p128-129t AKG,; p129br AKG,; p130t BAL,"British Library,London,UK"; p130-131 Corbis, Arvind Garg; p131b By permission of The British Library IOL.T 10951; p132c AKG; p133t Werner Forman Archive, BM; p133 BM,; p135br Mary Evans Picture Library; p136bl Jean-Loup Charmet; p137br Mary Evans Picture Library; p138bl BAL,"D.F.Barry,Bismarck,Dakota"; p139tr Corbis, Bettmann; p140-141 istockphoto.com; p141cr Corbis , Hulton-Deutsch Collection; p145 Magnum, Steve McCurry; p146l AKG; p146-147 BAL,"Galerie Daniel Malingue,Paris,France"; p147cr Jean-Loup Charmet,"Musée National de L'Education,Rouen"; p148-149b ET,"The Imperial War Museum,London "; p150tr, p150-151b, p151tr David King Collection; p152tr Mary Evans Picture Library; p152-153b"Special Collections Division, University of Washington Libraries Photo by Lee. Negative No.20102"; p154tl Hulton Getty ; p154bl Magnum, Abbas; p154-155t, p156t, p156-157b Hulton Getty; p158bl Corbis, Hulton-Deutsch Collection; p158-159b"The Imperial War Museum, London"; p159tr, p160-161b Hulton Getty ; p161b Magnum, Peter Marlow; p162t UNICEF; p162-163b Magnum, Koudelka; p164b Magnum, Bruno Barbey; p165cl Associated Press; p165 tr Magnum, Bruno Barbey; p166b Magnum, Abbas; p167bl Magnum, Bruno Barbey; p168 Magnum, Bruce Davidson; p169b Magnum, Raghu Rai; p170b SPL, John Mead; p170-171t SPL, Ed Young; p170-171 Deep Light Productions/Science Photo Library; p172-173t Magnum, Ferdinando Scianna; p173r Magnum, Rene Burri; p174t Magnum, Jean Gaumy; p175tr SPL, NASA; p175bl SPL, Ed Young; Computer Pic.© Oxford University Press; p176b Magnum, Gilles Peress; p176-177t Corbis,
"Paul Velasco,ABPL".

Key: BAL = Bridgeman Art Library; BM = The British Museum; V&A = Victoria & Albert Museum; ET = E.T. Archive; SPL = Science Photo Library;
     AKG = AKG London; MH = Michael Holford